The Qualcomm
Equation

The **Qualcomm Equation**

HOW A FLEDGLING TELECOM COMPANY
FORGED A NEW PATH TO BIG PROFITS
AND MARKET DOMINANCE

DAVE MOCK

ΛMACOM

American Management Association

New York • Atlanta • Brussels • Chicago • Mexico City • San Francisco
Shanghai • Tokyo • Toronto • Washington, D.C.

Special discounts on bulk quantities of AMACOM books are available to corporations, professional associations, and other organizations. For details, contact Special Sales Department, AMACOM, a division of American Management Association, 1601 Broadway, New York, NY 10019.
Tel.: 212-903-8316. Fax: 212-903-8083.
Web site: www. amacombooks.org

This publication is designed to provide accurate and authoritative information in regard to the subject matter covered. It is sold with the understanding that the publisher is not engaged in rendering legal, accounting, or other professional service. If legal advice or other expert assistance is required, the services of a competent professional person should be sought.

Library of Congress Cataloging-in-Publication Data

Mock, Dave.
    The Qualcomm equation: how a fledgling telecom company forged a new path to big profits and market dominance / Dave Mock.
        p. cm.
    Includes bibliographical references and index.
    ISBN 0-8144-0818-4
        1. QUALCOMM Inc.   2. Telecommunication.   3. Wireless communication systems.
    4. Spread spectrum communications.   5. Code division multiple access.   I. Title.

HE7797.Q35M6 2005
338.7'62138456—dc22

                                                                    2004022296

Printing number

10 9 8 7 6 5 4 3 2 1

Contents

--➤

THE FOLLOWING TRADEMARKED PRODUCTS ARE REFERRED TO IN
THE QUALCOMM EQUATION:

QUALCOMM®, QChat®, BREW®, Eudora®, OmniTRACS®, and QCTel® are registered trademarks of Qualcomm, Inc.

MSM6200™ is a trademark of Qualcomm, Inc.

NASDAQ® is a registered trademark of the National Association of Securities Dealers Inc.

Q Phone® is a registered trademark of Kyocera Wireless, Corp.

Globalstar™ is a trademark of the CDMA Development Group.

cdmaOne is a registered trademark of Loral QUALCOMM Satellite Services, Incorporated

CDMA2000® is a registered trademark of the Telecommunications Industry Association (TIA).

VideoCipher® is a registered trademark of General Instrument.

80286®, 80386®, and 80387® are registered trademarks of Intel Corporation.

Iridium® is a registered trademark of Iridium Satellite, LLC.

iDEN® and StarTac® are registered trademarks of Motorola, Inc.

GSM® is a registered trademark of GSM Association.

Walkman® and Betamax® are registered trademarks of Sony Corporation.

VHS® is a registered trademark of Victor Company of Japan, Ltd.

i-mode® is a registered trademark of NTT DoCoMo, Inc.

Windows® is a registered trademark of Microsoft, Inc.

UltraPhone® is a registered trademark of InterDigital Communications Corporation.

J2ME® and Java® are registered trademarks of Sun Microsystems, Inc.

Foreword

By George Gilder

In the search for innovative excellence, set aside the stories of Intel, Microsoft, and IBM. They have had their day. Shun the likes of Sony, Cisco Systems, Nokia, and NEC. They still fall short. Peruse these pages and you will come to the mounting realization that an American company from San Diego called Qualcomm is the best technology company in the world today. You will want to learn all the lessons of its awesome triumph, revere its founders, join the company, and own its stock.

In taking this attitude, you will not be alone. Over the next decade, all the leading players in communications and electronics will have to come to terms with this new colossus from southern California. There is no better place to start than with this definitive book of business history, business management, and technology strategy. Normally known as the source of the next generation of wireless telephony, Qualcomm is in fact the inventor of the exemplary twenty-first-century technology corporation.

I am a passionate advocate of fiber optics—the sending and receiving of messages over worldwide webs of glass and light that I call a "fibersphere," which can achieve bandwidths millions of times greater than those possible with copper wires. But without wireless access, the bounties of the fibersphere will remain indoor pleasures for the plugged-in and wired, the couched and tethered. To serve mobile human beings wherever they live, work, and travel, the fibersphere needs the atmosphere just as your lungs need air.

Your cellphone is a radio. So increasingly is your computer. By computerizing the cellphone, Qualcomm is creating a new way of accessing the atmosphere with radio waves. But the world is full of ingenious companies that excel in digital radio engineering and access technology. What distinguishes Qualcomm is its prowess in accessing the noosphere of the academy for advanced scientific ideas, then turning these cutting-edge ideas into practical applications.

The key founders of Qualcomm, both of whom have doctorates in electrical engineering, were Irwin Jacobs and Andrew Viterbi, paramount students and teachers of the information theory of Claude Shannon. A genius who worked at MIT and Bell Laboratories, Shannon began in 1948 with a narrow effort to gauge the carrying capacity of any communications channel in the presence of noise, but he ended up creating the fundamental science behind modern information technology. With crucial prompting from another Qualcomm founder, Klein Gilhousen, Jacobs and Viterbi extended Shannon's ideas into the engineering systems that are the underpinnings of Qualcomm's success. The essence of Qualcomm is that it is an information technology company based on a theory of information.

Shannon defined information in terms of digital bits and measured it by the concept of information entropy: unexpected news or surprising bits.[1] Unless a message changes your mind, it does not convey informational entropy. A basic principle of information theory is that it takes a low-entropy carrier (one with no surprises) to bear high-entropy messages (those that are full of surprises and news). Unless the carrier is predictable and relatively free of entropy, it will not enable the detection of surprising messages at the other end.

The epitome of a low-entropy carrier is the electromagnetic spectrum, from radio waves to light waves, a regular radiance of perfect sine waves limited by the speed of light and differentiated only by their hertz, the number of times they undulate every second. Because of its supreme regularity, the spectrum can bear a measurable modulation, a deliberate distortion that is detectable at a remote receiver. Because of its radiance, it consists of patterns of energy that can be enhanced and harbored, amplified and resonated over long distances down wires or through the air. As a result of these features, all the entropy of the information economy is rapidly migrating toward using the regular radiance of the electromagnetic spectrum for communications.

Qualcomm entered the wireless fray during the period when the industry was moving from analog transmissions, which use every point on the waveform to simulate the sound or image, to digital solutions (based on Shannon's binary bits), which convey only a numerical rendition of the message. Because it uses every point on the waveform, analog seems more efficient, but any interference or noise can distort the outcome—as in snow on a TV image or static on a radio—whereas digital messages remain robust as long as their two possible states are intelligible.

Having studied with Shannon at MIT, Qualcomm's founders were far better prepared to deal with the new era of digital radio than were the veterans of analog radar, telephony, and television who dominated most other wireless companies. In particular, Jacobs and Viterbi grasped Shannon's revelation concerning the relationships between information, power, and noise in digital systems. While added power improves the efficiency of an analog signal—you can hear the unexpected sound more clearly if it is louder—Shannon showed that more power degrades digital efficiency. If you receive a bit at all, it doesn't matter how loud it is—a bit is a bit. But a loud signal can drown out other signals around it. What matters for digital communications is not maximizing power but reducing it to the minimum that remains intelligible. The object is not to blast a particular signal, such as a television or radio program, over a long distance, but to maximize the total number of bits—the amount of entropy—that can be transmitted and received by all radios in the area. Qualcomm was the first wireless company optimized for this Shannon mindset in the Shannon era of low-power communications.

Crucial to every radio communication system are its air interface and its modulation scheme. The system must translate audio or video signals from a phone or computer into a stream of bits that are modulated onto radio frequencies in the air. There are four ways to share spectrum: You can divide it into time slots (time-division multiple access, or TDMA), divide it into frequency bands (frequency-division multiple access, or FDMA), divide it in terms of space (by the location and directionality of transmitters), or use Shannon's new way as developed and adopted by Qualcomm: piling up messages on top of one another in the same frequency bands while differentiating them by codes. Qualcomm's system, called code-division multiple access (CDMA), uses a spread-spectrum technology: Rather than dividing a spectrum band into narrow slices—frequency slots (FDMA) or time slots (TDMA)—CDMA spreads out the message over all the available spectrum all the time for every call or connection.

Qualcomm's founders initially developed this technology for satellite communications. It may have been Gilhousen who first saw its advantages for terrestrial systems. By eliminating the shuffling of frequencies between cells and time slots that afflicts other techniques, CDMA enabled other transmitters in a cell to exploit the routine silences in conversation and allowed "soft handoffs" to neighboring cells without changing the frequency or briefly dropping the call. Using all the assigned spectrum all the time also meant that CDMA was superior for sending data, which characteristically arrives in bursty transmissions that would overflow a single time slot but could be absorbed across a broad CDMA spread of spectrum. These insights started Qualcomm on its ascent to its current position as the world's exemplary technology company—and Mock tells the story superbly here.

A master of technology, Qualcomm over the years has become a many-sided miracle. In an era in which wireless is becoming the dominant mode of Internet access and telephone communications, Qualcomm is the world's leading source of wireless technology innovation. In an era of ascendancy for

Carver Mead's horizontal "fabless" model of the semiconductor industry, in which microchip designers pass on their output to specialized foundries for manufacture, Qualcomm is the world's number one fabless semiconductor company in revenues and profits. At a time when share value is increasingly based on intellectual property, Qualcomm is the global champion of intellectual property management, with a portfolio of more than one thousand patents for the implementation of its CDMA, generating royalty revenues of nearly one billion dollars each year.

Qualcomm is also rapidly becoming America's most effective supplier of broadband Internet links at a time when broadband is fast gaining momentum among customers. With the increasing use of handsets for still and motion photography, I expect about half of phone company digital subscriber lines (DSL) and a good many cable modem subscribers as well to eventually switch to Qualcomm's system for most of their Internet accesses.

Qualcomm is the worldwide leader in third-generation (3G) wireless networks and is expanding its technology portfolio through GSM (global system mobile) and other time-division multiple-access methods. With some twenty million current customers, Qualcomm is the most successful U.S. company in the ascendant domain of China, and it now has ten million subscribers in India. Qualcomm's GSM1x chipset, which links CDMA systems to GSM networks, enables the company to sell its technology to the entire mass of several hundred million users of GSM. Pervasive in Latin America and gaining in Russia, Qualcomm is the pivotal player in the emerging new world of ubiquitous voice and video communications.

Qualcomm began as a supplier of satellite technology and remains a leading satellite player. Not only does CDMA's use of global positioning technology to synchronize its cell sites put Qualcomm in the forefront of location-based services, but Qualcomm's OmniTRACS system maintains logistical communications with trucks, boats, and other vehicles around the globe.

Because its computer technology is hidden in cellphones, Qualcomm is not widely seen as the world's ascendant computer company, in both hardware and software. But it is. With its complex single-chip systems for handsets and base stations, Qualcomm produces some of the world's most complex and efficient computer chips. With its robust BREW (binary runtime environment for wireless) platform for applets and its pioneering Eudora e-mail program, it is a leading software vendor. Sixteen hundred software developers attended Qualcomm's 2004 BREW mobile software conference. As of June 2004, twenty-six device manufacturers were supplying 140 BREW-enabled models to thirty operators in twenty-one countries, and some thirty million total BREW handsets had have downloaded 130 million applications and services. Qualcomm also has an ever more resourceful port-folio of new technologies, such as software radio and QChat. But now the company is facing what is widely seen as a deadly challenge—a powerful in-ternational alliance of companies dedicated to overthrowing its newly domi-nant position in wireless.

Shaping the strategic consciousness of nearly all technology companies over the last decade has been Clayton Christensen's vision of "disruption."[2] In electronics, the prime example is the personal computer, which, though inferior to mainframes and advanced minicomputers, was a good enough product that sold for far less and thus ended up dominating the industry. At the outset, mainframes and minicomputers could hugely outperform the PC, but the PC offered cheap functionality for undemanding users and rapidly achieved economies of scale that dwarfed the established computer industry. With larger volumes, the PC industry moved up the learning curve and ulti-mately supplied higher performance as well, displacing mainframes and servers even in high-end 3D graphics and database access applications. In massively parallel configurations, PC microprocessors now perform even most supercomputer functions. By the rough index of millions of instruc-tions per second (MIPS), the PC ended up providing over 99 percent of all the economy's computing power. Because of the initial conditions of overshoot-ing and overpricing in mainframes and minis, the inferior technology of PC s could succeed first in disrupting and then in displacing the entire establish-ment of the computer industry.

The latest dazzlers in disruption, WiFi and WiMax, both promise to disrupt Qualcomm just as the company prepares to take over the wireless world. WiFi, the dominant standard for wireless local area networks, provides Internet links for computers in homes and offices and at hot-spot access points, such as coffee shops, hotels, and airport lounges. In *Wired* magazine, Nicholas Ne-groponte of MIT's MediaLab famously predicted that like lily pads on a pond—hardly noticeable until the very day they suddenly eclipse the water—WiFi hot spots would spread to cover the country and eclipse the Qualcomm regime for wireless Internet access. Then for mobile applications would come WiMax, which promises cell sites thousands of times larger than WiFi's hot spots and accessible from moving vehicles.

In promoting this new disruptor for Qualcomm and the wireless establish-ment, few analysts noticed that the leading proponents of WiFi and WiMax are Intel, Cisco, and IBM, the established leaders in computer networking that are currently under attack by Qualcomm and the "teleputer." With an esti-mated 600 million cellphones being sold in 2004, compared to some 200 mil-lion PCs, cellphones already outsell PCs by three to one. Cellphones already far outperform PCs as communicators and cameras. WiFi and WiMax, in fact, are desperate stratagems concocted by the PC and computer incumbents to fend off disruption from Qualcomm and the mobile teleputer.[3]

Neither WiMax nor other new contenders such as Flarion achieve better results in terms of the chief metric of spectral efficiency, bits per second per hertz. Spectral efficiency largely determines economic efficiency for wireless service providers. A decade ago, Qualcomm claimed, and proved, that it had far higher spectral efficiency than the incumbent systems. By spreading transmissions over a wide band, using digital codes rather than time slots to differentiate signals, and employing sophisticated-power control techniques at low power levels, Qualcomm's CDMA substantially beat the then-reigning technology of TDMA (time-division multiple access, embodied in the GSM standard). Qualcomm accomplished Peter Drucker's rough rule of winning in a technology market by being ten times better than the incumbent.

In true 800-pound-gorilla form, Qualcomm just keeps executing. Qualcomm's CDMA2000 was once thought to be threatend by W-CDMA (wideband CDMA), a competing 3G standard engineered by the Europeans and Japanese to be different from Qualcomm's preferred flavor while still retaining CDMA's inherent advantages. But now Qualcomm has mastered W-CDMA ahead of the competition; it has twenty-one customers for its W-CDMA chips (ten Qualcomm-enabled W-CDMA handsets are due by year end), and it will soon integrate W-CDMA with CDMA2000 EV-DO, GSM/GPRS, and Wi-Fi. The company projects that the W-CDMA handset market will grow quickly, from seventeen million in 2004 to some forty-five million in 2005.

In the wireless paradigm, serving teleputer camcorder phones everywhere, ubiquity is critical. While the WiFi hype continues, CDMA offers cells some twenty-five thousand times larger than an average WiFi access point hot spot. With broad coverage over the entire continent, Sprint and Verizon are making the entire nation a hot spot. Both Sprint and Verizon, though, sharply lag Korean carrier SK Telecom and Japan's KDDI in broadband deployment of CDMA2000 data services and in per capita data revenues.

Led by Intel, Microsoft, and Cisco, the personal computer industry has become a byzantine establishment afflicted everywhere with overshoot products, such as huge software operating suites, gigahertz microprocessor chipsets, motherboard mazes, proliferating network interfaces, and communications protocols too complex to integrate into smoothly performing systems. The computer industry comprises a sprawling standards committee of committees, and it has designed a gigantic camel that cannot thread the needle's eye of cheap, robust, and secure mobile services needed by billions of new customers around the globe. Meanwhile, a new teleputer industry, led by Qualcomm, is emerging to challenge the incumbent players.

Epitomized by the multipurpose cellphone handset or personal digital assistant, the teleputer is optimized for ubiquitous connectivity. As I described it years ago, it will be as portable as a watch and as personal as your wallet. It will recognize speech and convert it to text. It will collect your news and your mail, and if you wish, it will read them to you. It will browse the World Wide Web and download desired information. It will tell you the weather at your destination. It will conduct transactions, and it can load credit into an encrypted credit meter embedded in a microprocessor or onto a chip on a smart card that can be used like cash. It can pay your taxes or help you to elude them legally by documenting the location of transactions. It can take pictures or videos and project them onto a wall or screen or transmit them to any other digital device or storage facility.

However, it may not do Windows—certainly not in any conventional form. In fact, the teleputer is introducing a new software paradigm based on adaptable applets that are small enough and agile enough to download to a handset. As early as 1990, Bill Joy of Sun called for such a software model: "As we add more and more of these features to older systems," he said, "the complexity gets multiplicative.... I get this feature and that feature but the combinations don't work. What I'd really like to see is a system where the complexity goes up in a linear way but the power goes up exponentially."[4] In software, the complexity has long been rising exponentially, while the power rises additively. Niklaus Wirth, the inventor of Pascal and other programming languages, has propounded two new Parkinson's Laws for software: "Software expands to fill the available memory" and "Software is getting slower more rapidly than hardware gets faster." Indeed, newer programs seem to run more slowly on most systems than their previous releases did.[5]

In contrast, Qualcomm has introduced BREW (binary run-time environment for wireless)—a new operating system, developer platform, billing model, and authentication scheme, all optimized for wireless applications.

Using the BREW 3.1 client software and the user interface toolkit 1.0, operators and handset makers can develop an entire phone user interface, akin to an operating system that can be customized to suit the individual operator or manufacturer's requirements. This includes things like the features of the address book, the messaging menu, and even the color, styling, and shape of the icons. For enterprises, Qualcomm offers productivity applications for the sales force or for field force automation. Ironically, Sun designed Java for cross-platform neutrality, but in the cellphone domain, the system has broken down as different vendors adapt it to their own proprietary applications. Today Java-equipped handsets will not support BREW, but BREW-enabled handsets can support all Java applets.

The applet and BREW models both halt the elephantiasis in software and provide software that accords with Bill Joy's original vision. Since BREW and Java will soon be on more devices than Windows, these new small-works technologies represent a new software paradigm.

Qualcomm is positioned at the epicenter of the wireless new world, reaching out to revitalize all contiguous technologies. Dave Mock's *The Qualcomm Equation* gives us the definitive narrative and analysis of this supreme company.

Acknowledgments

I owe a tremendous amount of gratitude to scores of talented individuals who dedicated a significant amount of their time to aid in developing this book. Many shared their personal experiences and insight, provided references and materials, offered expert guidance, or reviewed the content for accuracy. Out of the hundreds of people who made this project possible, particular thanks are given to Anthony Loder, Bill Frezza, Bruce Ahern, Christine Trimble, Cherry Park, Casey Corr, Christina Briscoe, Dan Briody, Dave Hughes, David Clapp, Debbie Andersen, Debbie Casher, Dr. Irwin Mark Jacobs, Eric Linscott, Doug Ramsey, Esa Nurkka, Guy Hicks, Howard Goldberg, Ira Brodsky, Jackie Townsend, James Madsen, Jeff Hultman, Klein Gilhousen, Dr. Martha Dennis, Patty Goodwin, Perry LaForge, Romuald Ireneus 'Scibor-Marchocki, Scott Goldman, Tom Taulli and Steve Altman.

I'm especially indebted to Rich Kerr, Allen Salmasi, and Ed Tiedemann, each of whom gave an inordinate amount of personal time to provide detailed recollections and information on several occasions. I'm also grateful for the research assistance of Donna Berlier, who was instrumental in delivering much of the research and documentation that was difficult to track down. I'd also like to thank those who contributed their insight and experiences, but who wish to remain anonymous. I sincerely appreciate the trust and support of Qualcomm's employees and their partners for their willingness to lend support to this project.

I was also blessed with an outstanding editorial team: Charles Levine deserves credit for taking the raw script to a whole new level of style and substance. Thanks also to Barry Richardson, Jim Bessent, Jaqueline Flynn, and the whole AMACOM team for their exceptional work.

Finally, my heart goes to my wife Gina for her endless patience, understanding, and support.

Significant Characters

Hedy Lamarr—Born in Austria in 1913 as Hedwig Eva Maria Kiesler, Hedy Lamarr's acting career gained worldwide prominence with a nude appearance in the film *Ecstasy* in 1933. After a move to Hollywood, Hedy befriended composer George Antheil. The pair went on to develop the initial concept for what is today referred to as frequency hopping to help the Allies defeat the Germans in World War II. Hedy Lamarr died in Florida in 2000.

George Antheil—Born in 1900 in Trenton, New Jersey, George Antheil was an avant-garde composer with a passion for player pianos. He met Hedy Lamarr at a Hollywood dinner party and contributed his knowledge of synchronizing player pianos to their patented secret communication system, which employed frequency hopping. George Antheil died in 1959.

Claude Shannon—Born in 1916 in Gaylord, Michigan, Claude Shannon studied mathematics and electrical engineering at the University of Michigan before receiving a Ph.D. in mathematics at the Massachusetts Institute of Technology (MIT). Often referred to as the "father of modern communications theory," Shannon developed sophisticated theories on the capacity of communication channels. His groundbreaking work spawned a new age in communications theory and applications. A victim of Alzheimer's disease, Claude Shannon died in 2001.

Dr. Irwin Mark Jacobs—Born in 1933 in New Bedford, Massachusetts, Irwin Jacobs received an electrical engineering degree from Cornell University and a master's and Sc.D. from MIT. Jacobs founded Linkabit in 1968 and went on to become the founder and CEO of Qualcomm. The author of *Principles of Communication Engineering* and numerous technical papers and patents, Jacobs is a pioneer of modern communications.

Dr. Andrew Viterbi—Born in Italy in 1935, Andrew Viterbi immigrated to the United States in 1939. He attended MIT, where he earned a master's degree in electrical engineering in 1957. He also received a Ph.D. in electrical engineering from the University of Southern California in 1962. Viterbi cofounded Linkabit and Qualcomm with Irwin Jacobs and is best known for developing a decoding algorithm that bears his name, the Viterbi decoder.

Klein Gilhousen—Graduating from UCLA with a degree in electrical engineering in 1969, Gilhousen worked as an engineer at Magnavox before joining Linkabit in 1970. Gilhousen was a cofounder of Qualcomm in 1985 and is credited with developing much of the fundamental technology used in CDMA mobile communications.

William C. Y. Lee—After earning his Ph.D. from Ohio State University in 1963, Lee was employed at Bell Laboratories from 1964 until April 1979. Lee later joined AirTouch Communications (formerly PacTel Mobile Companies) in April 1985 and went on to assist Qualcomm in the early development and testing of CDMA technology in commercial cellular networks.

Allen Salmasi—After receiving bachelor's degrees in both electrical engineering and management economics from Purdue in 1977 and completing a master's in electrical engineering in 1979, Salmasi earned a master's in applied mathematics and did doctoral coursework in electrical engineering at the University of Southern California. In 1984 he founded Omninet Corp., which merged with Qualcomm in 1988. Salmasi's first product concept at Omninet—a satellite messaging system for the trucking industry—became Qualcomm's OmniTRACS product.

The Qualcomm
Equation

Introduction

The conversation was only a mild stirring for such a large crowd in such a small space. Even though dozens of people were engaged in conversation, many of them were repeatedly checking their watches and glancing periodically at the stage. Dr. Irwin Mark Jacobs would stride in at any moment to give the world a progress report on the state of the wireless industry and the latest developments in his company. When Jacobs arrived with a laptop in tow, the crowd settled down without provocation—almost as if on cue. As Jacobs unfolded the screen at the podium and lifted his eyes to look at the crowd, the audience fell into a hushed silence without so much as a word from the soft-spoken CEO.

Irwin smiled.

He opened the discussion in a soft, personal tone that one wouldn't expect from the CEO of a multibillion-dollar corporation. There was no square-jawed, authoritative demeanor, no chest-puffing diatribe from a prepared statement detailing an aggressive company strategy. His body language spoke of a humble stature; here was someone who fully believed in what he had to say, but was not sure whether anyone else shared his outlook. He seemed almost surprised that so many people were interested in listening.

Dr. Jacobs lightened the mood of an intense audience with a slight joke about having to keep a close watch on his laptop—only six months earlier, someone had stolen his portable computer as he mingled with reporters after a presentation to the Society of American Business Editors and Writers. The chuckles and the ensuing banter set the tone for the next forty-five minutes, in which Jacobs made it plain that he would answer any questions—because he had all the answers. But not before he demonstrated with numbers and the sleek gadgets lining his suit pockets that his company was revolutionizing the world.

The aura was unmistakable. To even the greenest of observers—even a neophyte reporter—it was obvious that Irwin Jacobs was not your typical CEO.

All the better, because his company, Qualcomm, is not your typical company.

It was a mere blip in time: a press conference at America's biggest wireless show of 2001, the annual Cellular Telecommunications and Internet Association conference and convention. Dr. Jacobs had appeared at hundreds of similar events to speak to a range of audiences about the explosion that was unfolding in wireless communications worldwide. But the crowd's reaction to his presence this year was quite different from that in many prior years. Walking into the same conference a decade earlier, Jacobs had been met with more discord and indifference than smiles. Ten years ago, Jacobs had been selling an invisible concept; today he was relishing the rewards of hard work. The skeptical mood of a decade ago was dominated by the question of *if* Qualcomm's solutions would ever be realized in a physical, commercial product; today, the only lingering doubt was *when* its solution would be ubiquitous.

From the time of its inception until today, Qualcomm has gone the full route from a completely unknown company from San Diego to a global kingpin in the wireless industry. Its success has been born from disruption—taking the standard approaches to problems and throwing them in the garbage. More than any other company working in wireless, Qualcomm pushed the most advanced, radical solution to provide efficient mobile communications to the masses. Its technology solution, called code-division multiple access (CDMA), which is based upon spread-spectrum techniques, has gone on to be synonymous with both the company and the art of advanced communications.

For its aggressive approach of disruptive development in the wireless industry, Qualcomm has attracted ire internationally, probably second only to that facing Microsoft. In the United States, Qualcomm's CDMA technology is identified as either the best thing that ever happened to wireless communications or the sole cause of everything that is wrong with wireless services today. Your cellular phone doesn't work on that highway? Blame Qualcomm. The United States is behind several other countries in terms of advanced wireless services? Blame Qualcomm. After all, the true pioneers are the ones with arrows in their backs.

FROM SMALL UNKNOWN TO GLOBAL POWERHOUSE

A mere decade ago, few people in the business world had even heard of Qualcomm. In fact, few people had even considered a company based in sleepy San Diego to be any threat, especially in the area of high technology. Silicon Valley was still considered the place where the brightest of minds gathered—one success story after another was being churned out at a seemingly unending rate. In San Diego, however, it was another story. There, everybody knew about Qualcomm and its highly regarded founder, Irwin Jacobs. When Qualcomm seemed to come out of nowhere in the early 1990s, local businesses simply saw it as another chapter in a long story—one with an almost too predictable ending.

The long process of building a strong base of business in the San Diego area was already in full swing. A steady growth in companies specializing in health sciences and communications was quickly accelerating, and more and more venture capital was pouring into the area. Qualcomm had assembled an exceptional team to pursue some of the most promising communications technologies.

Qualcomm hit the average U.S. citizen's radar screen in 1999, when its stock shot up by an amazing twenty-five times, from a low of just under $7 to an ending high of over $176, in a single year (see Figure I-1). Whether or not you were an investor, or even whether or not you cared about cellular phones, you heard about Qualcomm. Mainstream periodicals and news sources carried numerous stories of how this corporate American dream was playing out, producing many a millionaire (and a few billionaires) in the process.

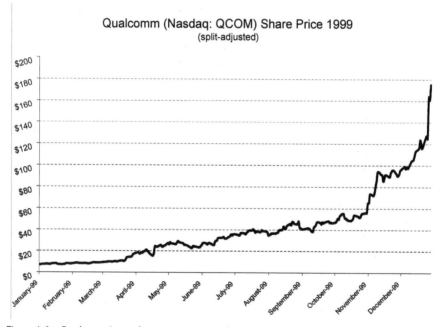

Figure I-1: Qualcomm's stock: every investor's dream

What fueled Qualcomm's meteoric rise in the market that year was the perception that the company held the keys to the future of mobile communications, and those keys would unlock a steady stream of money in the form of licensing royalty paid for use of the technology that the company had pioneered. Qualcomm had fought long and hard to protect its intellectual property through patents in numerous countries, not just the United States. Companies were already paying millions to have unrestricted use of its patent base. Late in 1999, Wall Street had concluded that at some point in the near future, Qualcomm would be deriving revenue from virtually every single mobile phone sold.

As with most stock stories of 1999–2000, what went up eventually had to come down. While the stock of Qualcomm has yet to revisit its highs of 1999, the company has continued to barrel forward at full throttle. The excesses of the all-too-often-labeled dot-com era caught up with everyone. But Qualcomm was no flash in the pan; there was a solid business behind this Wall Street darling.

While just about everyone knows the headline synopsis of the Qualcomm story, few know about the years of development and refinement that went into making the company a global powerhouse in communications. Many people figure that a few sharp people just got together, wrote a few good patents, and hired an aggressive team of lawyers to write up legal agreements. A different set of observers credit Qualcomm with mastering a technology that was so good that it sold itself. Heck, plenty of dot-coms were doing the same thing, making millions in the process. Nothing could be farther from the truth, though.

Qualcomm's prowess is now almost literally the stuff of legend. Because of the almost mythological stature of the company's founders—particularly Irwin Jacobs and Andrew Viterbi—anyone involved with it has almost automatically entered the engineering elite. In the late 1990s, it was commonplace for executives pitching a start-up company to venture capitalists to cite their hiring of ex-Qualcomm employees, as if that certified the start-up's engineering pedigree. Qualcomm was both feared and respected, and never underestimated.

The scale, breadth, and depth of the impact that Qualcomm has had on the global wireless industry is almost without comparison. Equally interesting to note, though, is that depending upon your frame of reference, Qualcomm has been either a positive or a negative agent of advance in the wireless market—or both. Qualcomm is commonly credited with bringing a highly disruptive technology solution to market—something that you don't do while making only friends. For every fan of Qualcomm, there's an equally fervent critic.

THE COMPANY NO ONE CAN DO WITHOUT

Qualcomm's crowning achievement is bringing one of the most sophisticated methods of modern communication to commercial reality. Its CDMA technology was a concept that had been reserved for secret military purposes before the company brought its advantages to the commercial cellular market. But there is often a subtle misrepresentation in the way that many people portray Qualcomm as the inventor of CDMA.

Qualcomm did not invent CDMA. It pioneered it.

Almost every press release by the company reminds the world that Qualcomm indeed pioneered CDMA technology:

> "QUALCOMM Incorporated (Nasdaq: QCOM), pioneer and world leader of Code Division Multiple Access (CDMA) digital wireless technology..."

Even though the company has *thousands* of patents granted or filed on the technology, it does not count itself as the inventor of CDMA.

This seemingly trivial difference actually has profound significance when it is viewed in the context of the success that the corporation has enjoyed. Inventors enjoy many things—prestige, honor, and peer respect. But it is very rare for the inventor to enjoy tremendous wealth along with these things. A pioneer has the constitution not only of an inventor, but also of a trailblazer—someone that not only dreams big, but dares to live it.

And when it comes to blazing into uncharted territory, Qualcomm is certainly an organization that not only talks the talk, but walks at a pace like none before it. What creates wealth for an astute inventor (or someone who simply knows what to do with inventions) is the application of novel concepts. The greatest inventions in the world bring no lasting value to the world if all they do is age on paper. Qualcomm's founders are most of all gifted in their ability to apply cutting-edge technology to practical problems, bringing more advanced products and services to everyday consumers.

Most inventors are so involved with the details of proving out their concepts that making money is a secondary thought (if it is even a thought at all). And when they do attempt to extract value from their creation, some inventors go about the task entirely backwards—they develop an idea first, then look for somewhere to apply it. A much more straightforward and rewarding approach is to fully understand a problem or need in a specific market, then apply an appropriate solution based on a novel idea.

The application of inventions to problems or limitations with current products or services is the key to success in this area. Qualcomm's success is derived from its successful application of CDMA technology to one of the fastest-growing markets this century has seen—mobile communications. Its effort in pioneering the use of spread-spectrum communications in the cellular industry sets it apart from all others. Qualcomm has achieved what many literally called impossible.

* * *

Hence, the primary focus of this book is on following how Qualcomm brought spread-spectrum technology to the global masses of mobile phone and Internet users. The story of Qualcomm, however, is one that admittedly cannot adequately be captured in a single book. Neither can the company's achievement be easily understood by looking at it from a few perspectives, such as its supporting technology or sales tactics. Nevertheless, this text strives to be a comprehensive case study for probably the best real-world example of disruption done right.

This text doesn't just focus on the happenings behind Qualcomm's doors, but also deals with events and dynamics outside the company. Disruption is just as much about the soon-to-be-overthrown competition as it is about the company that's violating the existing order. Without an understanding of the progress of the wireless industry as a whole, Qualcomm's tactics have little significance. Successful disruptive companies don't blindly push against barriers to entry; they methodically react to events and decisions to attack competing weaknesses that develop over time. Understanding what Qualcomm executives and engineers were (and continue to be) up against is fundamental to grasping the depth and talent of the corporation.

This book assumes that the reader has little or no knowledge of Qualcomm's business or the wireless industry in general. To give a thorough, high-level overview of Qualcomm and how it got to where it is today, this book is divided into two sections. The first section chronicles how the company took a radical communications concept and successfully applied it to the commercial wireless industry. The second section dedicates individual chapters to several significant characteristics of Qualcomm's business that made it successful. Since Qualcomm both pioneered a new technology and capitalized on it, the two sections are designed to give readers an overview of how the Qualcomm team successfully pulled it off.

The first section starts in Chapter 1 with the origins of spread-spectrum technology and introduces the visionaries who advanced the key concepts. The next chapter highlights Qualcomm's roots, its principal founders, and the company's early business focus. Chapter 3 covers what happened after Qualcomm shipped its first successful product, OmniTRACS, and began looking for another opportunity in the burgeoning cellular market. The next chapter focuses on how Qualcomm determined that its idea for advanced wireless communications would solve critical problems facing the industry at the time.

Chapter 5 covers how Qualcomm initiated its efforts to woo various companies in the industry to its solution, and the series of efforts that was necessary to overcome setbacks. Moving into Chapter 6, the discussion moves on to how the company got serious and committed significant resources to marketing its solution and its capabilities. Chapter 7 describes how, with the success of its first-ever prototype demonstration of CDMA, Qualcomm moved ahead quickly with additional funding to take its solution to the next level. Chapter 8 covers how Qualcomm put significant resources behind formalizing its CDMA technology in a standard and continued to rally more partners to its cause. In Chapter 9, the discussion moves on to Qualcomm's major battle over the formal acceptance of CDMA by the U.S. industry standards bodies while simultaneously looking ahead to other major opportunities in the PCS and satellite communications sectors.

Moving through Chapter 10, the book tells how Qualcomm bootstrapped its own industry by going into the manufacturing business. To reach its goals, the company had to enter almost every value-added niche in the business to assist vendors and network operators in adopting the CDMA solution. By Chapter 11, the story of the battle with competing standards reaches fever pitch, with Qualcomm aggressively courting PCS operators to adopt CDMA. Chapter 12 then concludes the first section by describing the company's success in finally breaking into the mobile communications market in a big way. With the adoption of CDMA by a majority of cellular and PCS providers, the road ahead was paved with assurances that CDMA would not be just a niche technology. This completes the story of Qualcomm's success at breaking into the wireless industry.

Obviously, the story doesn't end there, but the year 1996 concludes a major era for Qualcomm, the era in which it was fighting to secure its spot in the industry. After this point in time, many challenges obviously faced the company, but its position had changed from what many considered a wannabe to a solid contender with strong backing.

The next section of the book opens with a discussion of how Qualcomm managed the turbulent phases of demand for CDMA products. Chapter 13 discusses the process that Qualcomm went through in building the industry and then, once there, stripping major divisions away from the company to return to its core competency. In the next three chapters, 14 through 16, the technology licensing aspect of Qualcomm's business is dissected. Qualcomm is widely recognized as one of the most successful intellectual property (IP) companies ever, deftly developing a business around its core talent in advanced communications. Chapter 17 spends time discussing one of the hallmarks of the wireless industry—politics. Qualcomm's navigation of the global political battlefield had a profound influence on its success beyond the borders of the United States.

In Chapter 18, Qualcomm's battle to make sure that CDMA was the standard for next-generation networks is discussed. With the world rapidly moving toward third-generation (3G) devices, Qualcomm had to go to great lengths to ensure that it was adequately represented in the future. In Chapter 19, an important aspect of Qualcomm's character is discussed—the cultivation of its employee base. Rooted in innovation, Qualcomm has an employee base with many unique qualities, and the company takes great care in cultivating its most valuable resource. And finally, Chapter 20 caps the section with a brief look at some areas where Qualcomm is placing its bets in the future. As the wireless industry matures and creeps toward 3G, many more opportunities for disruption and profit lie ahead of the company.

Certainly this short text doesn't do justice to the collective efforts of the thousands of employees at Qualcomm who shared a vision of advanced communications for consumers via CDMA. Many more characters, stories, and events have had a profound influence on the path of the worldwide wireless market over the last few decades. And, of course, many more will profoundly influence the future as well. Yet the wireless world would be a completely different place today were it not for the talented team of engineers that made up Qualcomm.

PART ONE

The Radical Technology Solution

"True creativity is characterized by a succession of acts, each dependent on the one before and suggesting the one after."

—EDWIN H. LAND (1909–1991),
INVENTOR AND FOUNDER OF POLAROID

CHAPTER 1
Ecstasy, Pianos, Torpedoes
-‧-➤

The Beginnings, World War II to the Mid-1960s

Entire industries can start from a simple idea—a drawing scribbled on a nap-kin, or a hobby that unexpectedly grows into a full-time endeavor. Bill Gates dropped out of Harvard to play around with new computing devices. Bill Hewlett and Dave Packard started selling electronics from a makeshift work-shop in a single-car garage—now designated as a California historic landmark and widely regarded as the birthplace of Silicon Valley.

For every invention that is doggedly pursued until a goal is reached, dozens can be found accidentally or unintentionally. In 1968, a researcher at Min-nesota Mining and Manufacturing (3M), attempting to improve tape adhe-sives, considered a semisticky substance that held for an unusually long time despite its relatively low adhesiveness to be a failure. Then, years later, 3M found a blockbuster application for this tacky backing in its line of Post-it notes, the hugely profitable repositionable notepaper.

In 1886, John Pemberton, an Atlanta pharmacist, developed the original formula for Coca-Cola, using the coca plant and kola nuts, as a nerve tonic for people who were feeling under the weather or fighting an addiction. You can probably guess the rest of that story. Many novel inventions take decades to find a suitable use, while others never do.

But the founders of Qualcomm and the team that backed them had no such problems applying their radical communication solutions. From the outset, they knew exactly where they were going. No one knew how success-ful they would be, or how their ideas would be received in the marketplace, but there was definitely more purpose to their inventing than just getting a few patents under their name.

The story of how Qualcomm found its niche in advanced communications starts with the origins of what is called *spread-spectrum technology*. Clever engi-neers at Qualcomm devised ways to apply this new, radical, and advanced communications concept to everyday communication products around the world. But the theory underlying their work goes back to World War II, when communications came to play an increasingly vital role on the battlefield.

And in this case, the inventor was not someone most people would have expected. In fact, she was an entirely unexpected inventor.

THE MOTHER OF SPREAD SPECTRUM

A wide chasm can separate an inventor from a pioneer, and an accomplished visionary from a successful inventor. Visionaries conceive and enlighten, while inventors resolve and implement, and the two sets of characteristics are rarely found in one individual. The inner workings of spread-spectrum communications, upon which Qualcomm's code-division multiple-access (CDMA) technology was based, are derived from an earlier discovery by an unlikely source—a beautiful and insightful actress named Hedy Lamarr (see Figure 1-1).

Born Hedwig Eva Maria Kiesler in 1913 in Vienna, Austria, Lamarr's controversial nude appearance in the film *Ecstasy* in 1933 secured her an acting career that would eventually include appearances in many other popular features, such as *Samson and Delilah* and *White Cargo*. That same year, she married the first of her six husbands, Austrian industrialist Friedrich (Fritz) Mandl. Most people saw Hedy Lamarr as simply a showpiece for a powerful tycoon, like many other famous wives. But many would later be surprised to discover her interest and competency in technology and the science of advanced warfare.

Her marriage to Mandl landed her in the middle of interesting conversations on current warfare techniques, as her husband was an arms manufacturer who was doing more and more business with the Nazis. One topic he and his colleagues often discussed that interested Lamarr was the radio control of torpedoes. In battle, naval fleets launched torpedoes from their hulls and then used radio signals (from a plane or ship) to guide the speeding bombs toward their targets.

Unfortunately (assuming you were the one sending, not the one receiving, the torpedoes), jamming the radio signals was a common countermeasure that made the torpedoes far less accurate in reaching and destroying their targets. Since early communications were transmitted on a single frequency channel at a time, an enemy had simply to detect that channel and then

Figure 1-1

blast enough electromagnetic noise to effectively jam the signal (in much the same way that driving under power lines can render music or speech on an AM radio station incoherent). It was no secret that developing a means to avoid direct jamming would greatly increase the effectiveness of naval fleets, but a solution to the problem was elusive. While most of her husband's colleagues assumed that Lamarr had no clue about her husband's work, she later returned to the challenge of guiding torpedoes and showed that there was more to her than just a beautiful face.

Lamarr became increasingly repulsed by the Nazi regime and her husband's involvement with it, and in 1937 she decided to escape her caged existence. After fleeing Austria, Lamarr moved on to Hollywood after Louis B. Mayer of MGM convinced her to sign a movie contract with the company (when she adopted the name Lamarr). With a new life and a film career in full swing, Lamarr met popular composer George Antheil at a Hollywood dinner party. The two teamed up in what was to become one of the most unlikely pairings to support the U.S. war effort.

It turned out to be a natural fit—Lamarr's interest in technology was complemented by Antheil's knowledge of music fundamentals. The two started spending more time together—not courting, but rather discussing how to solve the problem of American torpedoes being jammed by Nazi signals. Antheil helped Lamarr discover through music the key to communication methods that were immune to the then-current jamming techniques.

Antheil had become well known for developing symphonies using several instruments and sonic mechanisms. Some works called for coordinating several automated player pianos, drums, gongs, and even airplane propellers. The artist never heard some of these symphonies, as synchronizing all these unusual instruments successfully was impossible at the time. But this did not deter Antheil from accurately describing how such synchronization could be done. Today, musicians and composers use powerful computers to play his symphonies. Though Antheil credits Lamarr with being the brains behind their joint developments, there's no doubt that his vision of synchronization influenced what was to become Lamarr's concept for discrete radio communication.

The initial concept for their torpedo guidance system was literally scribbled in pencil on an envelope from Antheil's home. A sketch of the communication method on the back was accompanied by a short description on the front. The basic idea for this novel concept, which eventually became known as frequency hopping, was thus immortalized on a scrap of paper. Lamarr and Antheil captured the main principles of a jam-proof communication system in a simple picture and little more than a hundred words. The essential idea entailed jumping from frequency to frequency to elude jamming. The challenge involved synchronizing the hops of both the sender and the receiver—

as in musical orchestration. The system could be scaled from relatively crude to ultrasophisticated, depending upon the degree of secrecy necessary and the intricacy of the technology used.

Lamarr and Antheil spent more time working out the details of how their idea would be implemented and pitched the concept to the National Inventors Council, which was headed by Charles F. Kettering. Started in early 1940, the council culled ideas from the general public and encouraged support for the war effort (especially from women). Kettering suggested that they continue to develop their idea into functional form, while others encouraged Lamarr to instead put her star power to use in selling war bonds (which she did very successfully as well).

Antheil and Lamarr's work culminated in U.S. Patent 2,292,387, "Secret Communication System," granted on August 11, 1942. The patent, filed under her then married name of Hedy Kiesler Markey, describes how a torpedo can be guided by a method of communication that hops among carrier frequencies at a regular time interval (one of the patent diagrams is shown in Figure 1-2). The synchronized changing of the carrier frequencies used by both the sender (a high-altitude airplane) and the receiver (an active torpedo) was controlled by identical player piano rolls marked with a unique sequence of eighty-eight possible steps (the number of keys on a piano).

"I read the patent. You don't usually think of movie stars having brains, but she sure did."
—FRANKLIN ANTONIO,
QUALCOMM COFOUNDER[1]

This meant that the torpedo could be steered by sending only small portions of the entire message on each frequency. Attempts to jam the communication would typically render only one of the channels useless at a time, and the information on the other channels would be enough to enable the torpedo to make the necessary course corrections to reach the target.

What Lamarr and Antheil gave the U.S. military and the world was the concept of *frequency hopping*, which broke the conventional mold of communicating over a single frequency—the method that had been used since the inception of radio. Today's spread-spectrum communications techniques are derived from this concept of using multiple frequencies to transmit information. And even though spread-spectrum technology contains many more novel elements, Lamarr and Antheil's elegant frequency-hopping concept remains an integral component of many spread-spectrum implementations.

Unfortunately, neither Antheil nor Lamarr made any money from the ideas captured in their patent, even though it is the basis for hundreds of others that followed. Out of a sense of patriotism, both decided to donate the patent to the U.S. war effort. Few people understood the profound implications of this discovery at the time, but it marked a transformation from narrow thought and opened up the wide world of spreading communications across frequencies. Even though no one could make the device described in the patent function at the time, the U.S. military classified the patent and held the concept under tight security for decades.

MILITARY APPLICATIONS

Very little is openly known about early military experimentation with the frequency-hopping concept that Lamarr and Antheil had so brilliantly laid out in their patent. Since the patent described a mechanical means of switching frequencies, the actual implementation of a device using the parts described was nearly impossible

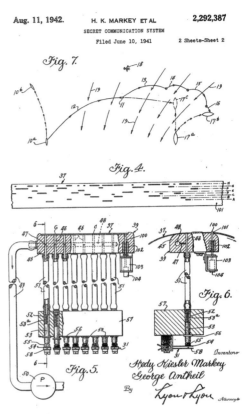

Figure 1-2

FREQUENCY HOPPING VS. SPREAD SPECTRUM

Frequency hopping was generally a sequential method, with information being transmitted on one frequency for a period of time (dwell time) and then hopping to another frequency.

Spread-spectrum techniques were developed from frequency-hopping concepts, but were more advanced. In spread-spectrum communications, information can be sent over multiple frequency channels simultaneously. Both methods use codes to make them resistant to jamming, but they use them differently. In frequency hopping, the code depicts the sequence of the hops, with the timing fixed. In spread spectrum, the code is included with each packet of information; all the frequencies are gathered in by the receiver, and then the codes are used to reassemble the information correctly. The two methods are often mixed, and there are variations of each, blurring the distinction.

because of the speed and accuracy required. Many people figured that the mechanical piano rolls could not be synchronized and switched fast enough to produce reliable communication. In addition, Antheil himself noted that the player piano mechanism described was probably a poor choice to use in pitching their concept to the high levels of the military. He figured that they had surely laughed at the notion of installing player pianos in their torpedoes. As far as anyone knows publicly, the United States was never able to frequency-hop a torpedo into a Nazi cruiser during the war.

One of the earliest known implementations of frequency hopping while it remained classified was in the mid-1950s. It involved two-way communication between aircraft and devices called sonobuoys—cylindrical devices that were dropped into the ocean by airplanes to search for enemy submarines by using sonic emitters and sensors to listen for submarines in the area. Several buoys placed in a pattern could triangulate the position of a submarine.

The Hoffman Radio Corporation was given a contract by the Navy to build the sonobuoys and the accompanying airplane radios, and the Hoffman engineers were given the Markey-Antheil patent upon which to base the design. The names of the inventors were removed from the document, and the information was given under extreme secrecy, with the U.S. Navy offering information only on a "need to know" basis. Since the patent was dated more than a decade earlier, the engineers at Hoffman figured that the advanced concept came from some brilliant engineers in the military or defense sector. Little did they know that they were exploring one of the earliest implementations of the brainchild of a beautiful actress and a creative composer.

Frequency hopping played a vital role in retrieving the data from the sonobuoys. The sonobuoy used a mechanical spool that had protrusions spaced around its circumference in a unique pattern. The protrusions activated individual switches as the spool rotated at a fixed rate, with each switch representing a different frequency. The airborne radio communicating with the sonobuoy carried an identical spool to match the frequency hopping, which took place at a rate of approximately thirty-six hops per second. To talk to multiple buoys, the plane's radio used several spools, one for each buoy, making communication with each buoy secure and undetectable.

This implementation of a mechanical device for frequency hopping was actually not far from what Antheil helped Lamarr convey in their patent using piano rolls. By today's standards, the sonobuoys used a crude and simple implementation of a complex concept, but they were sophisticated for their time, considering the challenge of synchronizing the communication. Many other engineers at Hoffman and elsewhere later went on to develop more products under military contract using frequency hopping, among them an unmanned surveillance drone that was used in the Vietnam War. This implementation in the 1960s, however, took advantage of new digital computing technologies rather than mechanical means for frequency hopping. All the while, the source of the original patent and the diagramed techniques was unknown to communications engineers. (Spread-spectrum technology was not declassified by the U.S. military until 1981.)

Over time, the development of the electronic transistor made the implementation of frequency-hopping techniques much simpler. The move from mechanical to electronic means of frequency synchronization fueled its widespread implementation. The concept of frequency hopping fit naturally with digital technologies, since the communication channel needed to change at discrete points in time. Though this was dramatically different from the conventional radio wisdom of the time, the necessity for jam-proof communications in the military drove ongoing work in spread-spectrum techniques.

It is certain that the U.S. military and its allies initiated scores of new implementations of frequency-hopping techniques in the decades following the original patent, many of them probably unknown to the public. The benefits of secure communication that also had improved immunity to noise and interference certainly made the technology a prime candidate for any new communication projects at the time. The first widespread military use of the technology that the public at large saw came in the form of covert communication between the ships forming the naval blockade during the Cuban missile crisis in 1962.

By the time the Markey-Antheil patent was on the verge of expiration in 1959, researchers around the United States were delving into all sorts of applications for frequency hopping. The Russian launch of *Sputnik I* in October of 1957 marked the beginning of the space flight era and galvanized the United States to move further into communications research. One of the organizations that had teams working on advanced communication projects was the Jet Propulsion Laboratory (JPL) in Pasadena, California. A mathematician there, Dr. Solomon W. Golomb, was working on what would eventually became the primary form of spread-spectrum communications used today. Of equal importance—at least for this story— was that Golomb had a very bright colleague on his team named Andrew Viterbi (see Figure 1-3).

Figure 1-3. Andrew Viterbi.

FRIENDS AND COLLEAGUES

After receiving his master's degree from MIT in 1957, Andrew Viterbi went to work for the Jet Propulsion Laboratory's Communications Research Section in the summer, starting out on the *Explorer I* project under director Eberhard Rechtin. He began working side by side with researchers and engineers implementing some of the first attempts at satellite telemetry—using orbiting satellites to transmit measurements, observations, and other data.

Overcoming the challenges of satellite communications impelled Viterbi to significant achievements in the development of phase-locked loops and digital modulation techniques. (Phase-locked loops were the hardware portions of a radio that tracked and locked on to a frequency that was carrying information of interest. Digital modulation encompassed a variety of techniques used to embed as much information as possible into a carrier signal, and also extract the information once it was received.) Both technologies were necessary for reliable and effective communication over great distances, and both were largely undeveloped and untested at the time. Viterbi's exposure to new digital electronics theory at JPL was to become the basis for a majority of his life's work.

> "By 1960 we were heavily into digital communications on the theoretical side and doing the first experimental work."
>
> —ANDREW VITERBI,
> QUALCOMM COFOUNDER[2]

In 1963, a year after finishing his Ph.D. work in digital communications at the University of Southern California, Viterbi became a member of the faculty at UCLA. As a professor, he was forced to broaden his horizon to include information theory, a related but separate area that he had not been formally educated in during his days at MIT and USC. Through his continued consulting work at JPL and the classes he taught on information theory, he developed a passion for this area, where coding principles played pivotal roles in reliable communication.

During Viterbi's time at JPL, he met many other researchers who were excited about the prospects of digital communications theory. Late in 1964, a visiting professor on sabbatical from MIT arrived at JPL, joining as a NASA Resident Research Fellow. This marked the beginning of a long and fruitful relationship between Viterbi and Irwin Mark Jacobs (Figure 1-4)—one that would change the world of communications forever through their cofounding of Qualcomm.

Viterbi and Jacobs had known of each other previously—they had shared an award from the National Electronics Conference for their presentations in 1963. But the time they spent together at JPL was the start of their working relationship. While both of them had been educated at MIT during the same time period, they had had different interests, and Viterbi had left for the West Coast while Jacobs stayed on the faculty of MIT. Jacobs's decision to stay was largely prompted by the groundbreaking work of one man—Claude Shannon.

THE FATHER OF MODERN COMMUNICATIONS THEORY

Claude Shannon is widely credited with some of the most profound advances in information theory. Sometimes articulated in very simple and unorthodox ways, Shannon's ideas for the most efficient methods of transferring information over any medium sparked a

Figure 1-4. Irwin Jacobs. *Courtesy Qualcomm Inc.*

new era. Being a mathematician, Shannon formulated his theories in terms that are mostly beyond comprehension by the layperson. But to those educated in engineering, the concepts that Shannon expressed in mathematical formulas were an astounding break from the traditional focus of communications. Above all, Shannon broke down many complex problems of the day into very simple parts—a skill that many people say set him apart from numerous other capable minds of the time.

Shannon's theories laid the groundwork for a new phase of exploration in communications by simplifying the approach to developing such systems. Shannon is often cited as being the one who could see the big picture in problems that faced communications engineers—the one who *could* see the forest for the trees. For instance, Shannon's strategies for finding a suitable means of coding a stream of information focused on first understanding the characteristics of the medium the information was to be transmitted through. In fact, Shannon was the first to completely characterize a variety of communication systems in measurable ways so that engineers could optimize them.

Shannon developed his information theories to take into account the secrecy, reliability, and capacity required in any communication system. Given the vital role that intelligence had played in World War II, many were interested in Shannon's theories of coding and encryption. But others were interested in using the fundamental concepts he laid out to characterize the capacity and information-carrying potential of telephone systems.

Perhaps the most important aspect of Shannon's theories was his description of information in terms of bits—simply 1's and 0's (*bits* is shorthand for *binary digits*). This binary code was the simplest way to express any content that was being communicated—whether it was a voice, a picture, or other data. His suggestion that all information could be transmitted, stored, and manipulated *digitally* launched a revolution in communications and spawned the Information Age. This era would go on to be one of the most important phases of the twentieth century, with many other great minds adapting his theories to real problems.

> "I like to find ways of understanding more intuitively what's behind the formulas."
>
> —IRWIN JACOBS,
> QUALCOMM COFOUNDER[3]

The young and bright Irwin Jacobs had originally intended to pursue studies in electromagnetics. But his exposure to Shannon's work while at MIT changed his mind. When Jacobs graduated and joined the faculty at MIT in 1959, his office was situated only a few doors down from Shannon's. Several instructors and students at the time recall that period as one of the most exciting and combustible learning environments they ever experienced. There were so many breakthrough ideas at MIT that were opening up the world of information theory that the nascent area was too attractive for Jacobs to pass up.

The mathematical models and formulas that Shannon was developing and presenting to the staff and students intrigued Jacobs. While these models and formulas were highly theoretical and complex, Shannon helped Jacobs and others see the eloquence and simplicity of his theories. After thoroughly digesting the theoretical aspects of Shannon's information theory, Jacobs joined another professor, Jack Wozencraft, to develop a senior-level course on information theory. The goal was to take the sophisticated theory and apply it to practical problems in the real world. While the course quickly became a graduate-level one, it didn't intimidate the engineering student body—students at all levels filled the seats at the seminars and classes.

Like many other MIT students and faculty, Jacobs took his passion for information theory with him when he visited other universities and events. He also went on to immortalize his work by coauthoring, with Wozencraft, *Principles of Communication Engineering* in 1965, one of the first textbooks to catapult Shannon's theories into the world of practical digital communications. Jacobs's training at MIT and his continual quest for practical applications of information theory set him up to make the transition from the world of academia and abstract mathematics to the realm of practical problem solving, working in companies that were building advanced communications equipment—creating the wireless revolution of the late twentieth century.

What earned Linkabit its reputation for excellence was not just the names on its company roster, but its tenacity and its commitment to solving some of the most complex issues facing the military and academia at the time. Jacobs brought a level of intensity to the organization that was rarely seen elsewhere. Linkabit's core team would work literally day and night on projects. One project in particular—to develop a modem for the army—had the team camping out at the facility for four days and three nights straight. Jacobs himself would work all day, then return after dinner with his four boys in tow, getting back to work with the rest of his team while the boys did their homework.

"Our first contract was with the Naval Electronics Lab in San Diego. We looked at error correcting coding and its application in naval communications."
—ANDREW VITERBI, QUALCOMM COFOUNDER[1]

Linkabit quickly excelled at applying the new science of digital information theory. One Linkabit first was a programmable modem for satellite communications. This was the first implementation of what is called time-division multiple-access (TDMA) communications, a technique that would later gain widespread popularity in mobile networks. The project involved a proof of concept for the army, which went off successfully thanks to round-the-clock work by the entire team. The modem also started what became a trend for Linkabit: The company actually built, tested, and proved out pieces of communication gear that people often told them were impossible to make. And many of the Linkabit naysayers were not just unskilled engineers or competing salespeople; their critics were sometimes regarded as the brightest minds in their respective fields. Sometimes Linkabit's own customers were the most doubtful that Jacobs and his team could actually make their revolutionary products work.

In 1971, after a year of challenges and excitement, Jacobs made the tough decision to leave the world of academia and move into the communications industry full time to organize the business. It was a decision that he never reversed or regretted. Even at this point, though, Jacobs could not imagine how fast Linkabit would grow—at an average rate of over 50 percent per year.

Linkabit continued to flourish, receiving many government and military contracts. The company quickly got involved in digital satellite communications, which had been made practical by the development of microprocessors. Andrew Viterbi's best-known legacy, the Viterbi decoder, an algorithm that reassembled an encoded signal sent through a noisy channel, was implemented in large-scale integrated circuits, which were advancing rapidly at this time. The company also eventually moved into what would become other very lucrative fields, such as developing for Home Box Office (HBO) encryption circuitry for satellite television broadcasting. The late 1970s were a time of rapid proliferation of cable and satellite television services, and an unbreakable method for subscriber security was in high demand.

After growing from three to over six hundred employees in just over ten years, Linkabit was purchased in August 1980 by M/A-COM, an East Coast conglomerate that grew out of Microwave Associates. Jacobs saw the combination of the two companies as ideal—Linkabit had the systems engineering talent, and M/A-COM built many of the components used in those systems. Dr. Larry Gould, the chairman and CEO of M/A-COM, and Jacobs saw a tremendous synergy between their businesses, and the first few years of their partnership were fruitful.

But Gould's time with M/A-COM was limited. Differences between Gould and other senior executives in the company led to a battle and to Gould's leaving the company and being replaced by new management. Jacobs soon found himself more at odds with the decisions of the new guard of senior management, who lacked the vision and direction that Jacobs had enjoyed with Gould present.

> "At that point it was clear that it [M/A-COM] wasn't going to be a very well managed company."
> —IRWIN JACOBS

Running a separate division of the larger company, Jacobs had to fight constant and tiring battles to get funding for projects that he knew would pay off. Many of these projects would need years of development—and significant up-front expenditures—before they paid back the investment. But the M/A-COM management didn't have the stomach for this level of risk in product development; it preferred more predictable product revenue streams in a much shorter time frame. Eager to finally realize commercial success from many of Linkabit's inventions over the years, Jacobs was continually rebuffed by a bureaucratic leadership.

While Jacobs's frustration with the management of M/A-COM was not unknown, his decision to leave the company caught many off guard. On the evening of April Fools Day in 1985, Jacobs walked into the facility with empty boxes. A short while later,

> "The management of M/A-COM just let go of the smartest man I had ever met. Of course I did whatever I could to stay associated with Irwin."
> —KLEIN GILHOUSEN,
> EARLY LINKABIT EMPLOYEE AND
> QUALCOMM COFOUNDER

his belongings in hand, Jacobs walked out of Linkabit for good. Martha Dennis, a Linkabit employee and a good friend, held the door open for Jacobs on his way out. He had finally had enough. The company that he had toiled for and nurtured for more than a decade, and that had grown to over 1,400 employees, was now completely out of his control.

WHAT NEXT?

Jacobs already had a track record as a highly successful entrepreneur and business owner, and he was in no hurry and had no dire need to go back to work immediately. But there was no way that a mind like Jacobs's could sit idle and just think about the tremendous technical advances that were happening without him. Not surprisingly, Andrew Viterbi felt a similar disenchantment with Linkabit and quit within a week of Jacobs.

Many other key Linkabit employees chose to leave Linkabit as well, because of their discontent with the new path that the parent company, M/A-COM, was taking. Many of the best projects that the Linkabit team had a hand in developing were being sold off to competitors before they started to see significant penetration in commercial use. The cable and home business of M/A-COM, which had developed the videocipher for HBO, was sold to General Instrument, which turned cable set-top box descramblers into a multi-hundred-million-dollar business in a matter of months. This project and others were major successes in the hands of the buyers, but M/A-COM's impatience and lack of vision killed Linkabit's chance to vindicate all its hard work and pioneering efforts.

> "When Irwin and Andy left, things definitely changed at Linkabit. It didn't have quite the same appeal. It wasn't growing."
> —MARK DANKBERG,
> LINKABIT EXECUTIVE,
> FOUNDER-PRESIDENT OF VIASAT[2]

With the fragmentation that occurred in 1985, Linkabit went down in history as having been a spawning place for much of the communications industry in San Diego. At the twenty-five-year reunion picnic for Linkabit in 1993, employees pieced together a corporate family tree for the company. At the time, four generations of companies were traced through ex-Linkabit employees and buyouts. Since the reunion, this heritage has expanded to seven generations (Table 2-1) as employees who cut their teeth under Irwin Jacobs and Andrew Viterbi fanned out into their own ventures.

A few months after leaving Linkabit, Irwin Jacobs was still pondering what he would do next. Retirement was nice, but he missed all the fun of developing cutting-edge technology with long-time friends who were practically family. He contemplated going back into academia, but during a European trip with his family, he finally decided to pick up where he left off with a new venture. Upon returning home, Jacobs rallied a tight group of Linkabit's elite to

TABLE 2-1 SEVEN GENERATIONS SPAWNED BY LINKABIT (AS OF 2003)

1st Generation	2nd Generation	3rd Generation	4th Generation	5th Generation	6th Generation	7th Generation
		Interactive Concepts 1983	WaveLogic (AZ) 1990 (R)			
		Sciteq 1984	Osicom Technologies 1996 (SO)	Sorrento Networks 1997	Torrey Pines Networks?	
		ComStream 1984	ComStream/SPAR 1992 (SO)	Radyne ComStream 1998 (SO)		RFMagic 2000
				Rockwell 1997 (SO)	Conexant Systems 1997 (I)	Entropic 2001
			Glencom (MI) 1994			
			Comsystem 1996			
			ComCore 1996	National Semiconductor 1998 (SO)	Vativ Technologies 2001	
			StarGuide 2001	Digital Generation 2001 (SO)	X-Digital Systems 2003	
		QUALCOMM 1985	Boatracs 1990 (T)	ARCOMS 1995 (M)		
			Solana Tech Dev 1995	Verance 1999 (M)		
			NextWave Telecom 1995	Control Point 1997 (RIP 2000)		
			Dot Wireless 1997	Texas Instruments 2000 (SO)		

1st Generation	2nd Generation	3rd Generation	4th Generation	5th Generation	6th Generation	7th Generation
			NeoPoint 1997–2002			
			DriveCam Video Systems 1998			
			Leap Wireless 1998 (SP)			
			Ericsson 1999 (SO)			
			Mobilian 1999			
			Kyocera Wireless 2000 (SO)			
			Axesstel 2000 (E)			
			Actona (Israel) 2000			
		General Instrument VideoCipher 1986 (SO)	Cornerstone 1986			
			MCSI 1989			
			Tiernan 1989	Tourmaline Networks 2000		
				Radyne ComStream 2001 (SO)		
				La Jolla Networks 2002		
Linkabit 1968	M/A-COM Linkabit 1980 (SO)					

(continued)

1st Generation	2nd Generation	3rd Generation	4th Generation	5th Generation	6th Generation	7th Generation
		ViaSat 1986	TrellisWare 2000 (SP)			
		MultiSpectra 1986–1991	TurboNet 1996	Correlant 1999 (R)		
		PCSI 1986	Cirrus Logic 1993 (SO)	Nuera 1996 (SP)	NetSapiens 2003	
				ADC Wireless 1996 (SO)		
				Rockwell Semiconductor 1997 (SO)		
				RC Networks 1997	Viadux 2002 (R)	
				Istari Design 1997	Conexant Systems 1999 (SO)	
				Ensemble 1997		
				Silicon Wave 1997		
				Analog Circuit 1998	innoCOMM 2000 (R)	National Semi-conductor '00 (SO)
						Staccato 2002
		Hughes Network Systems 1987 (SO)	Uniden 1994	WIDCOMM 1998		

1st Generation	2nd Generation	3rd Generation	4th Generation	5th Generation	6th Generation	7th Generation
			Commsolutions 1994	LSI Logic 1996 (SO)	VIA Telecom 2002 (M)	
		Indra Technology 1987				
		Linkcom (Israel) 1988				
		Titan Linkbit 1990 (SO)	Quality Systems Integrated 1994	CenterComm 1997		
			Tachyon 1997	Stracon		
			Lockheed 2003 (SO)			
		Primary Access 1989	3Com 1995 (SO)	Copper Mountain Networks 1996	Figure 8 Wireless 2001	
				AirFiber 1998		
		Milpower 1989				
		Orckit (Israel) 1990				
		Torrey Science 1990	Welkins Systems 1998	E-Monitoring Networks 1998 (R)		
		Commquest 1991	IBM/Commquest 1998 (SO)	Triton Net Sys 2000 (SO)	CarrierComm 2002 (SO)	

(continued)

1st Generation	2nd Generation	3rd Generation	4th Generation	5th Generation	6th Generation	7th Generation
		ComFocus 1991	Magis Networks 1999	Ellipsis Digital Systems 2000 Tahoe RF Semiconductor 2003		
		VideoFreedom 1993				
		Alantro 1997	Texas Instruments 2000 (SO)			
		Nomadix 1998	PacketAir Networks 2000 (SP)			
		Path 1 Network Technologies 1998				

Legend:

(SO) = Sold To
(R) = Renamed
(SP) = Spinoff
(I) = IPO
(E) = Equity—major share by Linkabit successor
(T) = Technology derived from Linkabit successor
(M) = Merger with

Source: Martha Dennis and Doug Ramsey

pitch the idea of a new company. The small group met in Jacobs's San Diego home to hear Jacobs's vision for a new company that would be what Linkabit should have become. Acknowledging that M/A-COM had fumbled projects with vast potential, Jacobs vowed to apply the best innovators to many of the same areas they had already recognized as major opportunities, plus a few new ones that he saw on the horizon.

In July 1985, Qualcomm was born. After the initial meeting in Jacobs's home (which Viterbi actually missed, as he was on a European cruise), a team of seven people decided to commit to Jacobs's vision: Jacobs himself, Andrew Viterbi, Adelia Coffman, Harvey White, Andrew Cohen, Klein Gilhousen, and Franklin Antonio. These seven were to become known as the original founders of Qualcomm.

FOCUS ON THE TECHNOLOGY

Qualcomm's founding was unique in many ways. The company basically hit the ground running upon its formation. Since all the people involved knew one another intimately and had worked side by side late into the night for years, there were very few elements of a start-up evident at the new company. Much of the focus and many of the projects that had been active within Linkabit at the time were in areas that Qualcomm was targeting as well, so it was almost as if the team had never left. What effectively transpired was that the cloud of conservative and misguided management was lifted from an exceptional team of innovators.

> "We didn't have a particular product in mind."
> —IRWIN JACOBS ON THE FOUNDING OF QUALCOMM

M/A-COM's continued perception that the Linkabit division was of limited value allowed Qualcomm to progress in these areas uninhibited by the threat of noncompetition litigation. M/A-COM simply had little interest in Jacobs's ideas and felt that his pursuing those ideas elsewhere posed no threat. This contrasts sharply with today's business environment, in which even a somewhat liberal management would be much more protective of its intellectual property and product lines if a large portion of its development team were to leave to start a competing venture. Fortunately for Jacobs, Viterbi, and the other ex-Linkabit

> "All the founders were familiar with each other and the type of projects, so Qualcomm really hit the ground running."
> —RICH KERR, EX-LINKABIT, QUALCOMM EMPLOYEE

employees, much of their experience at Linkabit could be used as a basis for the new company.

Many of the founders and early Qualcomm employees were personal friends as well—their families spent time together, and play often mixed with work. Impromptu social gatherings were common, both inside and outside the office. The technical geniuses that made up Qualcomm were certainly not the reclusive, antisocial nerds characteristic of other high-tech companies. These innovators thoroughly enjoyed their work; but they also enjoyed each other. Friendship and interaction did not have to be forced—they already existed.

> "Linkabit's DNA runs through this community like crazy. They created a culture of innovation."
> —JOHN CHIER,
> KYOCERA WIRELESS[3]

Of course the workplace interactions were not always pleasant, for, as the saying goes, familiarity breeds contempt. Because of their diverse and gifted minds, the engineers within Qualcomm had their share of differences. The predominantly male technical staff didn't harbor much personal resentment over differences of opinion, though, so most disagreements could be worked out and overcome. Fortunately, the egos had their limits.

> "We used to fight like brothers—we could disagree passionately one day and then come right back to work the next. There was just an amazing synergy there."
> —RICH KERR

Besides the embedded camaraderie, the other benefit that Qualcomm had from its founding was its Linkabit heritage and the names of its founders, particularly Jacobs and Viterbi. Both were well known inside and outside the San Diego area as the top minds in the area of advanced communications. Their reputations were golden: Jacobs as a pragmatic visionary who could bring great ideas to fruition; Viterbi for his deep intellect and cutting-edge theories. The rest of the core team was on the same level, with talents and abilities focused in different areas: Klein Gilhousen, Steve Morley, Roberto Padovani, Harvey White, Franklin Antonio, Chuck Wheatley, Butch Weaver, and dozens of others made up an all-star team.

The reputations of the core innovators at Qualcomm opened many doors to government contracts and satellite communications projects. More than half of the company's business was originally derived from government contracts, and the team was constantly filling out proposals for all the military and space projects in the southern California region. As a result of its Linkabit roots, Qualcomm had a technically superior team of distinguished researchers with tight ties to academia and the defense world.

Leveraging Partnerships

Within weeks of Qualcomm's founding in July 1985, Jacobs and his team were sought out by Allen Salmasi, CEO of Omninet Corporation, who had known the team previously at Linkabit. Salmasi and members of the Nazarian family had founded Omninet in 1984, after they fled from Iran, to develop satellite messaging for the trucking industry. A talented and insightful entrepreneur who was bent on commercializing satellite communications, Salmasi wanted to use satellite links to determine the location of long-haul trucks and enable communication with the truckers, which he knew would be a valuable service to the industry. After listening to Salmasi's idea, Jacobs saw a great opportunity in the proposed product and bid for the contract to develop it.

Omninet awarded Qualcomm a $250,000 initial contract to help design and implement the satellite messaging system, basically building the ground-based modem to carry out the communications. The contract was a big win for Qualcomm at the time, as the company had mostly been sifting through an assortment of smaller government contracts. Salmasi knew that Jacobs and his team had the technical talent needed to make his vision a reality, and he worked closely with Jacobs on the project. The partnership was based upon Qualcomm's developing the product and operating the messaging center while Omninet handled the marketing and sales end of the business.

The initial system design called for one-way communication from the dispatch center to the mobile trucks via satellite links. After several months of development, prototypes of the system were completed and functioned well. But as Salmasi marketed the product, he found that many customers were not interested in a one-way-only system. Several potential customers told him that the service had to be two-way to even be considered. Another company, Geostar, had a one-way system with a reverse link, from the truck back to the dispatch center; but Geostar fell into financial trouble, so Salmasi's initial idea of partnering with it to create a two-way service didn't pan out.

Qualcomm and Omninet then had to develop their own two-way solution. Developing a two-way satellite mobile system was quite a task for the team to take on, because many technical hurdles had to be overcome in order to achieve reliability. Outside the military, nothing quite like a reliable two-way satellite-based mobile system yet existed. Salmasi and Jacobs talked about the ramifications at length, and finally committed additional funding to the project. Salmasi provided the resources, and Jacobs committed his team's technical talent to get it done. Once Jacobs said go, the Qualcomm engineers went into overdrive.

So, in the middle of 1987 Jacobs gathered the members of the project team together for an all-day working meeting, from morning until dusk. Once they understood the challenges ahead of them, they organized and assigned work on all the outstanding issues, then rolled up their sleeves. By the end of the day, every major impediment had been addressed. It is estimated that more than twenty patent applications were born out of this remarkable meeting alone, with more than a dozen of them eventually granted. The team had to work fast, as Jacobs figured that he needed a working prototype in just a few months.

The seasoned ex-Linkabit staff came together under the Qualcomm name to produce technical breakthroughs at a rapid pace. The team turned problems upside down and inside out, kicking their brains' right sides into overdrive. One of the most creative solutions for the prototype involved the tracking antenna—a cheap and effective two-way antenna that was mounted on the truck. The antenna had a portion that moved to track the satellite, while the electronics and other components stayed fixed. The antenna worked surprisingly well, was easily manufactured and installed, and cost much less than expected.

REMOVING OBSTACLES

By 1988, what was soon to become the OmniTRACS product line was starting to come together. The staff at Qualcomm had prototyped and tested their two-way system, and the team knew that they were on to something big. They geared up for manufacturing the product by leasing additional space in a separate building in San Diego and began to look at expanding their team to handle the product flow.

But further complications arose that tested the flexibility and commitment of Omninet and Qualcomm. Salmasi and Jacobs increasingly found that trucking customers were not eager to commit to purchasing their product. Since much of the trucking industry was unaware of the advantages of tracking and communications on the road, the new product's benefits had to be explained over and over again. Even beyond this, the whole system seemed too complicated, because once a trucking firm bought the product, it had to run the service and receive support from somewhere else.

The Qualcomm team realized that they couldn't just sell a product; they had to sell a complete solution that included a dedicated dispatch and servicing center, with built-in redundancy for reliability of services to the customers' fleets. The whole system had to be sold as a package so that truckers and dispatchers could easily adopt the advanced service and realize its benefits. To provide this, Qualcomm made plans to staff a network operations center in San Diego to handle all services for the customers around the clock. The concept of packaging the product and the service together was well received by potential customers, but then internal issues appeared that complicated things further.

At this critical point, funds began to dry up. Qualcomm and Omninet had been developing their product for years now, spending millions along the way, but they still had no revenue to show for it. Jacobs knew that they had only to get the product launched for it to be successful, but additional financial support was necessary. In additional, their prospective customers (those who were actively involved in trials with prototypes) were increasingly asking for customized products. Negotiating product options often got cumbersome, and the three-way negotiations among the companies made customers uneasy about who was running the show.

Just as with several products at Linkabit, Jacobs felt that he had a winner if it could only live to see commercial availability—and Salmasi agreed. So late in the summer of 1988, Jacobs and Salmasi crafted a plan to merge Omninet and Qualcomm. The merger would recapitalize the com-

> "Each time we negotiated with customers, it had to be a three-way discussion. It took two or three times the energy and resources to make changes, which made the process very inefficient."
> —Allen Salmasi, Omninet founder, former Qualcomm VP, now CEO of Nextwave

pany through an offering of preferred shares at $5 each. By August, Jacobs and Salmasi were able to gather funding from several sources—mostly friends and family, as well as some of their own funds—to establish the new company. The preferred offering sold 713,000 shares, raising over $3.5 million to help bring OmniTRACS production online. Omninet and its affiliated shareholders ended up with roughly a one-half ownership in the new company, which bore the Qualcomm name.

Some employees and others associated with the company saw the merger as a desperate move by Jacobs that gave away Qualcomm to Omninet and others when he didn't have to. Since Qualcomm had contracted with Omninet, some thought that Jacobs should have just shut OmniTRACS down when the funds to develop it dried up and moved on to the next project. But Jacobs saw too much opportunity to pass up the chance. He believed that even a deal that seemed too expensive at the time would work out when the product reached a commercial stage. It was a huge gamble by a man with a lucid vision of the future.

A New Qualcomm Takes Shape

With the new company and its funding in place, and Jacobs at its head, creditors now backed Qualcomm's large equipment purchases for its manufacturing facilities. Jacobs's reputation went a long way in San Diego, and he was able to garner additional support from bankers, investors, and even potential customers. The company expanded its space in what is now Building A from roughly 25,000 square feet to over 60,000 square feet in the back part of the building—a portion it had been given first right of refusal on in the original lease. Jacobs had bet big, hoping that it would all pay off. And it seemed that he was right.

> "It did require money to finish the [OmniTRACS] development, to lease the satellite space, for marketing and sales efforts, and to get ready for manufacturing."
>
> —IRWIN JACOBS

In October 1988, Jacobs had cemented the first big contract for OmniTRACS with Don Schneider of Schneider National, one of the largest trucking fleets in the United States at the time. The deal would provide Qualcomm with sorely needed cash flow from product sales. On top of this, the recurring revenue from providing service through the operations center would be a steady source of income. The manufacturing line started buzzing, and OmniTRACS units went flying out the door. The dream had become reality, and many in the company were struggling just to keep up with the demand.

Of course, not everything went perfectly with the product launch. Since the Qualcomm team had worked in the development mode for so long, supporting products that were out in the field tested their flexibility. Major field demos were needed for customers, and a growing staff at Qualcomm had to get up to speed fast. An early test of everyone's mettle occurred when thousands of OmniTRACS units already installed in the field were found to be flawed: There was a low-level software bug that had to be corrected in all the field units. In a rush to correct the problem, essentially every employee in the company was given a plane ticket to a different destination around the country, with training and instruction on how to remove and replace a memory chip in these flawed OmniTRACS units.

But by and large the OmniTRACS product and the accompanying service was a huge success. The cash flow coming into the company did not make it immediately profitable, but it was able to support, refine, and grow the business until it eventually did achieve healthy margins. The Schneider deal, accounting for a full 50 percent of Qualcomm's revenue of $32 million in 1989, opened the doors for many more customers to follow. OmniTRACS went on to be a highly successful, long-term product for the company, generating product proceeds and substantial recurring service revenue.

Qualcomm had graduated to commercial delivery of a highly desirable two-way satellite communication system, and Irwin Jacobs was finally seeing the fruits from the talented team he had assembled over the years. But this success left Jacobs with a problem, the kind he liked having. A manufacturing line was no place for a skilled team of Ph.D.s to apply their talents. There were even bigger opportunities out there that beckoned for Qualcomm.

CHAPTER 3

Start of the Cellular Boom

--→

The Need for New Commercial Applications, 1980s

Linkabit had grown at such an astounding rate because Jacobs, Viterbi, and the rest of the engineering staff never stayed in one place for very long. Even while actively working on several projects, they were always eyeing other markets that were potentially bigger. At Qualcomm, they behaved no differently. Having founded the new company with no specific product or purpose in mind, Jacobs maintained a very open and fluid environment at Qualcomm. If an engineer came up with an idea for a novel application in communications, he could start working on it immediately—after hours when his normal work was done.

Ideas flowed constantly. No idea was shunned because of a different focus somewhere else within the company. There were plenty of applications sitting on the corporate back burner, and many of the core staff at Qualcomm continued to explore these ideas on their own time. Because most of the early company members were good friends, practically family, their work and pleasure lives often mixed. Problems that were mulled over at dinner or at social events were picked up and expanded upon the next morning.

This opportunistic approach to innovation kept Jacobs coming back several times to one area in particular—mobile voice communications systems. Though they had spent most of their early careers developing military communication systems, the engineers at Qualcomm had always kept abreast of the research and developments in the related commercial sectors, such as satellite telephony, wireless local loop (using wireless instead of landlines to connect houses to a public switched telephone network), and cellular telephony.

> "Irwin always maintained a research-style atmosphere at Qualcomm. He really encouraged people to fly ideas off the wall."
>
> —RICH KERR, EX-LINKABIT, QUALCOMM EMPLOYEE

In fact, within weeks after Qualcomm's founding in 1985, the team of seven had been contracted by Hughes Aircraft to review a proposal for a mobile satellite communication system. The FCC had ambitions to license a new commercial global communication service supported by satellites and had put out a request for system design proposals. Hughes, along with eleven other companies, had submitted proposals to the FCC; and Hughes wanted the opinion of the brightest minds in communications on ways to improve its design.

After looking at the system, Qualcomm suggested using spread spectrum as the basis for communication and showed how this technique—properly implemented using code-division methods—could boost the capacity of the system tremendously. Initially, Hughes balked at the idea, believing, as many others did at the time, that forms of spread spectrum could not be efficiently used in mobile environments. But after much discussion, Hughes agreed to fund Qualcomm's research and simulation tests based on spread spectrum—the principles of which Jacobs and his team were familiar with from their work on military contracts and OmniTRACS, and which in turn could be traced back to the brilliant early insights of actress Hedy Lamarr.

But the FCC continued to drag its feet on a decision about the implementation of a mobile satellite communication system. After reviewing twelve different proposals, the FCC actually recommended that the individual contributors form a joint venture to develop a single system. This greatly slowed down the process and reduced the incentive for Hughes and others to stay involved with the project. The option of implementing such a system on its own was seen as a tremendous undertaking, and it would face many regulatory and economic unknowns as well.

Qualcomm's tests of the concept worked well and proved that a system based on spread spectrum was feasible, but this did not overcome the numerous impediments to making the project successful that Hughes saw. After the initial feasibility and simulation tests, the idea died on the table as Hughes shelved the effort.

> "We were also very opportunistic. We kept our eye out for possible opportunities—not areas of little bits of change—but some places where we would be quite innovative. Something that would make a major change. Something that perhaps if we brought it to the market quickly enough would be a significantly sized market."
> —IRWIN JACOBS, QUALCOMM COFOUNDER

However, after successfully commercializing its OmniTRACS product, Qualcomm returned to the idea of using spread-spectrum techniques in a mobile environment. This time, however, it wouldn't be done with satellites. When Jacobs and Gilhousen were driving back to San Diego from a meeting with Hughes, the idea dawned on them that the same spread-spectrum techniques used in the satellite test project could be applied in a terrestrial mobile network. There were some issues to be overcome in this application, but it seemed feasible and a good problem to address. Now, nearly three years after founding Qualcomm, with cash flow from products coming into

> "Irwin's attitude was to just throw out a bunch of little projects and see where some go."
> —ED TIEDEMANN,
> SENIOR VP OF ENGINEERING,
> QUALCOMM

the business, Jacobs wanted to reopen the idea. There were many nascent markets in mobile communications—but the most promising opportunity was in the booming cellular industry.

GETTING TO THE POTENTIAL OF CELLULAR

Since their days at Linkabit, when they had actually developed an early-model mobile phone, Jacobs and the other Qualcomm founders had been watching the maturing cellular industry closely. The major telecommunications companies in the United States had been working with the FCC for decades to open up new forms of terrestrial mobile service, and the 1980s were a period of rapid growth for the newly deployed cellular networks. Qualcomm had noted that cellular networks held significant potential and promised a great future.

The cellular concept was first developed at Bell Labs in the late 1940s. Cellular communications was 180 degrees opposed to the conventional wisdom in wireless communication at the time. In a cellular system, mobile units transmitted signals at a very low power level, precisely so that they would not travel very far (signal strength diminished rapidly with distance). This meant that a person talking on a frequency channel would not be blasting her conversation over an entire city, but just within a small area. However, this necessitated erecting many more receiving towers around the city to maintain calls, making the system much more costly and complicated.

Cellular networks weren't commercially deployed in the United States until 1983, five years before Jacobs and his team turned significant attention to this market. But that cellular launch had come after decades of work—not just because the technology was difficult, but because the entire process of coordinating and regulating the commercial services had dragged on for years. Much of the delay was attributed to government regulation and the dynamics of trying to limit AT&T's monopoly in the communications industry.

With cellular networks locked in a perpetual limbo, up until the 1980s mobile communications in the United States were limited to an inherently inefficient noncellular system called the mobile telephone system (MTS). These early attempts at noncellular mobile communications via wireless, starting in 1945, suffered from severely limited capacity in any given area, as the early MTS, and even an improved version (IMTS) that followed, was built on a broadcasting paradigm, in which only a few sources of information could speak at once.

Contrary to the cellular concept, in these early mobile telephone systems, units transmitted their signals at very high power levels on separate frequency channels to avoid interfering with each other. These high-powered transmissions traveled for miles, allowing a person to roam over quite an impressive area. But the problem was that the caller's frequency channel was reserved over that entire area, preventing anyone else from using the same channel. Many of these systems, therefore, could support only a handful of callers in a major city at any one time. By contrast, the wired landline telephone networks at the time could support hundreds of thousands of simultaneous calls.

Cellular systems promised a huge boost in the capacity of mobile wireless by allowing callers to reuse frequency channels as long as they were far enough apart. Thousands of callers, rather than just a few, could then be supported in relatively small areas. For networks in the United States, a cellular standard called AMPS (advanced mobile phone system) was developed and put into use across all the then-deployed networks, starting in 1983 (see Table 3-1). While AMPS networks had many of the same characteristics as older broadcasting methods—such as using analog signals with no satellite support—the low-power cellular architecture gave them a tremendous boost in capacity. This network architecture finally mimicked the wired telephone network in its ability to support multiple access (simultaneous connections for numerous users), so it's no surprise that serious proliferation of cellular wireless services ensued.

BOOM TIMES FOR THE NEW CELLULAR

While Jacobs was meeting with the Qualcomm founders in his home in the spring of 1985, the wireless industry was already tasting the first real fruits of cellular success. The capacity of cellular networks was orders of magnitude above anything that had previously been deployed, opening the floodgates for all the professionals on waiting lists who were hoping to get a phone in their car.

But even with this great advance in capacity and the benefit of mobility, cellular networks were unable to keep up with the almost unreal level of consumer demand. When AMPS networks went into commercial service in 1983, no one knew quite how successful cellular mobile telephony would be in the United States. At first, the price of equipment and service was exorbitant, the hardware was bulky, and call quality was horrid compared to landlines—but people kept signing up in droves. A typical cellular phone cost more than $3,000 in 1983

TABLE 3-1   ON THE ROAD TO MODERN CELLULAR

Technology	Year Launched in United States	Mobile	Cellular	Uses Satellite	Uses Base Transceiver Station (BTS)	Analog/Digital	Transmission Method (TDMA/FDMA/CDMA)
MTS (mobile telephone system)	1945	Yes	No	No	Yes	Analog	FDMA
Military applications at Linkabit	1970s	Some	No	Some	Yes	Both	All
AMPS (advanced mobile phone system or 1G)	1983	Yes	Yes	No	Yes	Analog	FDMA
OmniTRACS	1988	Yes	No	Yes	No	Both	CDMA
2G	1992	Yes	Yes	No	Yes	Digital	TDMA/CDMA
3G	2000	Yes	Yes	No	Yes	Digital	CDMA

(Motorola's "brick phone" retailed for $3,995). As networks began expanding at a rapid clip, equipment volume soared, bringing costs down rapidly: The price of a cellular phone dropped to less than $1,000 in only a few years. AT&T's optimistic 1982 projection of nearly one million cellular users by the year 2000 quickly looked like a colossal understatement. By 1985, there were more than 200,000 subscribers to AMPS services in the United States; by 1988, there were 1.5 million. (And there were over 160 million mobile subscribers in the United States by the end of June 2004!)

The dramatic drop in the cost of mobile cellular phones throughout the 1980s was also due to the advancement of integrated circuits and related technologies. When the first U.S. cellular network went into commercial operation in Chicago in 1983, Intel was already developing its 80386 processor, just a year after the successful launch of its 80286 processor: The circuit density on the newer chip more than doubled, from 120,000 to 275,000 transistors. The performance of succeeding designs scaled rapidly as well, with clock rates and memory capabilities also growing dramatically.

"Analog cellular systems were reaching capacity much sooner than forecasted."

—SCOTT GOLDMAN,
FORMER CEO OF THE WAP
(WIRELESS APPLICATION
PROTOCOL) FORUM

During this period, the computer industry was in full swing and booming. Throughout the 1980s, as companies invested billions in integrated circuit technology, the nascent cellular industry was quietly piggybacking on the rapid development of more powerful integrated circuits. As foundries for the manufacture of complex integrated circuits went up, prices went down. Advances in semiconductors were bringing cellular communication, once a product and service only for the super rich, closer and closer to the common man.

But there continued to be a technology disconnect between cellular communications and the booming computer industry—cellular systems still sent information in analog format, not digitally as their computer counterparts did. While cellular equipment utilized some of the benefits of advanced digital circuits, it was still living in the past, sending and receiving analog signals the very same way a broadcast had been sent fifty years earlier. Stuck in an outdated paradigm, analog cellular systems could not enjoy the full promise of digital communications.

THE ANALOG BROADCASTING MODEL

As the name implies, broadcasting systems spew their radio information as far and wide as possible. That's the whole idea: to maximize the number of listeners. But privacy and broadcasting remained an oxymoron: One naturally canceled out the other. Unfortunately, the method used to broadcast information from a single source to millions of destinations was carried over into the first mobile telephony systems and used to link up thousands of sources with an equal number of separate destinations. Mobile radios in early personal communication systems—where security and privacy were issues—awkwardly followed this broadcast model. To combat the problem of too many people wanting to communicate at the same time, multiple frequency channels were assigned over a range of frequencies for people to use privately. As we'll see in Part 2, this paradigm proved more and more troublesome as personal communication services grew in popularity and the airwaves quickly became overcrowded.

In the first cellular networks employing AMPS, the fundamental technique used to transmit a person's voice through the air was called frequency-division multiple access (FDMA). This method evolved directly from the earlier MTS (mobile telephone systems) networks, which in turn copied the broadcasting technique of separating transmitted information by frequency. In broadcasting, a show or song transmitted by one station is carried by a strong signal of a known, fixed frequency. This carrier frequency does just what its name implies—it carries information. Another station that wants to air a different music program or show in the same area at the same time has to use a different carrier frequency. Listeners then tune their radios to the correct carrier frequency to extract the audio information sent by each broadcasting system. Early radios had dials that coarsely altered the receiver circuitry as they were turned; modern radios have more intelligent tuners that can lock on to broadcasts automatically.

The concept for the mobile telephone system that was introduced commercially in 1946 was not that far from the broadcasting paradigm. Basically, a downsized radio tower was placed inside an automobile, and then two radio stations talked to each other through high-powered broadcasts. The receiving circuitry was leveraged from the extensive development of the radios that millions of Americans already had in their homes. The techniques for tuning in to a carrier frequency for information were well understood, and components for radios were readily available, making them relatively inexpensive.

The first cellular networks of the 1980s adopted this fundamental concept of separating information based upon carrier frequencies (also referred to as frequency channels). While the idea of using low-power signals over much shorter distances was new, the carrier signal technique was a carryover from the past. In a mobile communications network, the conversations had to be separated somehow, and no other technique was yet deemed feasible: Frequency division was well understood, and the electronics used in this method were sophisticated and cheap. This traditional radio design architecture was firmly entrenched because of the sheer amount of time it had been in existence.

Thus the AMPS protocol used for the first cellular phones was largely frequency-based wireless. When a mobile user dialed a number to make a call, the phone signaled a local tower, called a base transceiver station (BTS), to set up a specific carrier frequency for the call. Once the BTS assigned two frequency channels (one to send information and one to receive it), a dedicated line was opened up to carry the two-way conversation. If the call was going to another cellular phone, then the local BTS nearest that mobile user would set up appropriate channels for that phone as well. The frequency channels used by the two mobile phones didn't have to be the same—they just had to be different from the signals used for the rest of the calls being made in each location (see Figure 3-1). While a lot more associated technology is necessary to support mobile calls, this radio access method was the most important piece in determining the overall capacity of a network for handling multiple callers simultaneously in any given physical space.

In a scenario in which multiple users wanted to hold different conversations in the same locality, the local BTS in the cellular system would manage each of the conversations on a different pair of channels. Once all the channels in a local area or cell had been allocated, new users were blocked from calling. Also, users that moved out of range of the closest BTS had to have their call handed off to another BTS. The AMPS networks passed mobile users from channels in one cell to channels in another cell through this handoff process. In this manner, callers could stay connected for as long as they

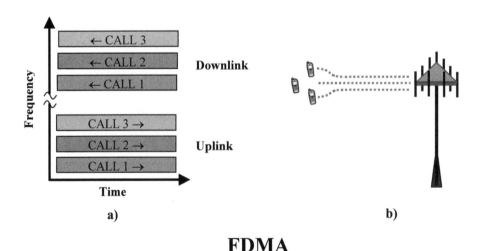

Figure 3-1: Frequency Division Multiple Access a) logically and b) pictorially

wanted while they were driving around—as long as the system wasn't fully loaded to capacity; if it was, the call could be dropped.

And as more and more people in the mid-1980s discarded their pagers in favor of cellular phones, the capacity of the networks once again became the Achilles heel of the whole system. The cellular structure of a network was originally a godsend for capacity, but now the limiting factor was the number of frequency channels available in any area. With the realization that significant amounts of additional spectrum would not be forthcoming anytime soon, network operators were literally begging their suppliers for a solution to the problem.

FACING CAPACITY ISSUES

More and more people were paying top dollar for wireless phones and services, but the network operators were finding it more and more difficult—and much more expensive—to maintain and grow their networks. The networks, especially those in dense urban areas, were strained beyond their limits, and operators struggled to expand them to keep up with demand. Once a particular area in a network became overloaded with too many subscribers, the network operator either dropped excess calls or invested money and equipment in expanding the capacity in that area. To increase capacity in an area of the network, the operator had to increase the capacity of the affected tower (called sectoring a cell), which was complex and costly, or install a completely new tower, an even more costly alternative.

Sectoring a cell involved installing more equipment on existing towers, a process that required many man-hours. But installing a new tower took even more time and was less predictable, because leasing land in the proper location could face major hurdles in many cities. Sometimes network operators needed a very specific location for a tower, but the landowner had no interest in seeing a large pole erected on his or her property. And even if an operator obtained suitable lease terms, the local municipality also had to approve the erection of a new tower. Then and only then could the network engineers go to work reconfiguring the network to accommodate the new tower site.

As more and more capacity limits were reached, this expansion process became a major headache and cost for the network operators. An easy way around all this work would be to simply open up more spectrum for additional call capacity—but this was much easier said than done. It was years before the industry could convince the FCC to open up any additional spectrum for the operators to use in dealing with capacity problems. This was finally done in 1989, with another 10 MHz being added on top of the then-current bandwidth of 40 MHz, but the allocation was not enough to stave off over-loading in the networks.

Another reason that demand continually outstripped supply in cellular networks was that the frequency channels (carrier frequencies) assigned to individual conversations were limited to single users. The voice information embedded in the carrier wave was still sent in analog format, so it could not be condensed, reduced, or otherwise limited in its size to make room for more users. This essentially meant that operators had little opportunity to squeeze more calls into the same band of frequencies allocated to them.

The disconnect between analog cellular and digital computer technologies had become starkly apparent. Cellular networks were stuck in an analog past, whereas computers were capitalizing on the digital future. Digital technologies used sophisticated computer algorithms to compress information into less space. Computer manufacturers were doubling the capabilities and capacity of their systems every eighteen months, whereas cellular networks could foresee no such gains in the immediate future. At best, they could project only modest improvements in capacity through changes in mobile phones and networks that would take much longer to implement. In contrast, wired communication methods between computers were quickly adopting digital coding and compression techniques to send massive amounts of information over thin wires.

Many in the cellular industry quickly realized that the incremental steps they were taking to tweak their analog networks to improve capacity would grant them only a temporary reprieve. What's worse, operators had still only scratched the surface in terms of consumer penetration: The wireless networks around the nation—especially in major cities like New York and Los Angeles—were to be flooded with new subscribers in the years ahead. Network operators needed a new technology that would give them several times the current subscriber capacity, plus new features. Additional spectrum and tricks with the current frequency-based wireless cellular technology were not enough to solve the problem. Something more radical, more digital, was needed.

And at that time, there were few people who knew more about digital communications than Irwin Jacobs, Andrew Viterbi, and the rest of the Qualcomm team.

CHAPTER 4

Cellular Goes Digital

—·——▶

Second-Generation Stirrings, Late 1980s

Qualcomm's roots went deep into digital communications. At Linkabit, the military contracts, satellite systems, and video scramblers that Jacobs and his team of engineers had worked on had pushed the boundaries of using digital schemes to encode and decode communications. Much of their practical work evolved from the theories of Claude Shannon, where the lowest level or piece of information was described as a bit—the core element of a digital system. These bits were now being handled at astounding rates of efficiency in ever more advanced microprocessors and digital communications chips.

As the analog cellular systems were quickly filling to capacity, device manufacturers were looking for the optimum way to overlay them with a digital replacement. With the advances in digital semiconductors and the parallel drop in prices, it was only a matter of time before analog methods would be regarded as archaic. Throughout the 1980s, the major providers of cellular equipment—AT&T, Ericsson, OKI Electric, and others—were developing equipment for cellular networks that took advantage of digital technology to expand capacity. They looked at several alternative methods of encoding voice information to take advantage of digital compression and to find the best way to make full use of the assigned frequency channels.

Since the analog cellular networks of that period were growing at breakneck speed, most of the early efforts at digital communication techniques built upon the current structure of these systems. Operators had to continue to support current analog users, and there was a great incentive to develop a technology that easily fit into the current wireless networks, at as little cost as possible. Because the spectrum that was used to send signals was fixed and regulated by the U.S. government, there was little flexibility to make changes in the frequency band used or the overall size of the band. The engineers had to figure out novel ways to squeeze more into what they already had.

This need for an evolutionary step into the world of digital communications led to the application of what is called time-division multiple-access (TDMA) technology to cellular networks. In time-based wireless communications, so-

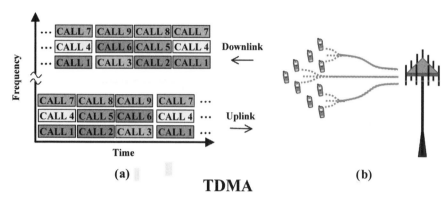

TDMA

Figure 4-1: Time Division Multiple Access (a) logically and (b) pictorially

phisticated electronics are used to include multiple separate conversations on a single frequency channel by separating them in time (see Figure 4-1). In a standard implementation, three callers could share a channel simultaneously because the circuits could switch small portions of their conversations into the channel at a very rapid rate. The receiving unit could then separate the three callers again at the other end, using the same method in reverse.

Digital coding is what enables TDMA to compress three conversations into one channel. Analog signals cannot be compressed directly, but if an analog signal is first converted to digital format, it can be compressed, and several signals can then be squeezed into the original space. This process of voice coding took place in a digital circuit called a vocoder. Advanced algorithms in time-based vocoders compressed the voice information from separate calls and fit them into separate time slots in what had previously been a single channel dedicated to one call. These digital systems could theoretically boost cellular network capacities by several times—something that was more than just mildly enticing to network operators.

Of course, Irwin Jacobs and the top minds at Linkabit (and then at Qualcomm) were intimately familiar with TDMA methods for communication. Linkabit had developed one of the first time-based modems for satellite communications and had used these techniques for many of its military contracts in the 1970s. It had also worked under a contract with International Mobile Machines (IMM) to develop an early time-based wireless telephone. But a time-based method was not the only way to do digital com-

> "Once we completed that contract, then it was possible to switch our attention over to CDMA."
>
> —IRWIN JACOBS,
> QUALCOMM COFOUNDER AND CEO[1]

munications, even though it offered the most promise early on. Further capacity gains in digital communications could be achieved by using more advanced methods of coding the voice, and Qualcomm had a few ideas up its sleeve there as well.

With a sizable staff now employed at Qualcomm to handle the production of OmniTRACS systems, Qualcomm's core engineering team was eager to take on the problem of applying efficient digital communication techniques to the cellular conundrum. Like a few others in the cellular industry, they believed that time-based wireless would quickly reach its limits in the booming cellular market, thereby making it an unacceptable alternative. They were considering something much more radical—something that capitalized on their digital coding experience with the Hughes project to get the most out of the spectrum assigned by regulatory bodies such as the FCC. Their suggestion for mobile networks, termed code-division multiple access (CDMA), was a true spread-spectrum technique that was a complete departure from other methods being considered for cellular systems at the time.

> "I remember when Klein came into my office and said what we were doing for satellite communications, we could do for terrestrial communications."
>
> —ANDREW VITERBI, QUALCOMM COFOUNDER[2]

A NEW FRONTIER

In September 1988, the Cellular Telecommunications Industry Association (CTIA) published a set of User Performance Requirements (UPR) that encouraged the industry to develop a digital wireless standard with at least ten times the capacity of the current analog networks, in addition to better reliability and quality. With the opportunity it saw in digital spread-spectrum technology, Qualcomm began to formally suggest that its code-based technology had merit in mobile communication applications and would meet this requirement. The company claimed that not only would this technology solve the capacity problems by making more efficient use of the frequency spectrum, but it would also offer higher-quality service and more advanced features for consumers.

Qualcomm started to pitch its concept of a code-based signaling method to cellular operators and manufacturers as an alternative to time-based methods. The proposal shocked many simply because it was so unconventional, departing from familiar concepts and methods. Jacobs and Viterbi were not surprised by the initial reaction: CDMA and spread-spectrum technology in general had never been greeted with open arms in the commercial sector.

Most people simply thought that spread spectrum was applicable only to expensive military systems that demanded secrecy, but not high capacity.

What Lamarr, Antheil, and other spread-spectrum pioneers had seen only as a method for secure communication, Jacobs and the Qualcomm team now realized was an ideal method for increased communication capacity. The Qualcomm elite envisioned what few others could see: that spread spectrum was the best method to maximize the capacity of the airwaves. Claude Shannon had shown Jacobs and others how to come closer to the maximum limit on carrying information, and it certainly wasn't with standard frequency division or its time-based variants. The essential insight that Jacobs and his team had was that by breaking each conversation into coded pieces (and reconstructing them on the receiving end), you could in theory cram in as many conversations as your equipment and computers could process until you approached the theoretical upper limit of the information-carrying capacity of your signal.

The implementation of CDMA—just like Antheil's piano roll concept—also went against all the conventional wisdom concerning radio design at the time. Antheil's suggested method for synchronizing a sender and receiver mechanically was unattainable with the technology available at the time. Qualcomm's suggestion that a form of spread spectrum be used was received in much the same way—this unorthodox method looked difficult, costly, and even impossible to realize using available computing equipment. The processing power and sophisticated digital techniques needed also seemed far beyond the capabilities of commercial technology.

Part of the resistance that Qualcomm was up against was simply the "this is the way we've always done it" mindset. Engineers in the industry had decades of experience in refining frequency-division methods, and this was what they were comfortable with. Time-based methods still encapsulated frequency division, so they were not too overwhelming for the industry to swallow. It was asking a lot of the average radio engineer to retrain him- or herself to think in terms of spread spectrum. Commercial designers were also not used to being on the cutting edge of technology the way those in the government sector were. In this environment, military-contractor-turned-commercial-product-developer Qualcomm was up against more than just a technical challenge in exploring commercial uses of code-based wireless; it had to convince the world that this was a real and practical approach outside of military use.

BREAKING ALL THE RULES

Even to some of the brightest in academia, for a long time spread-spectrum techniques (including CDMA) seemed to have little practical use in multiple-

FDMA, TDMA, AND CDMA

The three methods of sending wireless information while mobile were (in order of development) (1) frequency-division multiple access (FDMA), in which each conversation was transmitted over a dedicated frequency for each direction (see Figure 3-1); time-division multiple access (TDMA), in which each conversation was broken into packets, which were sent sequentially, along with other conversations, over a single selected frequency (see Figure 4-1); and (3) code-division multiple access (CDMA), in which a conversation was broken into individual packets, each stamped with an identity code, and sent out over a spread spectrum of frequencies (see Figure 4-2). To reduce the number of acronyms in the book, these three methods are interchangeably referred to as, respectively, frequency-based wireless (for FDMA); time-based wireless (for TDMA); and code-based wireless (for CDMA).

access systems such as cellular that had to support high volumes of users. This is not to say that no one explored the notion of using spread spectrum in mobile systems. As early as 1978, when the United States was just beginning to test AMPS networks (based upon simple frequency division), George Cooper and Ray Nettleton published a paper for the Institute of Electrical and Electronics Engineers (IEEE) suggesting spread spectrum as the ultimate solution for cellular systems because of its highly efficient use of the frequency bandwidth. But most engineers remained skeptical of spread-spectrum techniques—especially for use in mobile environments—and the cellular industry showed itself especially averse to Qualcomm's CDMA message.

So just what was it about CDMA that unsettled so many in the cellular industry?

Mainly, it was the suggestion of implementing high-rate frequency-hopping and spread-spectrum techniques inside commercial radios. This was more than just going against the grain; it violated the fundamental precepts of current radio design for consumer markets. On top of that, the complexity of transmitting code-based communications in real time made this technique appear to many engineers to be beyond the reaches of the current technology. Many said that code-based mobile phones would be too bulky and power-hungry for practical use because of the need for a higher level of processing power. It's not a far stretch to say that CDMA flat-out scared people.

But the intricacies of code-based wireless were not at all intimidating to the engineers at Qualcomm. They thrived on the elegance and simplicity of this method that appeared exceedingly complex to others. Jacobs and Viterbi clearly realized what Claude Shannon foresaw: that spread spectrum was the most natural means of communication in a shared space. When many people wanted to get their messages across with the absolute minimum of interference, code-based wireless was the way to do it. The concept certainly fit the problem, so all that was left to do now was to demonstrate an economic way of implementing the concept.

"It's magic if you don't get it."
—GEORGE GILDER[3]

Fortunately, the senior engineering staff at Qualcomm was very familiar with the pace of advances in semiconductor technology. These engineers had built many of their own communications processors from scratch for projects at both Linkabit and Qualcomm. Many companies, such as Intel and Texas Instruments, were now developing powerful microprocessors and digital signal processors, and the capabilities of these products were doubling every twelve to eighteen months. Qualcomm could see far enough ahead to realize that advances in semiconductor technology would enable cost-effective spread-spectrum communications in a suitable form.

Still, it proved amazingly difficult for Qualcomm just to explain how code-based wireless worked. What separated CDMA from other technologies was its use of unique codes, not time or frequency, to organize different conversations in a shared space. When the voice information from a caller was digitized and broken up, code-based systems assigned a unique code sequence to each user that was currently on the system. Just like Antheil's piano rolls (but much faster), the code sequence directed small snippets of the conversation to be sent across different frequencies at different points in time. The conversation was essentially blurred or spread across a wide band of frequencies (see Figure 4-2). The other users operated with a similar but slightly different code sequence, and the sequence was pseudo-random, meaning that it looked very much like background noise.

The receiving base transceiver station (BTS) on the other end of the wireless communication knew the code sequence assignments of each individual caller in the system. It could then rake in all the information in the band and use the codes to extract the individual conversations. The various cells in a code-based system were all synchronized with one another, so they could coordinate the code sequences to ensure that no mobile users got lost in all the noise as they moved from one cell to another. This system of wireless transmission can appear quite chaotic, as there are no hard rules on how and where in the frequency band the snippets of conversations can be sent. But again, incredibly advanced semiconductor circuits can sift through all the individual packets being thrown at them and extract the ones needed to complete each call. (Interestingly, receivers in CDMA systems were called rake receivers.)

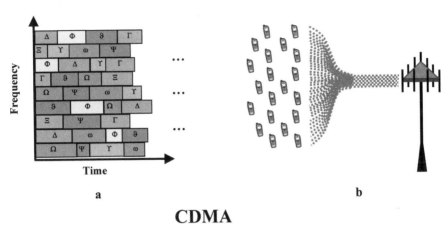

CDMA

Figure 4-2: Code Division Multiple Access (a) logically and (b) schematically

OVERCOMING IMPOSSIBILITIES

While the concept of code-controlled spread-spectrum communications wasn't too abstruse for skilled radio-frequency (RF) engineers at the time, Qualcomm's many critics complained that the technology that would enable this concept was just not ready. Additionally, the naysayers thought, the inherently noisy environment in which mobile phones operate would wreak havoc with code-based transmissions—it might look good on paper, but the advantages would quickly break down when code-based wireless was thrown out into the real world. Because CDMA's capacity could be negatively affected by radio noise in the environment, many saw its performance as unpredictable at best.

Early suggestions for using spread spectrum in mobile environments

> "One of the things that struck me was that, at that time, CDMA was not possible. The complexity of it all made it not possible."
> —RICK KORNFELD,
> PAST LINKABIT EMPLOYEE,
> QUALCOMM EMPLOYEE NO. 20,
> THEN PRESIDENT OF DOT WIRELESS
> (SOLD TO TEXAS INSTRUMENTS)[4]

were checked by several inherent problems. The theoretical capacity models of code-based wireless showed astounding results—until real-world factors such as fading and interference were added in. Many major problems appeared when more than a few mobile users were active, because of all the interference created in the common frequency band. And these issues were deal killers; if they weren't resolved or adequately tamed, the whole effort made absolutely no sense. Up until 1988, proposed solutions to these problems were incredibly complex and costly. In effect, many people came to believe that the idea of using CDMA (or spread spectrum) in mobile systems was absurd, with some even contending that the effort would prove to be not just commercially impractical, but impossible.

The biggest challenge that code-based wireless faced in a multiple-access system was one that is often referred to as the *near-far field effect* (or near-far interference) in communication systems. It's a component of all multiple-access systems in which many users want to communicate with one cell station (BTS). Since a radio's signal power drops off dramatically with distance, the signals from those that are far away, on the fringes of a cell area, would be very weak by the time they reached the BTS. If another mobile user was very close to the BTS, that user's signal would be very loud and would tend to drown out the signals from users who were farther away. Since code-based wireless users all shared the same band, these close-by "loud talkers" would dominate the electromagnetic airspace and block out all other signals. Since it was feasible for several mobile users to be close to the BTS, the capacity of a code-based system would be pitifully low in these situations, making it even worse than the prevailing analog networks.

This near-far interference problem associated with spread spectrum communication systems was probably the most significant factor that prevented the use of CDMA for years. Because traditional wireless communication kept callers separated in channels, mobile units were typically set for maximum power—the more power, the better. There was no need to worry about blasting anyone else out, since each caller was on a different frequency. Since users in time-based and frequency-based systems couldn't possibly overpower each other, this type of interference was a nonissue.

> "Several other issues come in and revolve around power control, but it's the killer."
> —KLEIN GILHOUSEN,
> EARLY LINKABIT EMPLOYEE;
> QUALCOMM COFOUNDER

But in code-based wireless, everyone used the same wide channel, so this interference had to be resolved in some way. Under the same maximum-power paradigm, code-based wireless systems would quickly break down.

The practice of using high-powered transmission was so ingrained in radio designers, and for good reason, that few sought to explore the possibility of reducing the power to lower levels. Maximizing the transmission power of a cellular phone helped to ensure a good connection. Since the signals from cellular phones degraded quickly, especially in hilly or obstructed areas, maximum power gave the strongest guarantee that a call would not be dropped. It was also important to maintain a healthy signal level when a call was handed off from one BTS to another, since this frequently happened at distances far from both towers.

In order to maximize the capacity of a mobile network using code-based wireless, though, the power of the signals emitted from the handsets had to be minimized. If any mobile user's handset was putting out too much power, the signal would drown out all the other users in the cell. So, the capacity advantages that Qualcomm cited for CDMA were severely affected by this issue of power control, and critics could imagine any number of noisy environment scenarios in which code-based wireless would break down. Some people viewed code-based wireless as applicable only to a controlled, ideal environment, at best, which never existed in a cellular system.

As if the issue of near-far interference wasn't enough to lead critics to dismiss CDMA outright, many of them also took code-based wireless to task on its ability to successfully hand off calls from cell to cell. Since the system would be coordinating conversations based upon high-rate code sequences, very accurate timing synchronization was required in the entire system. If the individual BTS towers were not accurately timed to a common reference, the code would go out of synch when a user was transferred from one BTS to another, leading to a dropped call.

In the analog systems used at the time and the proposed time-based systems, a hard handoff was used, basically a "break before make" connection: The call was terminated at one tower and then immediately picked up by the next tower. Much like trapeze artists swinging in a tight mode to enable an acrobat to be handed off from one swing to another, the process had to be coordinated carefully in advance of letting go. If the acrobat let go too early or too late, or if the other swing was not in place to receive the handoff, disaster resulted (or at least a gasp from the audience as an acrobat plunged into the safety net). In a cellular network, improper implementation of a hard handoff meant a dropped call and an angry customer. The handoff was also one of the more difficult aspects to get working in early cellular systems and required much tweaking to get it right. The code-based wireless proposal immensely complicated this handoff process, and many engineers shrank from the thought of compounding a problem that had taken many years of experience to get right.

The experts at Qualcomm suggested that the major drawbacks of code-based wireless in a mobile environment could be overcome with a few novel and well-designed solutions. The team had had plenty of practical experience implementing CDMA and spread-spectrum radios in several projects, including OmniTRACS, so they were confident that the theoretical capacity benefits of code-based wireless in mobile cellular systems could be maintained with their solutions. Even though many had sung the same siren song before, the technical clout of Jacobs, Viterbi, and Gilhousen was hard to dismiss.

But they had a hard sell in front of them. In addition to the need to prove that code-based wireless could work, Qualcomm also had to convince customers and many others in the communications industry that CDMA was really the future of telecommunications. The practical benefits of the technology still escaped most people (especially those without advanced engineering degrees).

CHAMPIONING A BRAVE NEW WORLD

Qualcomm believed that CDMA could be used effectively for cellular communications and that the major limitations could be overcome. But it had to spread the message fast—the industry was already well on its way to adopting time-based wireless (TDMA) technology as its future migration path. For code-based wireless to see the light of day within the coming decade, Qualcomm had to get the attention of the major network operators in the cellular industry. And nothing got the attention of network operators better than promising them a killer solution to the dearth of capacity.

Qualcomm's early calculations and theoretical models of code-based wireless systems showed vast improvements over the capacity of analog cellular systems. Early simulations showed that CDMA could potentially provide an astounding forty times the capacity of current analog networks. Jacobs and the other senior engineers presented these results at several industry events in 1988 and 1989 and waited for someone to find flaws in their assumptions. No one stood up to counter their claims (at least not yet), so they continued to preach their code-based wireless gospel.

While few people countered Qualcomm's proposal for a cellular world based upon CDMA, most contended that it was too little, too late. Too little because the company touting the technology was an unknown—the wireless industry had little connection with organizations that were primarily government contractors. Too late because the industry believed that it already had a digital solution—something that held a lot of promise for the network operators. For the most part, Jacobs and the rest of the Qualcomm team were simply ignored.

But much to the chagrin of many in the industry, Qualcomm didn't go away. The time-based wireless (TDMA) path that was chosen at the time fell short of the capacity improvements mandated by the Cellular Telecommunications Industry Association (CTIA). Qualcomm made a point of reminding its audiences that its solution exceeded this requirement, whereas TDMA failed miserably. The characterization of the fledgling but promising time-based wireless as subpar struck a nerve with many of the equipment vendors in the industry. For companies such as Ericsson and Nokia, which had mil-

WIRELESS TECHNOLOGIES AND STANDARDS

Many acronyms are used to describe various wireless technologies (methods of communication) and the standards that are defined to implement them. Often the acronym for a *technology* is interchanged with one for a defined *standard*, confusing the two. Frequency-division multiple access (FDMA), time-division multiple access (TDMA), and code-division multiple access (CDMA) are all technologies that describe fundamental methods for communicating signals, but they are not the defined standards that guide their implementation.

The European-based global system for mobile communications (GSM), for instance, is a defined standard that utilizes TDMA technology. Other standards include IS-95 (utilizing CDMA), personal digital cellular (PDC, using TDMA technology), and IS-136 (using TDMA). It would be incorrect to state that a network is based upon the TDMA standard. This book aims to keep this distinction clear, so that readers are presented with accurate information regarding wireless network implementations.

lions invested in time-division techniques, Qualcomm was basically calling their baby ugly.

On the other side of the world, the European Union had already decided that its member countries would build networks based upon GSM (global system for mobile communications, originally *groupe special mobile*), which also uses time-division (TDMA) technology. The EU had already done years of testing and validation of this technology, and had showed that time-based wireless techniques could boost network capacity by at least three times by most estimates. While the FCC was not keen on the idea of adopting a European standard and mandating it for U.S. operators, it also saw value in using time-based wireless technology as the protocol. The CTIA had been working with many U.S. companies to develop a time-based wireless protocol, even though it was clear that this protocol wouldn't meet the CTIA's mandate for capacity. The hope was that over time the technology could be improved, however, so that it would eventually meet the goal of a ten times increase in capacity.

THE BEGINNING OF THE END?

Despite Qualcomm's efforts to promote code-based wireless, the Telecommunication Industry Association (TIA)—with the endorsement of the CTIA—voted in January 1989 to select the time-based (TDMA) method of digital communication for cellular systems. Numerous U.S. companies had prototyped and tested time-based methods, and most of the network operators around the world felt comfortable with these more familiar methods. The announcement appeared to be a significant blow to Qualcomm, but, realistically, Jacobs and his team had known that the TIA would probably proceed with TDMA—it was the path with the least risk at the time.

The industry breathed a collective sigh of relief at this announcement. With the direction of standards settled, equipment manufacturers could now streamline their operations and focus on getting products into the market rapidly to meet the skyrocketing demand. The industry was busily reorganizing and realigning itself to get digital networks up and running as soon as possible. Much work lay ahead to develop a migration strategy for the wireless service providers so that digital time-based wireless could be integrated into their existing analog networks. With all the analog AMPS subscribers currently on the systems, the networks obviously had to continue to support them—you couldn't ask them to toss their phones and buy new ones. So companies went to work building equipment that would help networks handle both digital and analog subscribers and switch seamlessly between them.

With the advent of second-generation networks clearly upon the global wireless industry, the FCC and industry bodies in the United States (the TIA and CTIA) were all keen on the rapid adoption and development of their time-based wireless standard (technically termed IS-54). Strong standards embodied the collective innovation of a country and boosted leverage for trade, so all major industrial corners of the world dedicated sizable resources to this area. The other industrialized blocs—especially Japan and Europe—appeared to be well ahead of the United States at this juncture. No longer an orphan industry in telecommunications, wireless now embodied the future of communications, and the company that captured the lead in this race would be tough to catch.

With the endorsement of time-based wireless, momentum was clearly not in Qualcomm's favor. The floodgates were opened for spending to upgrade networks—but not for Jacobs's code-based systems. Barely into the first inning of the cellular game, Qualcomm was already buried behind a double-digit disadvantage. At this point, the industry wrote Qualcomm off: nice try, but too little too late. Even many code-based wireless advocates started looking to the next generation, at least a decade in the future. It looked as if it was the end of the cellular CDMA road for Qualcomm, which some people thought should return to satellite communications and government contracts. But not Irwin Jacobs. He had something else up his sleeve.

CHAPTER 5

Disrupting the Cellular Status Quo

Qualcomm Goes to Bat, 1989

In many industries, government regulation and political influence are the largest factors determining the success or demise of a product or technology. Since the whole purpose of the Cellular Telecommunications Industry Association (CTIA) was to help the cellular industry converge on a standardized digital technology, its word was essentially law. The momentum of consensus in the industry was strong, and companies that were not aligned with the decisions of the standards bodies, the Telecommunications Industry Association (TIA) and the CTIA, would be relegated to niche markets. No wonder, then, that most people felt that Qualcomm had had its legs cut out from under it by the CTIA's endorsement of time-based wireless.

But Qualcomm knew a lot about spread spectrum and code-based wireless that others could not yet see. After months of reviewing the benefits of CDMA in terrestrial mobile networks, Jacobs was confident that code-based wireless had a place in cellular. To him, finding the best way to bring others to recognize this inherent truth was the real trick. Setbacks such as the CTIA's endorsement of time-based wireless were only temporary obstacles to Jacobs—Qualcomm simply had to look for the best way around these roadblocks. To him, there was no question of going back and looking at other markets—cellular still presented a tremendous opportunity for Qualcomm's talent. So once the CTIA door closed, Jacobs met with his colleagues to look for open windows.

After some deliberation, the choice became obvious, mostly because it was pretty much the only one: Take the message directly to network operators in the hope that one or more of them would consider using code-based technology. One thing stood in the way of this approach: the chances that an operator could defy the CTIA's recommendation and proceed with an alternative approach to cellular services without being blocked by the FCC. A second obstacle would be the need for a significant influx of cash for Qualcomm's operations, but this was not Jacobs's concern: If code-based wireless was considered even a remotely possible alternative for cellular, the money would come from somewhere.

So, in early 1989, Jacobs paid a visit to the FCC in Washington, D.C., to ensure that if an operator did find CDMA compelling, it would be permitted to use it. As the FCC had been driving rapidly toward a deregulated telecommunications market, its answer was as Qualcomm expected: An operator could use any technology it wished. The only conditions were that the technology could not interfere with the existing analog AMPS networks and that the devices used needed the typical approval from the FCC for commercial sale. That was all Jacobs needed to know.

"That vote occurred in January, and here we came along in February and said, 'You missed a good thing here with CDMA.' Most people didn't want to hear about it."
—IRWIN JACOBS,
QUALCOMM COFOUNDER AND CEO

Encouraged by the prospect that they could effectively pursue a de facto standard, Qualcomm lost little time in continuing the development of the key components of a code-based wireless cellular system. Its approach, therefore, was more like a grassroots effort. If the organizational structure of the industry would not adapt quickly to compelling advances in technology, then power would have to be given to the minions. Change would have to be driven from the bottom up.

Emboldened by this refreshed approach, Qualcomm dismayed many companies in the industry by coming back only a few weeks after the adoption of the time-based standard and pressing with renewed vigor for cellular code-based wireless. With the industry consensus being TDMA, most companies ignored Qualcomm, figuring that the newcomer lacked the basic sense to know that it had effectively lost its chance. But through earlier discussions with network operators, Jacobs and others at Qualcomm knew that there was still a lingering dissatisfaction with the time-based option. Qualcomm capitalized on this underlying dissatisfaction and began to knock the TIA for failing to consider the very viable option of code-based wireless.

This early point in Qualcomm's break into the cellular market established its corporate character well into the future. To many companies in the United States, Qualcomm was viewed as divisive and rude—an outsider that (possibly unwittingly) would undermine the nation's chance of dominating global communications by disrupting the current consensus among American companies. The viewpoint inside Qualcomm was exactly the opposite—code-based wireless provided a unique opportunity for the United States to gain a huge advantage over other countries in the race to the wireless future.

Qualcomm's campaign therefore focused on the competitive advantages that its technology would bring to open-minded operators. The offer was intoxicating: The disease of capacity strain that affected the industry was a painful daily experience for the network operators. Here were several companies that were signing up thousands of paying subscribers every day and were dying for something to help them keep up with demand. Qualcomm was dangling more than just a carrot in front of the network operators; it was offering the whole bunch and the farm to boot. How could network operators not consider the possibility of code-based wireless nirvana, even if it were only partly true?

If one or more operators could be convinced to pursue CDMA technology in their networks, vendors would then be motivated to research the technology and provide equipment. For this to happen, due diligence would need to be done in order to demonstrate to operators that code-based wireless did indeed provide huge gains in capacity. Up until this time, Jacobs, Viterbi, and Gilhousen had theorized that CDMA could provide up to forty times the capacity of analog networks. But this was strictly calculated on paper; little real-world testing and measurements had been done with their power management and handoff solutions in place. Network operators needed far more than a scientific guess, since so much work lay ahead.

IT WORKS ON PAPER, BUT . . .

In February 1989, Qualcomm again began paying visits to several regional operators to pitch the idea that CDMA in cellular networks could provide tremendous gains in capacity. One of its audiences was the executives and chief engineers at the cellular division of Pacific Telesis (PacTel Cellular, which would later become Airtouch Cellular and is now part of Verizon Wireless). Identifying PacTel as a likely customer for code-based wireless, Qualcomm's top two executives paid a visit to PacTel's CEO, Jeff Hultman, to explain their solution. Hultman was also a member of the CTIA board and only weeks before had voted to approve TDMA as the official digital cellular standard, but with some reservations. Jacobs and Viterbi laid out their idea of applying code-based wireless to the cellular network environment, leveraging their experience in satellite applications and explaining their novel approach to transplanting the technology to a terrestrial system.

> "All of a sudden, one day, Irwin Jacobs and Andy Viterbi showed up in my office. Honestly, I don't even know how they got there."
> —JEFF HULTMAN,
> CEO OF PACTEL CELLULAR

While Jacobs and Viterbi were working to convince Hultman and others at PacTel that CDMA was the future, they already had a big fan in the audience, Dr. William C. Y. Lee, PacTel's chief scientist, who was already intimately familiar with spread-spectrum systems. With two key patents already under his belt from 1986, Lee knew the potential for code-based wireless, but he also knew its limitations, such as the near-far problem. His research had shown how powerful CDMA could be for use in covert communications with the clever use of frequency hopping and noiselike coding.

> "Our network in Los Angeles was bursting at the seams. We had 100,000 subscribers and were looking at picocell structures and possibly even turning away applicants it was getting so bad."
> —JEFF HULTMAN

Jacobs knew that PacTel was one of the operators that would be more receptive to CDMA, as it was keenly aware of the limitations of analog cellular. Its network in Los Angeles, with over 100,000 subscribers, was bursting at the seams, and it was particularly concerned with capacity and call quality—so concerned that it was seriously considering turning away new applicants. Lee and others at PacTel were evaluating new technologies for cellular networks and saw that the time-division solutions just wouldn't suffice if growth in the region continued. They needed something better, something that not only had better capacity capabilities but also was more scalable. Code-based wireless seemed to promise all this and more.

But Lee knew that applying code-based wireless in a mobile cellular environment added a whole new twist to the equation. Citing the near-far interference issue, Lee pointed out to the team, as others had, that the problem of power control remained a major obstacle in their way. Having painstakingly developed spread-spectrum system concepts that kept power minimized to the point where it blended in with background noise, Lee knew that just one mobile CDMA terminal blaring at full power could render all others ineffective. The transmission power of all radios in a network had to be tightly controlled if the system was to work at all.

But the keen minds at Qualcomm had already addressed this issue and had looked at several methods for resolving the near-far problem. In fact, many of the senior engineers in the company had been wrestling with the effects of near-far transmissions in spread-spectrum systems for years. Klein Gilhousen had worked extensively with spread-spectrum communications while he was at Magnavox, where the significance of advanced power control in satellite communications was recognized. But the problem of power control in a cellular system had a few added problems—most notably the high level of traffic in the communication channels and the necessity for a cheap solution, because commercial applications couldn't possibly afford to pay what the military was paying.

Both Jacobs and Viterbi assured PacTel that they could tame the interference problem and provide dramatic capacity advantages with code-based wireless. Intrigued by such a promising solution, Hultman invited Jacobs to keep PacTel apprised of Qualcomm's progress and return with a more detailed analysis of the solution. If Qualcomm could demonstrate in more detail just how it would implement CDMA in PacTel's network, and what exactly the technology would provide, he promised that PacTel would be quite interested, as long as other network operators supported the technology as well.

DEAL MAKER 1: POWER CONTROL

Within a few short months, Qualcomm had developed and refined a relatively simple method of power feedback control that could easily be implemented in cellular phones. The solution involved a background function that took place while a call was in process, a simple power monitor that dynamically changed the level of the signal output of a phone and a BTS during a call. Even though the near-far problem posed a complex puzzle, Qualcomm's solution actually surprised many by its simplicity.

A significant portion of the power-control problem was solved by using circuitry that was already being built into every cellular phone. The receive circuitry of a mobile phone had electronic components that took signals of varying strength and amplified or reduced them to produce a common, predetermined voltage level, which it presented to the next stage of the electronics. This circuitry was referred to as the *automatic gain control (AGC)* front end of a radio transmitter or receiver.

The clever minds at Qualcomm realized that almost all the information they needed for accurate power control of the handset was already there—the handset already knew how near or far it was from the BTS through the relative strength or weakness of the received signal. They deduced that all they had to do was monitor the AGC behavior of the cell phone's receiver frequently and mirror that behavior in the amplification of the transmitted signal: If the AGC saw weak signals coming in, it would crank up the transmit power. If the AGC detected strong signals, indicating that it was close to the BTS, the transmit power would be taken down. This solution formed the basis for what Qualcomm termed its "open-loop power control method."

When Jacobs and the team tested this solution, they saw that it resolved most of the near-far problem, but not all of it. They could still see scenarios in which the open-loop power control let handsets speak louder than they needed to, compromising the overall system capacity. They needed a more sophisticated tuning method to keep tighter control over the power emitted from individual handsets. At this point, they looked carefully at the other end of the communication, at the BTS, to see what opportunities existed there. The BTS offered more resources for implementing an advanced power-control solution, since it monitored the activity of all mobile phones in its area.

After a short study of the possibilities for power control at the BTS, Qualcomm came up with another novel approach to managing transmitted power. Basically, when multiple phones were in use in a given area, the BTS would measure all the signals it was receiving at any point in time to determine the quality and signal strength of each unit. Mobile users that were sending very strong signals were sent back a single-bit message telling them to turn their power down by a notch. Those that had weak signals that were becoming hard to resolve were told to kick the power up by a notch. This feedback would have to happen rapidly—several hundred times a second—to be effective, but this rate was well within the range of the electronics that were already being used in cellular networks.

This second stage of power control was effectively a closed loop, since the BTS fed control information back to the mobile phone based upon the output that it received from the unit. Adding this sophistication on top of the open-loop method installed in the handset effectively licked the problem of near-far interference. Klein Gilhousen, Roberto Padovani, and Chuck Wheatley documented the solution well and eventually submitted the findings in an application to the U.S. Patent and Trademark Office on November 7, 1989, depicting all the fundamental elements of efficient power control in a mobile CDMA network. This patent was granted to Qualcomm as U.S. Patent 5,056,109 on October 8, 1991.

In addition to the patented power-control method, Qualcomm also explored some of the finer points of this novel method to further improve the capacity of the system. Jacobs and his team realized that the BTS could also identify other forms of interference in a cellular environment, such as fading caused by a fast-moving mobile phone. In such a case, the signal from a mobile user tended to be confused and required higher power (a better signal-to-noise ratio) to resolve the information. But a motionless unit was not subject to a fading signal and could be accurately understood by the BTS with a significantly lower signal level. In such a scenario, the BTS could command the stationary units to drop their power further than normal to offer room for more users in the cell. Again, the process had to happen quickly, but Qualcomm felt that this was well within the capability of electronics at the time, and would become even easier to incorporate in the years ahead.

Emboldened by the results from simulations with its novel power-control method, Qualcomm paid visits to other network operators and returned to visit Hultman and Lee at PacTel as well. The advanced approach to power control that Qualcomm presented to PacTel and other operators made CDMA a more powerful, flexible solution. Rather than having the fixed, hard capacity offered by TDMA, code-based wireless took advantage of network characteristics to provide a soft capacity—one that was optimized for the terrain and conditions. With these algorithms in place, Qualcomm suggested that a code-based wireless cellular network could indeed meet the overall capacity limits the company claimed. Lee of PacTel, for one, was impressed. The other operators were initially skeptical, but NYNEX (in New York) and Ameritech (in Chicago) showed interest in CDMA similar to PacTel's.

Still, one lingering fear was that the solution would not work in all environments. If the power could not be tamed in every single handset of a system, applying code-based wireless in a cellular network was a waste of time and an exercise in futility. If the power of any single handset got too high, all the other handsets using the same cell would crank up their power in order to be heard. As each handset bumped up its signal strength, the others would continue to match it in order to overcome the noise, and so on, and so on. Many engineers could easily envision a worst-case situation in which things would quickly get out of hand if the power-control algorithm were not extremely stable in all environments—especially when mobile units were at the far extremities of a cell. While no one could demonstrate that Qualcomm was wrong on these matters, the proliferation of doubts and "what if" reasoning led to fear and uncertainty in most audiences.

DEAL MAKER 2: SOFT HANDOFFS

Taken by itself, the power-control solution that Qualcomm developed was fatally flawed. If it operated in conjunction with the current method for handing off calls in the then-deployed AMPS networks, or even that proposed for other digital networks, it would not work. The whole power-control scheme would fall apart when a user was moving between cells, because the handoff communication in then-current networks was far too slow for the power control to be effective. Additionally, in a time-based or frequency-based wireless system, users switched frequency channels when they changed cells. But in a code-based wireless system, the user utilized the same frequency band in all cells, so the method for moving from one cell to the next was not clear-cut.

To deal with this issue, Qualcomm suggested a more sophisticated method of handoff, called a "soft handoff," that would be implemented in conjunction with its power-control solution. The soft-handoff method suggested was a "make before break" process, where a user has a call maintained on two separate towers at the same time before the call is actually moved from one to the other. In fact, several cell towers could be processing a single call simultaneously if the user were within range of each. The system would constantly monitor the signal strength at each tower and use the one with the best signal to maintain the connection. At any point, though, another tower could take over and let a tower with a weaker signal drop out. Qualcomm saw that this method led to greater assurance that callers would not be dropped and to much smoother handoffs—users probably would no longer notice what was happening (hard handoffs in analog systems were usually accompanied by an audible pop or other irritating noises).

A KILLER COMBINATION

Designed to work together, the power-control scheme and soft-handoff method would achieve breakthrough performance, whereas one or the other by itself would provide nothing. By overhauling the old, standard methods of handing off calls, Qualcomm could avoid costly and complex solutions in other areas. Once again, thinking outside the box led Qualcomm's engineering team to see what others had failed to grasp.

But to the audience of engineers listening to Qualcomm, the new methods meant another level of technical complexity. The techniques that Qualcomm was suggesting seemed too intensive for the system, especially the phones, to manage in real time. To be successful, the soft handoff required precise synchronization among the various base stations in a network. Because several towers could be processing a call simultaneously, the system had to know the relative delay in each signal (which is dependent upon the user's proximity to each tower). To hand off calls smoothly from cell to cell, the voice information from a caller had to be correctly parsed and reassembled in short order. Improper or distorted timing would make the handoff process audible again, as the caller would hear echoes or gibberish when the channel was switched between cells.

The solution that Qualcomm suggested for coordinating the precise timing necessary to support handoffs involved using GPS (global positioning system) satellite signals. Each cell tower would have a GPS receiver in it, so that its clock could be referenced to a standard time. When different towers received a single caller's signal, they could time-stamp the information and align it to present a seamless handoff. The GPS system was not fully developed at that time, but the plan was for the system to be fully open to civilian and commercial use. If there were any doubts about the viability of using the GPS system for synchronization, Qualcomm suggested that any number of sources for accurate timing were available, such as signals from local television stations.

In every area where concern was expressed, Qualcomm fired back with something that was not only a solution to the problem, but a solution that improved upon the current situation. Its power-control and synchronization solutions not only mitigated functional problems facing network operators, but made cellular service better for the consumer. Effective power control would boost the efficiency of phones operating on batteries, and the soft handoffs would improve the quality of the connection, with fewer calls being dropped and less distortion. Qualcomm claimed that not only would an operator using CDMA reap the benefits of capacity, but it would have a key differentiator in the form of superior service to its customers—an added bonus that made the package all the more attractive.

KNOCKOUT PUNCH

Qualcomm was not just counting on one or two inventions to make the capacity of CDMA several orders above anything else available. In addition to power control and soft handoffs, Qualcomm developed breakthrough techniques in a third area of digital cellular systems—voice coding, or the process of converting a caller's voice to digital bits and back again. The efficiency of the voice coders (vocoders) in a digital cellular system had a direct impact on the capacity and quality of the network.

Having strong roots in information theory, Jacobs and Viterbi were especially interested in communicating the information contained in speech in simple and elegant ways. The quagmire of cellular systems gave them and the rest of their team a great opportunity to apply to the cellular environment what they had learned from Claude Shannon at MIT. One central point of Shannon's teachings centered on the efficiency of communicating a single thought, feeling, or bit of information. In essence, a good system should expend only the absolute minimum of energy needed to communicate a bit of information—any more would be wasted energy that would sap the overall capacity of the communication medium.

Qualcomm knew that typical voice conversations contained significant dead time—times when only one or neither party was talking. Surprisingly, this dead time makes up roughly 65 percent of the average communication via telephone. When information was not being transferred during a call, power was being wasted to send "nothing." Qualcomm took advantage of this element of the nature of communication between humans to further improve the capacity performance of CDMA.

To do this, the company developed what it called a variable-rate coder (VRC)—a digital voice encoder (vocoder) that could process voice information at four different levels of accuracy (9,600, 4,800, 2,400, and 1,200 bits per second). The higher, more accurate rates gobbled up more of the capacity of the whole system, while the lower rates produced lower-quality speech but conserved capacity for other calls. This vocoder had intelligence embedded in it that allowed it to sense when dead times in conversations were occurring.

When no activity was detected, the vocoder reduced the processing rate of the information. Dropping the rate dramatically expanded the system's capacity without degrading the voice quality (it was basically akin to pushing the mute button on a stereo). On top of the capacity gain, muting the quiet times during a conversation scored major points with users by cutting out much of the annoying background hiss and hum. It worked so well, in fact, that during demonstrations, many test users thought their lines were going dead because of the absence of noise.

This variable-rate encoder helped to increase the overall capacity of code-based wireless systems by a factor of three, so it was a key component of the solution. Like the other solutions that Qualcomm developed, it was additive and had little impact on the quality of the service provided. When coupled with many other innovations for handling voice conversations in a cellular network, Qualcomm's CDMA showed clear promise for meeting the capacity demands of service providers and providing better quality to customers.

"For some people it was initially a problem—the line was so quiet that people thought it was dead."
—KLEIN GILHOUSEN,
EARLY LINKABIT EMPLOYEE;
QUALCOMM COFOUNDER

CHAPTER 6

Spreading the CDMA Message

Turning Points, Late 1989

While Jacobs, Viterbi, and the rest of Qualcomm's senior technical team were out championing code-division multiple-access (CDMA) wireless to network operators and vendors, the San Diego headquarters was working overtime to keep the company operating. Huge bills were being racked up for OmniTRACS capital equipment and increased salary expenditures. Lines of credit were being used, and various loans from directors and affiliates were being burned through rapidly. It quickly became obvious that another round of private placements was necessary to keep the doors open. Another preferred stock offering of 2.5 million shares was planned for April 1989—enough to bring in almost $20 million to the company.

An offering of this size would have to capture some major new investors, not just friends and family with extra savings lying around. Qualcomm approached many of the major investment banks, and the company caught the eye of Peter Sacerdote, a partner with Goldman Sachs. While Qualcomm had originally hoped that Goldman's favorable due diligence on its business prospects would help it gain favor with other banks, too, Sacerdote was more interested in getting a bigger share of Qualcomm for Goldman. When the offering went through in April, Goldman ended up taking half, infusing $10 million into the company.

It was almost as if Jacobs had it planned all along: The money showed up. The prospects for OmniTRACS and code-based wireless proved compelling to outside investors, enabling Qualcomm to move to the next stage. In order to see code-based wireless succeed commercially in mobile communications, a business had to be built around the technology and products that were being developed. To begin with, a mass-market public relations campaign would have to be initiated.

Coming from the world of academia, Jacobs and Viterbi had little problem explaining the complex concept of CDMA to like-minded engineers and scientists. But the engineers at Qualcomm and many other groups in the industry that were promoting code-based wireless found the differences in their approach difficult to describe to laypeople. Operators who couldn't understand Qualcomm's code-based wireless technology lacked the confidence to invest in its development, so education was key. With the new funding in place, Jacobs approached Greg McQuerter, owner of a local PR firm in San Diego, to help the company champion code-based wireless technology to the masses and explain its benefits.

Starting on a shoestring budget, McQuerter began a project that would eventually span several years. In addition to developing a communications plan, McQuerter worked nonstop to put Jacobs and other high-level executives on panels and in discussion groups, as well as having them write technical bulletins on code-based wireless. To maintain visibility in the industry, Qualcomm engineers were placed in numerous industry standards groups, committees, and panels as advocates of CDMA. Developing the message was important; but rapidly disseminating it to all corners of the market was crucial.

McQuerter developed several strategies to communicate the benefits of CDMA simply, so that even nontechnical people could comprehend them. One such analogy—likening various forms of communications to a cocktail party—was actually a common metaphor to describe the problem of communicating in a noisy environment. A clamorous cocktail party aptly depicted the difficulty of making a message heard over background noise. McQuerter and Qualcomm expanded on the cocktail party scenario to include the types of wireless technologies that could be used for multiple-access communications.

THE NOISY COCKTAIL PARTY ANALOGY

To make them easier to understand, the various wireless technologies in mobile networks were likened to a social event at a large mansion. If the communications at the party were based on frequency division (FDMA), each one-on-one conversation would take place in a separate room. While you were in a room talking with a friend, no one else could join you there, so you and your friend could each hear each other just fine. And since you were alone in the room, you could speak as loudly as you wanted without disrupting anyone who was conversing elsewhere.

The room represented your assigned frequency channel, and you could use it for as long as you liked. No one else could come into your room and hold another conversation until you were done. Other conversations that were going on simultaneously would be taking place in other rooms, on other frequency channels. But if the mansion had only twenty rooms, only twenty conversations could be held at once. If there were hundreds of guests who wanted to talk, the party would be a drag for many, because they would just plain be left out.

A better party to attend would be one based on time division (TDMA), because it would allow more people to hold conversations simultaneously. Let's say those same hundreds of guests were to drop in on a time-based party. Here, several couples could enter a room to have one-on-one conversations, but the pairs would have to take turns talking. One pair would talk for, let's say, thirty seconds, then would stop to allow the next couple time to talk. The couples would rotate their conversations so that more than one pair could be in the same room talking. Since they were confined to the time periods they could talk within, no one would talk over someone else and disturb the conversation. Like the FDMA party, everyone could talk as loudly as he or she wanted, but the capacity for conversations would be increased—as long as each pair of conversants followed the rules, many more conversations could be carried on at the same time, through rotation.

But even the time-based party was somewhat limited in the number of guests it could accommodate. If you put ten or twenty couples in each room, they would have to wait an awfully long time before they could talk. Let's say that it was practical only to have three couples in a room. So even this cocktail party had its limitations.

While no one would really ever host a party this way (based on FDMA or TDMA), a spread-spectrum environment is more analogous to a real cocktail party—in other words, it is much more similar to the natural way in which humans communicate. In a spread-spectrum party, everyone shares the same space; no one is cordoned off in separate rooms. But the background noise level is much higher in this scenario, and it can often be difficult to be heard. However, CDMA solved this noisy party problem, especially for those suffering from "cocktail ear"—mostly older people with degraded hearing, who had difficulty understanding speech in a noisy environment.

At the code-division party (where all the cool people go, of course), more people are allowed to flood into any one space at the same time to hold discussions. At this party, though, each pair speaks in a different language. This way, their conversations are encoded in each couple's dialect. All couples can talk simultaneously, as the separate language makes it surprisingly easy to hear your partner. Because you would be keying in on the nuances of your spoken language, all the other languages would just sound like gibberish in the background.

Even though thousands of dialects were available for couples to speak, there was still a limit on how many could be spoken at the same time—basically the limit that resulted from the overall noise. If there were fifty couples, all talking different languages, it could get too noisy for anyone to hear. So at the CDMA party it was important to regulate how loudly everyone spoke, to make sure that the maximum number of couples could be heard. By using code division, conceivably ten or fifteen couples in the room could talk at the same time—far more conversations than any of the other methods allowed.

The cocktail party analogy also demonstrated another key aspect (and benefit) of code-based wireless. As more and more people talked, the noise level kept increasing, slowly degrading the ability of conversants to hear each other. Code-based wireless slowly degraded in much the same way, whereas other technologies, such as frequency-based and time-based wireless, simply cut users out—either blocking them from entering the conversation or dropping them in mid-speech. This softer limit of code-based wireless turned out to be a much more palatable feature than dropped calls, which both the cellular industry and consumers abhorred. Qualcomm's PR campaign went on to trumpet this soft limit of code-based wireless as vastly superior to the hard limits of other technologies.

The cocktail party explanation of various core methods of wireless access continues to be used today to explain differences in technology and to point out the merits of CDMA. This analogy actually goes further back than Jacobs or Qualcomm, to Claude Shannon, who in 1949 had made the same connection between the complex mathematics governing code-based communication and this real-life social experience.

> "If more people were there, gradually the noise level would increase on each channel. But everyone could still talk, even though it might be a pretty noisy 'cocktail party' by that time."
>
> —CLAUDE SHANNON,
> THE FATHER OF MODERN
> COMMUNICATION THEORY[1]

Shannon was extremely gifted in his ability to see the simple nature of complex concepts, and he could clearly see that code-based wireless elegantly used the available resources to hold the maximum possible number of independent conversations. Coding communications and spreading them over the total available bandwidth would be limited only by the total noise of all the conversations collectively, which Shannon believed to be the most "democratic" use of the available resources (spectrum). Every information source or caller was treated equally, with no one hogging a disproportionate portion of the resources. McQuerter and Qualcomm successfully used this analogy to explain code-based wireless to the masses.

WHAT MADE CODE-BASED WIRELESS BETTER?

Early in the presentations of code-based wireless (CDMA) to the cellular industry, a dual-front approach was used in dealing with various segments of the industry. Code-based wireless provided benefits at all levels of the value chain—manufacturers, service providers, and end customers—and Qualcomm needed to get its message of a package solution across effectively. Jacobs and his technical team knew how to communicate the mathematics and engineering effectively, but consumer benefits and warm fuzzy things needed to be sold to the industry as well. It was McQuerter's job to sell CDMA to the world, and in order for him to do that, people had to understand all the major benefits that made CDMA such a compelling alternative for cellular. Several advantages of the technology were identified and touted in literature and white papers disseminated to the industry. The following were identified as the compelling reasons for network operators to adopt the technology:

BENEFITS FOR THE NETWORK OPERATORS

1. *Enhanced and flexible capacity*. Code-based wireless was a far more efficient method of radio communication than other proposed methods. It utilized the limited spectrum resources that were available more efficiently than either time-based (TDMA) or frequency-based (FDMA) methods in terms of maximizing the number of simultaneous conversations that were possible. Code-based wireless promised at least ten times the capacity of current analog networks. The maximum number of callers in any given code-based wireless cell was not fixed or strictly bounded, either—it had a soft limit. Basically, CDMA permitted a temporary decrease in the quality of connected calls in order to squeeze more users into a heavily loaded cell. This gave network operators the option of choosing lowered voice quality in situations in which this was preferable to dropping calls or blocking them altogether. Time-based and frequency-based methods had no such provisions—they had hard capacity limits that could not be transcended.

2. *Better security*. Wireless conversations on analog equipment were easy to eavesdrop on, and phone numbers could easily be stolen. The coding methods used in CDMA made it impenetrable to illegal taps—after all, code-based wireless was originally developed for secure military use. This promised to save network operators significant sums of money (and system capacity) that would otherwise be lost due to fraud.

3. *Full frequency reuse*. Time-based and frequency-based wireless systems were similar to analog networks in that frequency channels had to be carefully allocated. Two cells right next to each other could not use similar frequency channels because of interference, so complex and inefficient methods of frequency assignments were necessary. In code-based wireless systems, all frequency channels are used in all cells, so no such planning is necessary.

4. *Easy transition from analog.* Code-based wireless systems were designed to fit on top of analog networks, using as little as 10 percent of the spectrum capacity of the network to implement digital CDMA. For this reason, network operators could continue to support the large base of users who still owned analog phones, while simultaneously offering advanced digital code-based wireless services over the same area. Dedicating even this small amount of network resources to CDMA could double the overall capacity of the network. Other time-based wireless technologies would require far more resources to provide the same level and capacity of digital services alongside legacy analog users.

5. *Reduced number of towers.* It was theorized that code-based wireless networks could provide comparable coverage with fewer BTS towers than analog networks. Early estimates promised network operators that with a CDMA system, they could even achieve superior coverage with one-half to one-fifth as many towers as they would need with other systems, cutting the cost of upgrading to code-based wireless tremendously.

Code-based wireless also brought a number of advantages to the end users—consumers who were eager to cut the cord and go wireless. Of course, whatever intrigued the end customer was also important to the network operators, and any technology that differentiated their services to consumers was highly sought after.

BENEFITS FOR THE END USERS

1. *Better voice quality.* Customers would be drawn to code-based wireless phones because their sound was so much clearer than that of phones using other technologies. A major complaint about analog service was its poor voice quality, especially in dense areas with high interference. Americans had already been spoiled by the high quality of wireline networks, and the quality of analog wireless services fell far short of this standard. Code-based wireless showed that it could potentially provide voice quality on a par with that of wireline services, something that dazzled those accustomed to the inferior analog connections.

2. *Enhanced privacy.* Eavesdropping on analog cellular calls was often splashed in the media, leaving many consumers apprehensive about using cellular services. Code-based wireless promised bulletproof security, so consumers need not worry about sensitive information being intercepted.

3. *Better connection quality.* Code-based wireless employed soft handoffs of mobile calls, resulting in fewer pops, clicks, or other disruptions to calls while

moving. Other methods used hard handoffs and were prone to these nuisances, as well as to the possibility of the call's being dropped altogether. With better error-correction methods, code-based wireless was also more resistant to other enemies of radio transmission, such as fading and interference.

4. *Longer battery life.* Code-based wireless technology was smart enough to drop the power consumption of a phone when less power would suffice, thereby extending battery life. Both analog and the newer time-based wireless phones wasted power and had comparably shorter battery lives. Consumers using code-based wireless phones would be talking longer and recharging the phones less often.

The enhanced capacity of networks was by far the biggest selling point of CDMA and the one that network operators around the world were keen about. The current analog networks were bulging at the seams with more and more subscribers, and the industry could foresee tremendous growth going forward. But competition in the industry was also expected to grow, so the added benefits of improved voice quality and security meant a lot to customers and their service providers. Providing unique services and qualities would set a network apart from the competition and give it a leg up in a booming market. This message was therefore critical to selling CDMA to the world.

YOUR NEW BEST FRIEND

While Qualcomm was working diligently on solutions to the issues confronting cellular code-based wireless, PacTel was investing in research teams of its own. It wanted to know whether the gospel that Qualcomm was preaching was for real—since it seemed, after all, too good to be true. William Lee and the PacTel technical staff had confidence in the theory behind CDMA, but they felt that the practical application and commercial timing of the technology were still open to debate. On top of this, they had to know whether mass production of code-based wireless handsets and infrastructure was economically feasible in the time frame they needed—PacTel couldn't wait for code-based wireless to mature while time-based wireless solutions implemented by its competitors stole away its hard-earned customers.

By April 1989, PacTel began to look seriously at the commercial viability of code-based wireless technology, the advantages it provided, and the inherent risks involved. The decision to adopt a digital technology was no small matter—it could mean success or bankruptcy for a company—so PacTel took its time doing due diligence and making several visits to Qualcomm for meetings. PacTel's CTO, Craig Farril, hired consultants from the Palo Alto firm Pittiglio, Rabin, Todd and McGrath to explore all aspects of code-based wireless technology as a cellular solution, and wanted to completely understand its strategic implications—technical, economic, and otherwise. In a rapidly growing industry like cellular, decisions at key inflection points such as this were all the more important.

The lead consultant working for PacTel, Perry LaForge, had developed skills and experience in evaluating new product launches for the cellular industry, so he felt ready for the job of looking at the potential of code-based wireless. If the technical features indeed panned out, PacTel needed to know what other factors would be important to consider in a possible pursuit of commercial code-based wireless services. It needed to look at all angles of the problem—industry momentum was against CDMA, so PacTel had to know what it would take to leapfrog the industry and make CDMA commercially successful.

The consulting team did a thorough analysis of the state of other digital technologies as well as where Qualcomm was in the development of CDMA. While code-based wireless was still very early in its development, LaForge and many others saw that time-based wireless (TDMA) networks such as those using the European global system for mobile wireless (GSM) standard were fraught with problems as well. Time-based wireless would not provide the capacity that PacTel needed, and GSM handsets were taking longer to produce than had been hoped. The consultants concluded that code-based wireless had the potential, and that the window of opportunity was there. But PacTel would have to move fast—very fast.

PROVING GROUNDS

After presenting its power control solution to PacTel, Qualcomm asked for financial assistance in developing the code-based wireless (CDMA) system concept for a cellular network. Impressed with Qualcomm's ingenuity and with their confidence in CDMA's commercial prospects now bolstered, PacTel agreed to fund further development. But further funding held one challenging condition—Qualcomm had to produce a working prototype, not just a lengthy presentation and a paper report. The cost to create a prototype code-based wireless phone and supporting base stations in 1989 was a cool $2.15 million.

The presentation and demonstration were set to take place in San Diego just six months later, in November 1989. An initial outlay of $1 million was granted by PacTel to Qualcomm to pay for the development of the prototypes. Later in the year, Qualcomm approached PacTel for additional funding to cover cost overruns on the system, but Qualcomm had to bridge this cost itself, banking on future funding. From that point on, the Qualcomm engineers once again went into overdrive, working day and night to develop the prototype system. Qualcomm knew that first impressions were critical at this juncture, so Jacobs and the team invited as many members of the industry as possible, including manufacturers and operators from around the world, to attend the scheduled demonstration and see firsthand that CDMA was real and it worked.

At each and every industry conference and symposium between April and November, Qualcomm sent senior-level representatives to speak about code-based wireless and invite members to the demonstration. Jacobs made a lengthy presentation at the Cellular Telecommunications Industry Association (CTIA) show in Chicago in June, outlining the advantages of CDMA over the frequency-based and time-based wireless cellular systems. The presentation was not warmly received, as the industry had already been through a lengthy battle over the decision between advanced frequency-based wireless methods and the newer time-based wireless. Many in the audience reiterated that in January 1989, the CTIA had officially given its support to the development of a standard based upon TDMA: Qualcomm was six months too late.

The thought of reopening the huge can of worms of standards was not even a consideration for the CTIA and many of its member network operators and vendors. Millions of dollars had been spent in the previous two years developing new technologies and lobbying for their approval by the standards bodies and within the CTIA. The thought of reopening the evaluation process once again made people squeamish—they wanted to move on, putting the past behind them. The cellular industry was running away from them, and spending more time haggling over standards would be like leaving free money on the table for someone else to pick up.

In addition, while the promise of code-based wireless preached by Jacobs was intriguing, there were too many

> "The cell sites they wanted to use for the demonstration in our San Diego network were Motorola's and they didn't want us to touch them. We kept calling and negotiating, but they just flat out refused to do it."
> —JEFF HULTMAN,
> CEO OF PACTEL CELLULAR

unanswered questions—too much remained to be proven. Jacobs acknowledged all the concerns and simply asked for an RSVP to Qualcomm's demonstration later that year. No one had found any fatal flaws in Qualcomm's code-based wireless design, so the proof of concept with a working prototype was necessary to answer the skepticism.

Back home in San Diego, the Qualcomm engineers worked round the clock to get the initial system up. The hardware prototype was big and bulky—several times the size expected for a consumer product (see Figure 6-1). But the phone and transmitting station only had to work—no points would be given for aesthetics. The engineering staff leveraged as much product design as they could, constructing code-based wireless phones by modifying existing phones they had already developed. Equipment was packed into vans to drive around Qualcomm's campus to test calls while moving, a critical element of the demonstration.

PacTel assisted the effort by assigning Lee and several other staff members to work at modifying PacTel's network in San Diego to accept the prototype code-based wireless gear assembled by the Qualcomm engineers. The base stations in Qualcomm's location were Motorola-built, but PacTel's CEO Hultman received a flat denial from Motorola when he requested permission to modify the sites for testing purposes. Motorola had no interest in supporting a competing solution, and Hultman had to place multiple phone calls and finally threaten to remove all Motorola equipment from PacTel's network to get the go-ahead.

Figure 6-1. *Courtesy Qualcomm Inc.*

During preparations for the trial, pizza deliveries and runs to the coffeepot were the norm, as many of Qualcomm's engineers were putting in twenty-four-hour days. All the senior staff worked alongside the engineers in the labs. To keep some sanity in the equation, some engineers took breaks to go mountain biking in the local hills, returning an hour or two later to park their bikes and get back to work. Jacobs himself would go home for dinner, only to return afterward to rejoin the team. By the time November 3 rolled around, the system was ready. And so was a large audience, including some 250 representatives from network operators and vendors from around the world.

Jacobs started out the morning by introducing himself and his company to an audience that included more than a few skeptics. Near the conclusion of his speech, as Jacobs outlined what they would be demonstrating that day, he received a signal to keep talking. Something had obviously happened to the prototype system, but without knowing any details, Jacobs could only nod and continue his speech. A chill went up the spine of the Qualcomm engineers and technicians working behind the scenes: The GPS (global positioning system) synchronization in the test vehicle had failed. With limited time to engage the few satellites, the system had to be reset, as one of the most momentous prototype tests in modern history was about to begin.

Qualcomm and PacTel engineers worked frantically to get the GPS receivers reinitialized—something had gone wrong with the first attempt, and they weren't sure whether the problem was theirs or the DOD's (Department of Defense, the owner of the GPS satellites). Since the GPS system was not yet fully developed at this time, with less than half of the planned twenty-four satellites in orbit, Qualcomm's demonstration was timed specifically to take advantage of the few satellites within range of San Diego. A reset was not a big deal—they had done it hundreds of times before—but the perceptions created by protracted problems would not bode well for their first-ever demonstration. Fortunately, after a short period, they got the receivers to lock in with the GPS system, and the demonstration was on. The thumbs-up was given to Jacobs, and he moved quickly to present the system. Several times that day, Irwin Jacobs and Allen Salmasi would ad lib their presentations to several groups before trips in the test vehicle, but other than slight delays, there were only minor problems.

The rest of the afternoon was spent driving the van around, making calls, and showcasing elements of CDMA's design to the attendees. By the end of the day, the first demonstration of practical code-based wireless in a cellular system was labeled a huge success. The trial demonstrated that code-based wireless exceeded a capacity improvement of at least ten times analog AMPS systems, and the voice quality of the code-based wireless calls was remarkable. All the major features and benefits of code-based wireless were verified in the demonstration and accompanying simulations. It was a stunning victory for Qualcomm.

CHAPTER 7

New Technology Never Sells Itself

Winning Acceptance One Demo at a Time, 1989–1991

The successful completion of early prototype systems by Qualcomm was a huge shot in the arm for all advocates of code-based wireless (CDMA). The confidence that pervaded Qualcomm after these initial successes was incomparable. If there had been any doubt—either inside or outside the company—that code-based wireless cellular could be done, the results were in. It was only a matter of whether you believed they were real. Surprisingly, many people who did not attend the demonstration expressed their disbelief, with some even suggesting that the tests were faked. Inside the company, though—and for those attending the demonstration—there was no doubt.

One of the biggest smiles at the demonstration was on the face of PacTel's William Lee. The validation of Qualcomm's code-based wireless approach to cellular bolstered Lee's visibility to the various levels of senior management within PacTel, whose support he had been wooing. The trial had won them over, and PacTel agreed to further fund Qualcomm's development of code-based wireless, in addition to taking an equity position in the company.

While the early response from the trial was very positive, Qualcomm knew that it was still a long way from seeing CDMA in commercial use. Soon after the completion of the San Diego trial, many in the industry were calling for tougher tests of the technology, claiming that the San Diego area was close to an ideal environment for cellular signals. Many critics of the technology claimed again that while code-based wireless might perform adequately under good conditions, it would quickly break down in difficult environments. A dense, downtown area would provide a true test of its performance—someplace like New York.

FROM WEST TO EAST AND BEYOND

The next demonstration of Qualcomm's prototype was held three months later (February 1990) in New York City, one of the toughest cellular markets in the United States. Its high-rise buildings and dense concentration of businesses made cellular service particularly difficult. Skeptics and proponents alike were curious to see how well the technology would perform in an environment fraught with multipath interference and RF noise. NYNEX Mobile, one of the observers at the San Diego trial, hosted this event. And once again, invitations were spread throughout the entire wireless industry, domestic and international.

The demonstration in New York went off without a hitch, and Qualcomm's code-based wireless once again proved its capacity benefits and immunity to noise.

Due in large part to the success of the San Diego and New York trials, Qualcomm was able to win the commitment of six leading operators and equipment vendors: AT&T, NYNEX Mobile, Ameritech Mobile Communications, Motorola, OKI Electric, and PacTel Cellular. Over the next several months, these companies collectively committed more than $30 million to the continued development of code-based wireless into commercial-capable equipment within the next two years. The goal of the development funding was to perform a large-scale field validation of CDMA. The trial would closely mimic the commercial operation of a real network, including multiple phones and base stations spread over a wide area. To implement this level of testing, Qualcomm would have to develop custom integrated circuits to make phones that were reasonable in size for commercial use.

With this two-year plan ahead of the team, things were beginning to look much brighter. Qualcomm now had a strong contingent of operators and equipment vendors willing to work with it to bring code-based wireless to commercial life. All the hard work of spreading the message of code-based wireless—and following it up with successful demonstrations—was paying off. With two successful demonstrations under its belt and more planned in the months ahead, Qualcomm charged ahead at industry events and meetings to build on the early momentum of interest in CDMA.

The new development agreements, along with an additional preferred-share offering, provided critical funding to Qualcomm, enabling it to pursue the development of commercial grade code-based wireless equipment aggressively. This critical endorsement by a large contingent of the U.S. cellular industry also bolstered Qualcomm's prospects internationally, with several network operators and equipment manufacturers now paying closer attention to the CDMA dark horse. Along with the renewed technical push, Jacobs quickly put the new cash infusion to work by launching a renewed marketing effort. Qualcomm's name now held legitimacy in the global cellular market: It was no longer just a government contractor that had lost its way and wandered into the wireless industry.

THE KOREAN CONNECTION

While adoption of code-based wireless in the United States was Qualcomm's primary focus, the company had always realized that certain international markets held tremendous opportunity for wireless communications. While the United States badly needed CDMA to solve capacity problems, other regions of the world with less-developed telecommunications were fertile markets as well. And Qualcomm knew that if it could penetrate the world en masse, the economics of code-based wireless would rapidly fall in line with those of the competing alternatives utilizing time-based or frequency-based wireless technology.

So, from its first days, Qualcomm sent out invitations for demonstrations and symposiums to companies around the globe. Perhaps Qualcomm's most significant international partner was actually one of its first, the Korean Electronics and Telecommunications Research Institute (ETRI).

By 1990, the southern Korean peninsula had developed analog cellular networks that were well received by Korean subscribers. The sole network operator, Korea Mobile Telecom (KMT), had a government-instituted monopoly on the market, and its mobile communications business performed well—unencumbered by competitors taking up physical or air-wave space. But the equipment providers that had developed the network infrastructure and mobile terminals were largely foreign entities, such as AT&T, Nokia, Northern Telecom, and Motorola. Domestic developers and equipment providers had almost no share of their own market, let alone any significant customers outside the country, forcing them to pursue other industries such as personal computers.

As the 1980s ended, with global bodies approving next-generation standards for digital wireless, the Korean government's Ministry of Communication (MoC) realized that domestic manufacturers would end up in a similar position in the coming generation of wireless technology. The digital technologies that were gaining global momentum were being dominated by European, American, or Japanese entities, and it looked as if Korea would once again lack any meaningful

> "Korean companies had no market share in phones or infrastructure—it was all Nokia and other foreign companies. If they had gone TDMA, they'd still be shut out because they would have been behind the development of all the other competitors developing TDMA products. But if they went with CDMA, they could be early suppliers and establish themselves as the leading manufacturers in their market."
>
> —STEVE ALTMAN,
> EXECUTIVE VP AND PRESIDENT,
> QUALCOMM TECHNOLOGY LICENSING

participation in its own domestic market or in the global trade in communications equipment.

To counter this trend, in 1989 the South Korean MoC initiated an effort to study ways for domestic manufacturers to play a leading role in the domestic communications market as well as provide a significant presence internationally. To achieve this, the government would work to unite universities and research bodies with local companies in order to develop technologies that would afford Korea advantages in the supply of equipment and services. The effort initially began with ETRI looking at improved analog and time-based wireless technologies from companies such as Motorola and Northern Telecom, but the level of development in this area was already sufficiently advanced to exclude a meaningful Korean role. With a limited amount of intellectual property and experience with the then-entrenched wireless protocols, Korean manufacturers and researchers were again at the mercy of foreigners for development.

In August 1990, the Korean government and members of ETRI were introduced to the concept of using CDMA in cellular systems through

> "Allen Salmasi was instrumental in making a lot of the openings for us to go in and do technical presentations."
> —IRWIN JACOBS,
> QUALCOMM COFOUNDER AND CEO

William Lee of PacTel during a sponsored seminar in Seoul. In addition, Allen Salmasi's tireless pursuit of key players in Korea was also successful in opening doors at ETRI and the MoC, giving Qualcomm the chance to explain the benefits of code-based wireless. Immediately, Salmasi realized the clear synergy potential between the two bodies—Qualcomm needed international endorsement for CDMA, and Korea seriously desired a role in global telecommunications. By becoming an early adopter and leader of digital wireless services using CDMA, Korea would gain a decided advantage over other regions.

Over the course of several months, Salmasi and Qualcomm's chief license negotiator, Steve Altman, made several trips to Korea to present the technology and negotiate terms for a joint venture. The nascent technology was viewed by some in the Korean organizations as a high-risk alternative, but Qualcomm repeatedly pointed to the initial successful trials. Hen Suh Park, PacTel Korea's representative director, with Lee and other PacTel representatives in the United States, kept negotiations going between the MoC, ETRI, and Qualcomm even when things looked bleak.

The negotiations with ETRI and the Korean government were long and difficult. Explaining how code-based wireless could work technically and perform well commercially became tedious and repetitive. Even those who granted that Qualcomm had the technical expertise to make the technology work questioned whether it made business sense to build networks in Korea based on yet another foreign technology. On top of this, the risk associated with commercializing the new technology in a timely manner was a reason for hesitancy for many in the MoC. Qualcomm had to demonstrate to the Korean government that its code-based wireless technology would indeed meet all the government's needs and requirements, and offered to build incentives into the agreement that answered each party's needs.

After several rounds of intense talks, Qualcomm finally entered into a joint development agreement with ETRI in May 1991. The agreement specified several phases of development and implementation of prototype networks intended to fully demonstrate the capabilities of the technology.

The deal was carefully structured to benefit both parties and address the concerns of Korean leaders. Designated Korean manufacturers would have full access to Qualcomm's intellectual property and would receive added technical support from Qualcomm's engineering team during the development phases. While it would receive a royalty for each product sold that used its technology, Qualcomm was required to donate 20 percent of its royalty income to ETRI to fund further research. This closed the loop of innovation and education in the Korean market and effectively developed a means by which Korea could move toward homegrown competency in mobile communications.

Direct access to Qualcomm's intellectual property and expertise would give Korean manufacturers a lead in developing the new technology and a huge head start over competitors. In return, Qualcomm would benefit from the dedicated development of its prototypes into commercial equipment. Having significant proficiency in core network design (involving the control and switching elements of a wireless network) meant that Korean manufacturers would develop this portion of the new network. Qualcomm, in turn, would provide the necessary technology for the air interface between the mobile units and the base stations.

To further dilute the risk to both Qualcomm and Korea, the agreement provided flexibility at each stage of development to modify the collaboration if either party did not meet certain goals. The initial funding gave Qualcomm $2 million to start the first phase of the project, and each succeeding phase would begin only after the Korean government's approval of the performance of the system at the previous step. Ultimately, the deal promised Qualcomm $17 million over the two-year span of the contract.

The ensuing success of the joint development of code-based wireless in Korea proved to be a boon for both Qualcomm and Korea's mobile communications market. By 1993, the deal started to bring in substantial licensing revenue for

Qualcomm and guaranteed a strong Asian presence for code-b[...] works. Korea was also be at the forefront of wireless services, d[...] best that wireless had to offer consumers. The country's ad[...] would end up being not only a proving ground for this adva[...] but also a valuable marketing asset that showcased advanced wireless services to other network operators around the world.

ANOTHER CORE COMPETENCY: CUSTOM ASICs

Because Qualcomm was at the forefront of communications theory and implementation, it had developed considerable expertise in VLSI (very-large-scale integrated computer circuit) and ASIC (application-specific integrated circuit) technologies, which were developing rapidly at the time. Even though the computer industry was booming in the 1980s and companies like Intel were rolling out advanced processors every eighteen months, the chips that were being developed were not well suited for advanced communications. The efficient mathematical cores required for digital communication functions were still lacking in the available components. (Intel's computer processors did not have a sophisticated math coprocessor until the 80387 chip was introduced in 1988.)

At Linkabit, engineers had to develop custom processors and other integrated circuits to carry out their breakthrough communication ideas—there were no off-the-shelf semiconductors that were capable of the performance and efficiency they demanded. Viterbi's hallmark decoder was implemented in a large-scale integrated circuit device custom-built under an early contract at Qualcomm, and many of the novel solutions developed were impossible without customized ASIC semiconductors. The engineers at Qualcomm were not just great systems integrators; they started at the lowest level and manipulated transistors to achieve their goals.

This talent in semiconductor design and its ongoing development would now come into play at what was a critical juncture for Qualcomm in its effort to advance the commercial application of CDMA. The chips that were needed to make the new technology work did not exist except as prototypes. So Qualcomm faced the dilemma of manufacturing the chips itself, because it now had to take the technology to the next stage and produce commercially usable cell phones along with network signal processing equipment. While some within the company thought that manufacturing chips would be a money-losing venture, the decision to pursue ASIC development was to play a key role in the commercial realization of Qualcomm's technology.

The scale of semiconductor manufacturing necessary for commercial implementation of CDMA in the cellular market was several orders of magnitude ʋove anything Qualcomm had done with semiconductors in the past. Qualcomm had a team in place in an ASIC division in 1989, but it was far too small to take on the task of designing several new ASICs for cellular CDMA. The team had developed the semiconductors used in OmniTRACS units and several of the earlier projects, including the Viterbi decoder chip, but the volume on these was well below the millions required for cellular. The complexity of the cellular communications task was also much greater, as it would require several chips working together.

Venturing into semiconductor design at this level was a big risk, but no other vendor could come on board quickly enough to fill this need—Qualcomm had to do it itself. The new funding from operators and manufacturers would permit a modest budget for the expansion of the ASIC division, so Jacobs sought to put together a plan for developing the division. Jacobs knew that if Qualcomm was successful in developing the code-based wireless ASICs, this would also give the company a critical supplier advantage if and when the new technology was adopted in the cellular industry.

Rich Kerr, another Linkabit employee who came to Qualcomm early on, teamed up with Roberto Padovani to develop the ASIC division into one that was capable of delivering all the circuitry necessary to implement CDMA.

"We sat down and designed all the ASICs in about three or four weeks."
—RICH KERR,
EX-LINKABIT,
QUALCOMM EMPLOYEE;
DEVELOPED THE QUALCOMM
ASIC DIVISION

They estimated that they would have to take the existing chip team of three up to about thirty, so this involved hiring dozens of skilled engineers in a very short period of time. The team went on whirlwind tours of San Jose and other concentrated talent pools to interview dozens of applicants a day. By February 1990, Qualcomm had a skeleton team in place and a new building to house them. The team went to work immediately to define the task of implementing code-based wireless in custom chips, all the while looking toward full manufacturing capability in the future. Qualcomm would take the route of being a fabless semiconductor company—that is, it would contract with outside foundries to actually manufacture the chips by the million. However, Qualcomm would perform all the core engineering, development, and testing of the designs.

Jacobs's goal was to have functional ASICs scoped out, fabricated, tested, and qualified in time to be used in a major 1991 demo that was being scheduled. By demonstrating to the industry that code-based wireless could indeed be implemented in commercially viable hardware, not just in prototype, Qualcomm would gain tremendous leverage over a large population of naysayers whose chief criticism was of the hardware complexity. With the development costs covered by the buy-in of the six early supporters, Jacobs had no problem approving Kerr and Padovani's budget for ASIC development—time was a more critical factor. As in many of his early experiences in Linkabit, Jacobs was not frightened by large up-front costs—he knew that the eventual return would dwarf the sunk costs.

This internal semiconductor development was to give Qualcomm a huge advantage over other vendors in the future commercialization of CDMA. Semiconductor design—especially RF semiconductor design—is still, even today, as much art as science. No sophisticated tools for the development and testing of RF chipsets and systems were available for engineers in the 1990s; it was all done by experience and feel. Having the right people with the right experience was critical, and many of Qualcomm's competitors would struggle to implement CDMA in their own chipset designs.

CHAPTER 8

Creating a Common Interface

Devising and Testing, 1990–1991

While the decision to develop competency in the manufacture of code-based wireless (CDMA) components and systems offered many advantages to Qualcomm, it opened up new issues as well. Speed in making the new technology function commercially was now critical, but the network operators would balk if Qualcomm were the sole supplier of equipment. Qualcomm had to balance the speed of developing new equipment with the necessity to quickly get other manufacturers moving ahead with their own CDMA-based designs.

Along with staging early prototype trials, Qualcomm worked hard behind the scenes to negotiate joint ventures with major manufacturers of cellular infrastructure and handsets. It used the leverage of the network operators who now favored code-based wireless to encourage equipment suppliers to come on board. Since the equipment suppliers basically moved in the directions that their customers (the network operators) indicated, they would need some prodding. Qualcomm offered to supply its customized CDMA chips (application-specific integrated circuits, or ASICs) to manufacturers to incorporate into their equipment, alleviating a costly portion of the development. But there was still a high level of risk involved, especially for major manufacturers with established businesses in other technologies.

> "Jeff [Hultman, CEO of PacTel] wouldn't write any checks until other carriers were interested."
> —ALLEN SALMASI,
> OMNINET FOUNDER, QUALCOMM
> VP, NOW CEO OF NEXTWAVE

Motorola in particular pushed Qualcomm to lessen the risk of investing in the development of code-based wireless equipment. Like many other vendors and operators, Motorola asked for performance guarantees, exclusive rights, and milestone targets in return for making a commitment to the technology. Since Motorola had a strong vested interest in competing cellular technologies, like N-AMPS (narrowband advanced mobile phone system, which was still analog), it was difficult to get Motorola to acknowledge that CDMA was important to the company's future. It was a delicate balance for a sales pitch—make sure your target is not threatened by your offering, but make sure it understands that your product is essential to the company's future.

AT&T was another early licensee of Qualcomm's code-based wireless technology for manufacturing into infrastructure equipment. Like Motorola, AT&T had a vested interest in time-based wireless (TDMA) technology, and CDMA threatened this revenue stream. Again, money talked: AT&T had to be guaranteed firm orders for equipment before license agreements were signed. By August 1990, Qualcomm had worked with Ameritech and NYNEX to craft a purchase agreement with AT&T for their networks.

> "We recognized at that time that the carriers that funded us would not go forward with a single source for CDMA technology."
> —STEVE ALTMAN,
> EXECUTIVE VP AND PRESIDENT,
> QUALCOMM TECHNOLOGY LICENSING

AT&T then signed a license agreement with Qualcomm, which provided it with some immediate funding for development as well as guarantees of future royalties. With two major vendors now under license, Qualcomm had much more leverage in negotiating with other vendors. The message could now be pitched as one of playing catch-up: Vendors who stalled on license agreements risked being overrun by early licensees.

But having multiple sources of equipment for CDMA networks opened up an even bigger problem: compatibility. Network operators liked to have the option of purchasing various pieces of equipment from multiple parties. It was common, for instance, for an operator to have its network supplied by one vendor while others supplied mobile terminals. This competition guaranteed the lowest cost, but it also necessitated clear standards for protocol development. Each vendor had to design equipment to the same specifications, or else chaos ensued. All elements of a network had to talk with one another and play nice together—there was no room for custom hooks or proprietary protocols.

Qualcomm's CDMA technology as yet had no published standards—a fact that many operators were quick to point out. As Qualcomm was developing CDMA at the time, the protocols and methods were entirely proprietary to it. This had to change rapidly: Multiple equipment vendors had to be given a common boilerplate for code-based wireless implementation. The specifications for the operation of a radio technology like CDMA were commonly referred to as a common air interface, or CAI. Qualcomm had only loosely developed an internal CAI for its initial trials, but a more detailed, formal document was now urgently required.

Methods for developing a reference document for CDMA's common air interface were discussed between Qualcomm and its main partners, PacTel,

NYNEX, and Ameritech. Since the CTIA (Cellular Telecommunications Industry Association) and TIA (Telecommunications Industry Association) had more interest in furthering the standards of a time-based wireless (TDMA) digital cellular system, the team had little choice but to begin the development of a de facto standard by themselves, without formal endorsement at this point in the game. The group decided to hold several meetings to emulate the process of standards development within the TIA, and it ultimately produce a document that could be quickly adopted by the standards body at a later time. The group decided to forgo all the bureaucratic steps, such as open comment forums, that could drag out the formal process: It needed to formalize a standard document in record time.

With the dedicated help of numerous operators and equipment vendors, Qualcomm and its invested team of network operators worked to publish the first formal version of the CDMA CAI in July 1990. This first document, known as the Green Book of CDMA, was distributed to Qualcomm's partners and advocates to invite input on the protocol and its improvement. In the coming months, the CAI for CDMA underwent numerous revisions to include the suggestions of numerous interested parties. Prior to the upcoming November 1991 capacity demonstrations, the CAI went through three revisions—the Blue Book, the Red Book, and finally the Gold Book.

With formal documentation of the common air interface in hand, Qualcomm was confident that the code-based wireless infrastructure and mobile units could be commercialized quickly, possibly within twelve months. The advocates of CDMA continued to lobby the CTIA for endorsement of the technology and its published CAI—at the very least, to make it an option for operators that wanted to deploy a digital cellular technology. While the CTIA and many others in the industry continued to spurn code-based wireless in favor of other paths, the Qualcomm group continued to press ahead. The technology worked incredibly well, and once the industry saw CDMA in action under real-world loading conditions, all the doubts would be removed. Qualcomm now had the technology, the money, and the talent to get there. It also had to keep public confidence in code-based wireless high.

SELLING THE INVISIBLE

While many people came to know Qualcomm for its technical excellence and the engineering wizardry of its founders, its success as a business had just as much—if not more—to do with its ability to rally a significant faction of the industry and evangelize the solution. The new technology did not sell itself, and the plan for marketing and funding during the years that followed to make CDMA commercial would prove equally challenging for Qualcomm.

In the cellular industry, no company could develop a technology, product, or service in a vacuum—without a solid understanding of the dynamics of the industry, the major players, and the industry segments. In the case of telecommunications in general, and cellular communications more specifically, services were provided to consumers through a complex coordination of individual companies. The model for the cellular industry continues today to be a complex "wireless food chain" with intertwined interests. Successful companies continue to be the ones that understand the industry well and leverage the strengths and weaknesses of each sector of the market. CDMA had no chance in the market if Qualcomm couldn't get companies at every level to buy into its benefits. Qualcomm also had to be smart in how it played competitors and customers against each other.

Qualcomm wisely courted the network operator segment first: those companies that were in direct contact with the wireless consumer. The network operators were the ones who were most keenly aware of the advantages and limitations of each technology—and how each succeeded or failed commercially. The message that Qualcomm brought to operators was one that they wanted to hear: better capacity, better coverage, and better service quality. Demonstrating the possibilities of CDMA to the network operators was key to driving the rest of the industry and dictating what form of technology was eventually supplied to their customers. Qualcomm was successful in winning the endorsement of a strong contingent of U.S. network operators at this early stage in the development of digital wireless technology.

> "One problem with bringing the technology to commercial introduction (as with other technologies) was that the handsets always lagged. So we decided we'd better continue to develop the equipment commercially so that when the standard was complete, we could quickly launch equipment."
>
> —IRWIN JACOBS

But as stated previously, the key ingredient to successfully breaking into the cellular market was getting equipment manufacturers on board early. It was common to have new network launches delayed because of lack of equipment, especially the mobile units. Even though Qualcomm could test prototype systems extensively, full due diligence required commercial-grade equipment coming off the assembly lines of various manufacturers. Equipment manufacturing often lagged behind the development of the network architecture and protocol standards, leading to many delays in service launches. While Qualcomm had the necessary technology (and documentation) in place, it needed to give manufacturers incentives to move quickly toward product commercialization. Qualcomm's furnishing ASICs for inclusion in products was seen as one key element to this. But since they had vested interests in other digital technologies, manufacturers needed more business incentives, not just technological incentives, to pursue CDMA.

The biggest challenge with CDMA at this early stage—as with any new technology—was that Qualcomm was essentially selling a promise to prospective companies. No full-scale, heavily loaded networks were in operation to demonstrate the functions and benefits achieved through code-based wireless. Much of the value of the new technology had been proven only in limited tests, and the full advantages of the solution were only extrapolated from the tests. Whether the predictions were considered valid or not, the benefits were still hypothetical, and this provided an easy excuse for critics or operators with cold feet.

PREPARATION FOR CAPACITY TRIALS

Qualcomm had claimed that it solved all the problems associated with CDMA in a cellular network. But solving the problems and making code-based wireless work was not the whole answer: It had to work well enough to provide the capacity benefits envisioned and marketed by Jacobs, Salmasi, and the other CDMA advocates. Operators wanted to test CDMA in various real-life conditions—rural areas, dense suburbs, hilly terrain, heavily loaded systems, and so on—before committing to the new technology. The trials planned for November 1991 (referred to as the CAP 1 trials) contained all the elements necessary to fully demonstrate a commercial cellular network.

The trials took place over several days in November 1991 in San Diego on PacTel's actual network. PacTel supplied locations in its base stations where Qualcomm could install its CDMA equipment next to the existing analog gear. PacTel also modified its current frequency allocations in the area so that a portion of the band could be used for the trial. In all, the test included five cells, divided into nine separate sectors, and seventy mobile units. The dozens of mobile units moved simultaneously through the different sectors, testing the ability of Qualcomm's patented soft handoff, which so many critics doubted. The plethora of mobile units also created the first true test of system capacity—the voice quality of multiple units was assessed while they were grouped in the same cell sector. It was a step up from early prototype tests of the technology, in which radio frequency (RF) noise was injected into the environment to simulate multiple users congesting a cell.

The capacity trial was also a major step in demonstrating commercial-like equipment to the industry. Equipment manufacturers were keen to "look under the hood" to assure themselves that the CDMA units were something that they could indeed manufacture in a reasonable size and shape (called a form factor). The development of Qualcomm's custom ASICs played a big role here. Jacobs showcased the technology implementation at both the chip and the subsystem level, to convince manufacturers that it was feasible to manufacture in the near term.

The Qualcomm ASICs team ended up developing five separate chips, each controlling a separate family of functions in the process of completing a code-based wireless call. With the new chips now functioning, Qualcomm quickly assembled the base station equipment and mobile units. The base station equipment was located in PacTel's cells in a variety of areas around Mission Bay that were chosen to test CDMA in a variety of tough environments—hills, downtown high-rises, highways, and over water.

ANOTHER CASH CRUNCH

As the trial date approached, though, Qualcomm once again was challenged financially. The money invested by the six major participants in the trial had initially looked sufficient to complete the preparations, but with so much else going on in the company, especially with OmniTRACS production, it was difficult to see how things would work out financially. Juggling all the money that was coming in and out of the company proved tricky. Cutting off funding for CDMA development was out of the question, so resources had to be shifted from other areas of the business or from lines of credit. Many employees in Qualcomm worked extensive overtime—without extra pay—to help prepare for the trials.

> "People worked there more for the excitement than the pay."
> —RICH KERR,
> EX-LINKABIT, QUALCOMM EMPLOYEE

The team was also contemplating the next financial step after the trials. With a large-scale trial under its belt, the next step would certainly include scaled-up manufacturing capacity for additional trials and tests. In discussions with its current partners, Qualcomm soon realized that it couldn't ask them for additional funding. Additional private offerings could be sought, but a more viable option for the level of funding they envisioned, in the range of $50 million, would be to position the company for an offering to the public. In 1990 the public markets had suffered their worst plunge since Black Monday of 1987, with the broad market indexes dropping over 20 percent in a single day. But in 1991 the markets had already fully recovered and sentiment had once again turned positive. The current strength in the public markets, if it was maintained, would give Qualcomm one of its best opportunities to raise the amount of money it needed. As the trials approached, an IPO became the clear choice.

The timing of the IPO was carefully coordinated with the CAP 1 trial demonstration, which would go a long way in selling shares in the company. The public sale was therefore scheduled for December 1991, right after the trial and the results analysis. With the world having been made aware of the benefits of CDMA, the company felt that it would have no problem getting funding from public sources—assuming, of course, that the trial was a success.

Only a month before the trial, Qualcomm's accounts were once again drained dry. At the end of September 1991, Qualcomm had only $125,000 in cash—not even enough to meet its payroll through the year. This latest cash crunch did not worry Jacobs; he figured that the money would come from somewhere. He wouldn't allow the cash crunch to impede the development process for the CDMA trial and ASICs. There was no question about it: Qualcomm would successfully complete the project it had been funded to do, and the money would be found somewhere, even if it came from Jacobs's own pocket.

Qualcomm had literally invested everything in the CAP 1 trials. All of its development funding had been bled dry. With most of the engineering staff exhausted from prolonged lack of sleep, adrenaline was about the only thing keeping them going. In the pretesting leading up to the trial date, Qualcomm and PacTel were relieved to see the system working as planned. They only had to avoid any major glitches during the operation and presentation. Fortunately, only a few problems occurred during the days of testing, and the CDMA consortium was able to reschedule and complete all the necessary testing and data measurements.

To capitalize on the publicity of the trial and get the most out of the money that had been invested in CDMA so far, PacTel and Qualcomm prepared to capture not only technical data from the trial, but "soft" information as well. The success of the trial would be determined not only by bits, MHz, and other technical measures, but by end–users' perceptions of quality as well. The quality of voices heard in calls would be vital to the perception of CDMA. Since voice quality was difficult to quantify, Qualcomm set up ways for users to compare the voice quality with code-based wireless to the voice quality with other technologies. Many of the vehicles rented for the drive-around tests were loaded with a variety of other cellular phones to compare voice quality in various areas of the test.

PacTel's project consultant, Perry LaForge, worked with the public relations staff at both Qualcomm and PacTel to build upon the image of code-based wireless and make an exceptional presentation of the technology for the world to see. For use in marketing and at trade shows, extensive video footage was taken as various mobile units traveled around the city during calls. The companies captured testimonials from numerous influential industry veterans praising the quality of the voice connections and expressing excitement at making mobile calls on this new one-of-a-kind system.

All the technical data from the trial were compiled by Qualcomm and the participating operators in preparation for a formal review of the data during a CTIA-sponsored forum. The technology forum was held on December 4th and 5th to review a detailed analysis of the capacity calculations and other metrics pertinent to the trial. During the presentations, Qualcomm showed that it had proved that its code-based wireless solution could indeed provide capacity enhancements exceeding ten times the capacity of analog networks. The new system also performed soft handoffs and power control accurately enough to keep calls from being dropped while mobile in a wide variety of environments. The five ASICs produced by Qualcomm met all functional requirements and performed within expectations for power consumption. For comparison, Qualcomm presented all the current information on field tests for competing technologies as well—TDMA and Motorola's N-AMPS.

The technology forum was a great opportunity to once again impress upon the industry that CDMA was a viable path for operators to take for implementation of digital cellular networks. It had now been proven to meet all the user performance requirements laid out by the CTIA—unlike the competing TDMA—and Qualcomm could have equipment commercially available in twelve months. All the information that operators and vendors needed was now laid out in front of them, and the CTIA board of directors had all the facts in hand to move forward with CDMA in the United States. The Qualcomm team, along with its partners, left the event with a new level of confidence—it had reached a major milestone with the successful wide-scale demonstration of code-based wireless, something that many had thought was simply impossible. Critics of the technology had little ammunition against CDMA at this point, and more doubters were being converted each day.

The CTIA was to convene a board meeting in the next year to take a position concerning digital wireless technologies. Even with the holidays coming, many informal meetings and discussions were taking place behind the scenes. Everyone was eager to know what the board would recommend: Would CDMA be given equal footing with TDMA? Or would it even possibly be chosen to take the place of the time-based variant that failed to meet the UPR (User Performance Requirements) document? Anything seemed possible, but the industry would have to remain in suspense through the holidays to find out.

IPO Oversubscribed

Internally, Qualcomm wasn't wasting any time considering the CTIA's review of CDMA—it had to keep going no matter what. With the triumphal success of the CAP I trials, everyone within Qualcomm was looking forward to the upcoming public offering. Roughly 20 percent of the company would be offered to the public: 4 million shares, 3.2 million domestically and 800,000 internationally, at a price of $16 per share. This more than doubled the valuation of the shares of some of Qualcomm's early investors; the last two rounds of preferred shares had been offered at $8 per share with a one-to-one conversion into common stock.

The IPO went off as planned on December 16, 1991, and the demand was great enough to dole out the shares allotted for oversubscription (an additional 480,000 shares domestically and 120,000 internationally). By the end of the trading day, the stock closed at $17.625, netting Qualcomm roughly $68 million—enough to last the company another fifteen months. The strong opening day would be followed by many more good days, and after two weeks the stock was up over 50 percent. The public support was a strong endorsement of CDMA and instilled more confidence than ever in Qualcomm's team. Now flush with new cash, Jacobs and the rest of the senior officers could take care of unpaid bills and once again turn their concern back to the technical challenges. The passing into the New Year would indeed be quite a celebration for Qualcomm.

As it turned out, though, Qualcomm was very fortunate in the timing of its IPO—a delay of a mere three weeks might have put a damper on enthusiasm for the shares. The CTIA held a board meeting on January 6, 1992, and the group unanimously chose to once again endorse time-based wireless (TDMA) as the choice for digital cellular networks in the United States. While the board could not fault the performance of CDMA, it questioned the time necessary to deliver commercial equipment. In the opinion of the CTIA board, it would be at least 1994 before any other alternative to TDMA could be sufficiently developed. The board saw time-based wireless as having the potential to deliver commercial equipment by the end of the year, giving it at least a two-year advantage in commercial deployment—a critical aspect in moving the industry forward with digital cellular technology.

Once again, CDMA was shut out. Qualcomm's stock dropped several dollars that week, erasing some of the earlier gains as investors and industry watchers fretted over the company's future.

CHAPTER 9

Becoming a Wireless Standard

––·–··–►

Going the Extra Mile to Acceptance, 1992–1993

The decision by the Cellular Telecommunications Industry Association (CTIA) left Qualcomm's code-based wireless (CDMA) sidelined in the minds of many people outside the company, but the CTIA made several additional recommendations that Qualcomm saw as very positive. The CTIA board recommended that the Telecommunications Industry Association (TIA) set up the structure for a wideband spread-spectrum standard (WBSS) that would be developed alongside time-based wireless (TDMA). This recommendation was accompanied by an instruction to formally start an open forum for a WBSS system. The stipulation was added, though, that the work on another standard could not in any way dilute or slow the effort to proceed with TDMA. At the time of the AT&T breakup in 1986, the wireless industry in the United States had begun moving more toward a technology-neutral stance, leaving voluntary standards adoption up to the marketplace. This required the collaborative development of standards within the TIA, which had been set up to coordinate this development of standards within various segments of the telecom industry, yet to set no policy or favor any one standard over another. It was simply an open forum for developing, documenting, and approving voluntary standards for companies to follow.

The resolution from the CTIA board had a number of implications for Qualcomm's technology. Many in the CTIA (and the industry as a whole) were concerned about developing a standard based upon CDMA because of Qualcomm's nearly 100 percent control of the technology. The open forum process was designed to get contributions from multiple parties into a spread-spectrum standard—even the name of the forum, WBSS, was meant to avoid favoring Qualcomm's version of spread spectrum. The U.S. policy on technical standards was consistently moving toward balanced contributions from a number of companies, so opening up the spread-spectrum technology to the rest of the industry was not a surprise.

But the side effect of the open forum proceedings was extensive delay in making CDMA a published standard. Qualcomm was certain that it would have to slog painfully through the process, in which companies—especially competitors favoring TDMA—could bicker and argue in a large committee setting. Many of the advocates of code-based wireless could easily see the subversive motive here: While the open forum was politically necessary in the eyes of the CTIA, it would offer TDMA supporters a great opportunity to stall CDMA and gain more ground, possibly killing the chances for code-based wireless altogether. As had been shown by the European development of its GSM standard, consensus could take years to develop in an open committee. As a relative newcomer to the cellular industry, Qualcomm would have to rely heavily on its partners' knowledge of standard setting around the world to navigate the politically charged environments.

DIFFERING APPROACHES TO DEVELOPING A STANDARD

The processes involved in developing technical standards (and cellular standards in particular) varied dramatically from region to region around the world. The interaction between the CTIA and the TIA in the United States was completely different from the way in which the European bodies set standards. Many regions of the world were also very early in the process of deregulating their telecommunications markets, so the level of political influence in standard setting remained high.

Since the U.S. wireless industry was still largely viewed as an extension of the much larger telecommunications industry, the policies that were in place for traditional landline services set the norms for the wireless industry throughout the 1970s and 1980s. The breakup of AT&T and the push against monopolistic control of telecommunications crept into wireless regulation as well, but not before an effective duopoly (licensing only two network operators in each market) had been put in place for first-generation networks. However, the rapid growth of cellular services and the unique component of spectrum management started to break this policy paradigm by the end of the 1980s.

First-generation analog networks were universally based on the advanced mobile phone system (AMPS) standard, simplifying technology compatibility concerns. This single standard was not seen as heavy-handed government policy, though, as there was really no serious commercial alternative to AMPS at the time of its deployment in the early 1980s. But since licenses to operate systems were granted to only two operators in any given market, the bare minimum of competition was effectively implemented on a regional scale.

In contrast, the European countries learned their early lessons in wireless standards the hard way. The first generation of cellular networks in Western European and Nordic countries used six different technical standards. Users who wanted to roam across borders saw their phones turn into paperweights as incompatible networks prevented them from functioning. Complaints from users and a big push to transform Europe into a global economic power were to change the landscape for standard setting in the coming digital generation, though.

Qualcomm's CDMA push took place right in the midst of the European Union's formative years. The pan-European body was moving rapidly to develop an environment in which member nations were well represented in local and global markets. This distilled down to a technology policy that favored a common interface standard, developed through broad collaboration among European companies—not necessarily encouraging the most advanced technology. The emphasis in the EU's Conference of European Posts and Telecommunications (CEPT) was on developing a single, unified digital standard for all of Europe and beyond. The cost of this approach, of course, was time: CEPT spent much of the 1980s developing the standard.

But the EU went beyond standard setting to implement public and economic policies that effectively blocked alternatives to the selected standard. The choice of what was called the global system for mobile communications, or GSM, as the standard for mobile wireless communications, though voluntary, was coupled with spectrum and roaming policies that were designed to make alternative standards much less attractive. The EU provided political and economic incentives to foster the adoption of this single standard, essentially guaranteeing consistency in implementation across member countries.

In 1987, more than a dozen European countries had signed on to a memorandum of understanding outlining the development and adoption of GSM mobile networks. As more and more nations signed on to the memorandum, the nations that remained uncommitted to a particular mobile technology had less and less incentive to hold out for an alternative. While GSM was a voluntary standard, member countries of the European Union had no realistic alternative. In a sense, GSM can almost be characterized as a forced de facto standard.

At the start of the 1990s, the United States and Europe were thus on starkly different paths for the development of wireless communication systems. The United States was opening up to more of a technology-neutral stance, where operators could effectively choose whatever standard they wanted, if it showed merit. The belief was that market-driven efficiencies in technology development would benefit the end users, American consumers. In contrast, the EU saw benefits for its populace coming from a different source—the seamless interoperability of dozens of networks spanning much of the industrialized world.

While the European bodies sought to spread the GSM technology around the world, the United States—like many other non-European nations—was not particularly interested in the EU standard. Since GSM had been developed largely within European companies, American companies did not have a large market share in equipment or services for this standard. And since spectrum assignments in the United States differed from those in Europe, the FCC saw far less benefit from supporting a global standard in GSM than from developing better digital standards under free-market policies. American innovation and the opportunities arising from it were favored over global consensus in cellular technologies, and the belief was that superior technology would make American products attractive for export.

It was in this open approach to technology standards that Qualcomm saw an opportunity. The FCC and industry bodies consistently remained open to multiple alternatives for standards, preferring to allow the free market to choose appropriate technologies. With the CTIA board decision, the standards process was within striking distance for Qualcomm, but first it had to get through the open forum debates. Qualcomm felt that the CAI was mature and that input from other companies was unnecessary—after all, no one else knew even a fraction of what Qualcomm knew about making CDMA work.

ALL ROADS LEAD TO ROME

Qualcomm still believed that CDMA could be deployed in an operating network by the end of 1992, but a formal standards process would certainly delay this, possibly for years. Rather than fight or complain about the CTIA decision to support TDMA, Qualcomm met with the consortium that had supported the CAP 1 trials to hammer out a plan for rapid standard setting. The common air interface (CAI) specification, in its fifth revision, was fairly stable and was in suitable form to present in the open forum as the template for a WBSS standard. Qualcomm hoped to push the CAI through the debates as fast as possible and get the group to buy into the development of the standard in a much shorter time frame than was typical.

Lots of companies now claimed to be developing code-based wireless and spread-spectrum variants, but only Qualcomm asserted that its version was a complete system that could be implemented immediately. While no other companies took the official stance that CDMA was primed and ready for second-generation networks, many nonetheless had input into the forum to establish a WBSS standard. Whether they truly wanted to have a part in the development of a spread-spectrum system or just wanted to stall the process, any attendee of the open forum meetings could voice their input. To make sure that only relevant suggestions were debated, Qualcomm had its gurus regularly attend the meetings to short-circuit any meaningless maneuvering.

A series of meetings took place in the spring of 1992 to address questions on a WBSS option for digital cellular systems. After the first meeting in March,

Qualcomm thought that it had come fully prepared for the next meeting, in April in Niagara Falls, but the team was knocked for a loop when an objection was raised to the mere suggestion of distributing the Qualcomm CAI document. A Canadian representative argued that the technology described in the document constituted sensitive information—spread spectrum was a military technology that needed export approval from the U.S. State Department, and so distributing the document at the TIA standards forum would violate U.S. export laws. As Qualcomm had no quick answer to this allegation, no formal presentation of the CAI was possible. Little productive work came out of the April meeting and Qualcomm ended up distributing the document to parties outside the gathering.

Then Ed Tiedemann, Qualcomm's lead for the standards effort, flew directly to Washington, D.C., to resolve the issue of disseminating information on CDMA to the TIA standards group. Tiedemann, another MIT graduate, who had come to Qualcomm in 1988, pressed the Commerce Department, the National Security Administration, and the State Department for a resolution of the issue. He soon found himself going in circles, as the Commerce Department didn't see it as being within its jurisdiction to issue a declaration for export control. To break through the runaround, Qualcomm enlisted the help of a Washington, D.C., law firm to deal with the bureaucracy and eventually succeeded in obtaining an appropriate release to allow distribution of the CAI in the next meeting.

With the minor obstacles out of the way, the committee continued soliciting input on the WBSS specifications. Qualcomm's CAI was the centerpiece of the discussion, but two other companies, Ericsson and SCS Mobilcom/Telecom, offered alternatives for implementing certain parts of the system. Both organizations argued that their intellectual property had a place in the standard and should be considered ahead of Qualcomm's solutions. SCS was pushing a different implementation of code-based wireless using a wider frequency band, while Ericsson was arguing over many of the finer points of the technology's operation. Many of the details of the components of the standard were brought up with the obvious intent of delaying the process, so Qualcomm quickly countered any technical objections that were unfounded. As the process wore on, more attendees were beginning to see that Qualcomm really knew what it was doing with code-based wireless, and that it had most of the solutions to making it a fully functional standard.

"What became more and more evident is that Qualcomm held all the solutions to the technical issues with CDMA and that their system was the way to go."
—PERRY LAFORGE,
EXECUTIVE DIRECTOR OF THE CDG
(CDMA DEVELOPMENT GROUP)

But many of the critics and those with a vested interest in TDMA technology were not silenced. Ericsson continued to fight against approving the standard based largely on Qualcomm's design. SCS ended up merging with Interdigital, a significant time-based wireless player, in October 1992. Qualcomm and the other code-based wireless advocates had finally pushed the process almost to completion in early 1993. In April 1993, ballots went out to the participants. Of the twenty-eight participants in the TIA forum, twenty-one voted in favor of the interim CDMA standard, four objected, and three abstained. Of the no votes, two were from major TDMA backers—one from Ericsson and one from Interdigital.

To further complicate the process, on the last day for submitting votes, April 16, Interdigital filed a lawsuit against Qualcomm and OKI, claiming that some portions of the CDMA standard considered in the ballot would infringe on patents that it held. Interdigital had already stated that it refused to license what it claimed was its essential intellectual property (IP) in the CDMA standard to others, a primary requirement in the TIA standards process. Ericsson and Motorola also claimed ownership of essential IP in the standard, although they agreed to license the technology on reasonable and nondiscriminatory terms.

To resolve the no votes on the standard and address Interdigital's claims, the TIA ordered a second round of voting through a default ballot process. The industry participants had to submit comments on the conditions of the no votes and were given the option of changing their vote in light of the recent claims. When the ballot was taken again in June, two participants who had abstained in the first round voted to approve the standard. Between the two votes, Qualcomm had countersued Interdigital over the patent claims, and the participants had examined the claims to verify what constituted essential IP in the standard.

After the second round of voting in June and the receipt of the comments on Interdigital's claims, the issue of ratifying the standard went to the TIA Technical Standards Subcommittee (TSSC), where the group evaluated the process to determine if there was consensus among the participants. As the final arbiter, the TSSC would have to weigh the merits of the dissents in the voting process, and determine whether there was sufficient reason to send the standard back to the open forum process. After a few tense weeks, in July 1993 CDMA's cellular implementation was officially approved for publication as an interim TIA standard, IS-95. Along with the approval, the TIA published a notice to manufacturers that Interdigital still claimed intellectual property rights in IS-95. The lawsuit from Interdigital hung over the CDMA standard, but the approval was an enormous victory for Qualcomm nonetheless—code-based wireless now had parity with time-based wireless as an official industry standard.

CELLULAR INROADS

While dozens of Qualcomm's staff members were involved in the effort to keep the standardization of CDMA on the fast track, an equally strong team was pushing hard to get the technology at least in a test phase with cellular network operators. PacTel could be counted on, but it pushed Qualcomm to get a buy-in from a large portion of the industry, in North America and internationally. By no means would PacTel develop CDMA as an island amidst a sea of TDMA networks.

Thanks to the successful CAP 1 trials and the continuing demonstrations of capacity gains from code-based wireless, Qualcomm successfully negotiated several significant trials in the United States and abroad. In May 1992, Qualcomm supported CDMA tests with Deutsche Bundespost Telekom in Germany for possible cellular and other wireless applications. A month later, it started a trial of cellular applications of code-based wireless with carrier Swiss PTT in Switzerland. In the United States, Bell Atlantic Mobile Systems (BAMS) was testing code-based wireless in vigorous environments around Washington, D.C., looking to stress the technology to its limits. The tests concluded with BAMS jubilantly stating that CDMA met or exceeded its expectations in terms of improvement of capacity, voice quality, and handoff performance.

With good news coming out of the continued trials, Qualcomm's consortium of partners continued to push the benefits of code-based wireless technology to the industry. Aggressive public relations efforts were launched to spread the message through white papers, sponsored forums, and convention presentations. For its part, Qualcomm opened its doors to any interested visitors and went to extensive lengths to not only publish but disseminate all the technical data on CDMA and the results from recent trials. Jacobs, Gilhousen, Viterbi, and others published papers in the IEEE and other organizations, detailing the technical attributes of code-based wireless and proving its benefits. They even invited outside companies to come to Qualcomm's facility with test plans to try to break CDMA. Qualcomm's certainty about code-based wireless was reflected in this open-door policy.

> "We were very open with the testing—giving people the data to go check it for themselves—just to get as much understanding and support in the industry by being very open."
> —IRWIN JACOBS,
> QUALCOMM COFOUNDER AND CEO

The heavy PR push and open technical communication hit its first serious paydirt in September 1992, when US West New Vector announced that it would not only adopt CDMA to upgrade its analog networks, but also sign outright purchase agreements with Motorola and Northern Telecom. The announcement gave Qualcomm firm commitments for the very first installation of a code-based wireless network in Seattle, Washington, by the end of 1993.

Thanks to a more than 60 percent increase in marketing expenses, Qualcomm made even more progress in 1993. BAMS agreed to go with CDMA in March, planning to have its digital networks in commercial operation by late 1994 or early 1995. With PacTel, which was looking to install code-based wireless in its Los Angeles network, and ALLTEL also supporting CDMA, Qualcomm was gaining much-needed momentum in the cellular market. On top of its successes in cellular, Qualcomm was increasingly looking at opportunities in other types of mobile communications networks, especially personal communications systems.

THE NEW BUZZ—PERSONAL COMMUNICATIONS SYSTEMS (PCS)

The continued proliferation of cellular phones and the rapid advance of the technologies involved around the world was captivating the minds and imaginations of not only the industry, but the public at large. With the rapid advance of digital technologies, and the advanced features they promised, thinking about personal communications opened up possibilities beyond the current cellular implementations. Prior to the late 1980s, cellular communications always meant a car phone—the portable units were just too bulky to be carried in anything but a large briefcase. In addition, being power-hungry, the units lasted only a short time.

But by the 1990s, digital technologies foretold a day when a phone would be small enough and light enough to be carried around everywhere—and a mobile phone number would no longer identify a car or a location, but a person, wherever that person chose to be. This new vision of personal communications devices broadened the industry's thinking to include a whole host of digital telephony services. Besides typical voice calls, new digital devices could be capable of paging, transmitting, facsimile, and short messaging as well.

In the United States, the industry had pressed the FCC to consider these new types of services as being not simply an extension of existing cellular services, but rather a whole new breed of advanced communication capabilities, based on digital methods, with a far superior quality of service. Cellular services at the time had limitations in the mind of consumers—poor coverage, poor voice quality, and very high prices. Digital services had the potential to mitigate all these issues.

The drawbacks of cellular services prompted the FCC to begin working with the industry in the early 1990s to define a method for developing this new type of personal communications services. The rapid adoption of cellular phones by consumers and the resulting capacity strains on the networks

PCS VS. CELLULAR

To the consumer, there was essentially no difference between cellular and PCS (personal communications services). In the early 1990s, the FCC (and the cellular industry) attempted to develop and brand a new class of digital wireless services, called personal communications services, to put a new face on cellular. Early cellular had a somewhat bad reputation: It was seen as having poor voice quality, lots of dropped calls, and high costs, and it provided only voice. PCS was envisioned as being everything that was good about cellular without the bad—and adding data services such as messaging to boot. To accommodate PCS, the FCC opened up new frequency bands to handle the subscribers who were flooding into cellular bands (which contributed to the degraded service). Cellular services were carried over the 800-MHz band; PCS, over the 1,900-MHz band. So technically speaking, a cellular phone operated at 800 MHz, while a PCS phone operated at 1,900 MHz. But network operators with cellular licenses simply upgraded their networks, incorporated nearly all the features of PCS (such as digital transmission and data), and cleverly marketed the resulting system in such a way that consumers ultimately didn't know the difference. For instance, SprintPCS was all PCS (no cellular at all), while AT&T Wireless was predominately cellular in many markets. But consumers would never know this from the services each company offered.

meant that new swaths of spectrum needed to be opened up for these services. As the FCC identified two higher-frequency bands for personal communications services (PCS), companies began to apply for experimental licenses to test equipment at the new frequencies. Qualcomm, of course, was an early applicant, and in 1992 it tested CDMA PCS with PacTel in San Diego and with American Personal Communications in Baltimore–Washington.

In addition to the industry visions for PCS services, though, the United States and other countries were looking at a whole host of mobile communication alternatives. Wireless local loop (WLL) architectures—in which wireless communications are used in the last mile of a network—were seen by some as being the future of all communications, especially in underdeveloped nations where the landline telecommunications infrastructure was limited or nonexistent. WLL was seen as a compelling economic way to connect residences in rural areas or those that were not serviced by telephone wires. Seeing opportunity here as well, Qualcomm developed a line of handsets and infrastructure called QCTel for use in WLL applications, and looked at countries, such as India, China, and Brazil, where WLL was an attractive alternative. Qualcomm aimed to have a full WLL product line available by 1995.

As digital technology developed rapidly, a new outlook began to take hold in the telecom industry. While cellular services had sometimes been considered the cash cow of communications, many companies now began to think that

WIRELESS LOCAL LOOP (WLL)

Wireless local loop is a technology aimed at solving the "last mile" challenge in communication to homes and businesses. In a typical telephone or data communications system, the last length of wiring (usually about a mile) to homes or businesses from a central switch is called the local loop. This is the most expensive and cumbersome portion of any network to install, maintain, or upgrade, since it can include millions of individual circuits.

To avoid the cost of upgrading or replacing the local loop with new wiring or fiber optics, wireless links can economically be implemented at the central switch and in the premises of the home or business owner. The last mile of service is then carried through the air at a negligible cost, rather than over a physical wire.

Wireless local loop is especially useful in developing countries, where it can significantly reduce the cost and complexity of building new or expanding old phone systems.

PCS, WLL, and other mobile services could not only succeed but overtake cellular services in terms of their potential for global proliferation. The capabilities of the new services would be much more attractive and would encourage subscribers to analog services to move to digital technologies much more quickly. Cellular was increasingly seen as the precursor of much bigger things to come.

Over this same period in 1992–1993, the strategy of many players evolved from simply modifying their current networks to trying to land new spectrum in order to expand their base even further. But the granddaddy of all communications projects was embodied in concepts for truly global connectivity via satellites. As euphoria over personal communications spread rapidly, the popular party talk turned to serious ventures to launch satellite constellations for global telephony and data services.

WIRELESS FROM YOUR IGLOO

With all the bustling activity around Qualcomm's headquarters in 1991, one would hardly believe that the company had any free time to entertain new ventures. Jacobs and the other founders were thinking big by taking on cellular communications with CDMA, but they had already tasted the extreme potential of global communications through several of their satellite projects at Linkabit. Communication anywhere in the world was the ultimate dream—no more cellular dead spots. And why should it be any surprise that a team of technical gurus who had cut their teeth on advanced satellite communications would come back to join in the race for a global communications system?

Early in 1990, Loral Space & Communications was looking for an entry into the satellite communications market. Several companies had already banded together to develop plans to build satellites and launch them into orbit, promising commercial services before the end of the decade. Loral was already familiar with Qualcomm from earlier work the two companies had done on military satellite projects, and it thought that Qualcomm would be the perfect partner to develop a sophisticated and competitive solution.

Jacobs, Viterbi, and a full complement of Qualcomm's senior engineering staff had pioneered communications and telemetry solutions in early satellite systems, so commercial satellite service was only a small stretch for their talent. Loral was eager to catch up with Iridium, a LEO (low earth orbit) satellite venture unveiled in 1990 by Motorola, Lockheed Martin, Raytheon, and several other partners. The Iridium system was riding the new wave of enthusiasm for global personal communications, with visions of swanky executives talking on phones while perched on Mt. Everest or checking in with their stockbroker from a deserted tropical paradise. Loral signed up with Qualcomm in 1991 and pushed a competing concept called Globalstar to the public, offering a technically better solution based on Qualcomm's code-based wireless.

The Globalstar communication system would be made up of forty-eight satellites launched into a low earth orbit. The network would provide voice, data, and various media and messaging services to subscribers almost anywhere in the inhabited world (between 70 degrees north and south latitude)— as long as you had a view of the skyline. Satellites would communicate with terrestrial gateways strategically located around the world, where the connection to traditional communications would be made. One advantage of the Globalstar system was that the phones would use cellular networks when they were in range, saving the users money on airtime charges. The satellites in the Globalstar system could also communicate with each other, becoming giant relay stations in the sky.

With the announcements of the Iridium and Globalstar systems, the great communications space race was on. Investor enthusiasm for the ventures was initially very strong, despite the inherent risk involved in satellite ventures. Both ventures were able to obtain significant funding from large corporations—Globalstar signed up nearly a dozen partners in 1994 alone, who committed $275 million to the venture. The media were strongly polarized on the ideas of these networks in the sky—many criticized the rosy business models being painted by the consortiums, while others hailed satellite communications as a no-brainer revolution in the making.

Much work lay ahead before the actual building of the satellites, though. A web of regulatory issues had to be settled—not just in the United States, but around the world. The Iridium and Globalstar ventures had to identify the operating frequencies that were best suited for their services and get all the major regions of the world to agree to reserve that portion of the spectrum. In addition, they had to negotiate agreements for location of the terrestrial gateways. The complex web of service rates in various countries made it nearly impossible to predict how much customers would have to pay for phone calls from remote locations. With a booming cellular industry, though, it was hard to believe that people would not sign up in droves for such an amazing service.

Qualcomm invested its intellectual talent in CDMA and satellite communications in the Globalstar system design. The satellites in its system would be much less complex than those in Iridium, making them more reliable. Most of the communications would be processed in the terrestrial stations, leaving the satellites to simply pass the processed information over great distances. While many people questioned the viability of two incompatible satellite networks, Qualcomm and Loral believed that the merits of CDMA would once again win out in the open market for services. A lot of work lay ahead, though, before the first call would be made.[1]

CHAPTER 10

Marketing in Tandem with Technology

Building Partnerships, 1993–1994

As Qualcomm's code-based wireless (CDMA) was going through the final stages of standardization, the cellular network operators were getting their first taste of large-scale trials of alternative digital technologies. As it turned out, the interim time-based wireless (TDMA) standard, IS-54, had some problems of its own. While the FCC and many players had seen time-based wireless technology as being far more mature than code-based wireless, the implementation of that technology that had been chosen for the North American standard still had some flaws. As the systems were being tested, numerous bugs in the protocol came to the surface. While the GSM standard adopted throughout Europe showed good progress in commercial testing, the American variant was fraught with shortcomings.

The teething problems that the time-based wireless tests were experiencing were nothing dramatic—no real show stoppers emerged. But the problems were significant enough to delay progress and cut into some of the promises of capacity and quality to be afforded by the standard. The TDMA networks were actually being tested at a higher stage than the CDMA networks, but this fact was often lost in the discussions of results that ensued. One of the biggest showpieces of TDMA's success—the adoption of the technology by McCaw Cellular—was now coming back to bite it, as many problems with dropped calls and voice quality plagued McCaw's trials in Florida.

> "The capacity [of IS-54 networks] wasn't as much as hoped, and trials showed quality was not as good."
> —ED TIEDEMANN,
> SENIOR VP OF ENGINEERING,
> QUALCOMM

As the results from the various trials of CDMA and TDMA—some of them side by side in the same market—came back, a massive PR effort from both sides ensued. In 1992–1993, as the rubber was now meeting the road, advocates of each technology spent millions to highlight the benefits of that technology and emphasize the failures of all competing standards. While most people had figured that things would continue to smooth out in the industry as a majority of operators moved to time-based wireless, the conventions and trade shows were now buzzing again with controversy and technical reviews.

To most people outside the wireless industry, CDMA technology and its relative merits seemed to be purely a matter of the science of wireless communication: The various wireless technologies should be subjected to straightforward scientific and mathematical analysis to determine the most compelling choice. Unfortunately, wireless communication was often more art (or even magic) than science. Those on the inside knew that there was nothing straightforward about wireless communication. And achieving the predicted results and performance was more the exception than the norm. All systems had to undergo extensive tweaking over time to optimize performance. The elusive nature of wireless technology and the difficulties inherent in producing quantifiable results clouded a straightforward comparison between CDMA and TDMA—for insiders and outsiders alike.

The human aspect of the perception of quality also made comparing technologies difficult. The voice quality of calls was dependent upon the vocoder implemented, something that was independently chosen and plugged in to the overall standard. Time-division systems were theoretically able to increase the capacity of AMPS networks by a factor of three to six, depending upon the vocoder used. But a higher compression level in a vocoder degraded the quality of the voice information being sent. When the compressed information was decoded in the receiver and the voice recovered, the intelligibility of the speech was greatly affected by the compression rate. So voice quality had to be balanced with the need for capacity in cellular systems.

In the United States, the Cellular Telecommunications Industry Association (CTIA) initially recommended that the industry standardize on the three-times vocoder in order to get the best voice quality in communications. The thinking at the time was that the vocoder technology would continue to improve over time, and that at some point in the future, a six-times vocoder that would have less impact on the voice quality would be implemented. In both GSM and IS-54 wireless systems, a three-times vocoder yielded better voice quality, but a six-times vocoder had a capacity advantage because of the higher compression. Various trials being done in the United States and abroad were using different encoders, muddling the overall perceptions of the performance of time-based wireless.

The code-based wireless trials occurring at the time used mostly high-capacity encoders—the 8-Kbps version that gave decent but not exceptional voice quality. But tests using a low-capacity 13-Kbps option produced astounding voice quality, and this vocoder largely won over the operators that heard it perform. The press value of this voice quality was invaluable in promoting CDMA, as many operators were optimistic about implementing a cellular system that was near-wireline quality. Such a system could give code-based wireless network operators a distinct and distinguishable service offering against the competition, so it was very attractive.

During this phase, another key attribute of Qualcomm's business began to develop significantly: the marketing of its technology. The code-based wireless system solutions developed by Jacobs, Gilhousen, Viterbi, and the rest of the team certainly had to work superlatively. But CDMA also had to be seen as the choice of a wide array of companies, not just Qualcomm. Selling code-based wireless to the industry was just as important as developing the technology itself, and it became especially important at this phase. With TDMA now showing signs of struggle, the advocates of CDMA banded together to capitalize on the opportunity.

> "All the carriers were in there looking at the tests saying, 'wow—we could blow away TDMA capacity and still have wireline quality.'"
> —RICH KERR,
> QUALCOMM EMPLOYEE #61

While the backers of time-based wireless continued to defend their struggles as normal maturation—claiming that code-based wireless would certainly face the same dropped call and capacity problems if it had commercial products available—the CDMA advocates continued to pound on the disappointing performance. As a comparison, they continually pointed to the successes and continuing improvement of the code-based wireless technology. The consortium of CDMA advocates had great success in marketing the new technology to the industry at a time when even the most optimistic observers still considered it a long shot.

The delays experienced in implementing TDMA during 1993 and 1994 gave many operators a chance to step back and reevaluate their technology choices going forward. The industry wasn't moving into digital technology as rapidly as many had initially thought, so they could take more time to consider alternatives. The main advantage attributed to TDMA by the CTIA, time to market, also seemed to be evaporating, as underscored by the CDMA consortium. Qualcomm and its partners were able to move several additional companies closer to adopting code-based wireless by committing to trials or licenses of the technology.

By the end of 1993, the partners that had long been toiling to get code-based wireless accepted in the industry decided to formalize their efforts. The CDMA Development Group (CDG) was founded in December 1993 to do the job that it had always been doing—evangelizing for the code-based solution to an unsettled cellular market. The collective resources of dozens of companies were pooled to make a more organized and effective push into global markets. The role of the CDG was critical, because CDMA needed the leverage of a powerful organization to lobby for change around the world, where a code-based alternative was becoming increasingly popular. It was necessary to get people out of a time-based mentality and get them to see the merits of code-based wireless. With the coming opportunities in the personal communications services (PCS), satellite, and wireless local loop (WLL) markets, the CDG would play a vital role in bringing CDMA in as the technology of choice.

FROM TECHNOLOGY INCUBATOR TO CONSUMER DEVICE MANUFACTURER

Successful companies always have to deal with two sets of challenges. During the early phases of a company or a product line, the challenges stem primarily from breaking into a new market, with the bulk of the company's resources being spent on capturing customers and gaining industry acceptance. At a certain point along the maturity curve, however, resources must be shifted toward supplying products—basically, following through on customer wins. Then a whole different set of strains and challenges can result if the company had too much success in the first phase—when the company has basically sold more customers than it was initially set up to supply, with the result that demand far outstrips supply.

With the renewed hope of converting more network operators to CDMA, Qualcomm was faced with the likely scenario of tremendous demand for chipsets and systems. Jumping into the commercial wireless industry meant providing products by the millions—in time frames of months, not years.

Since the beginning of its quest to commercialize code-based wireless, Qualcomm had been faced with the question of manufacturing equipment. Certainly, it could rapidly develop breadboard mock-ups and prototype equipment very well. The collective genius of the engineers in Qualcomm was very creative in transforming ideas into functional designs for hardware and software. But producing commercial products that were consistently built, economical, and aesthetically attractive to consumers took another set of skills altogether.

As code-based wireless began to gain traction with network operators and equipment suppliers, the question of manufacturing came to the forefront. With no outside pressures, Qualcomm certainly would have stayed within its core competency of system design and engineering and avoided large-scale manufacturing. But continued hesitancy on the part of equipment manufacturers to take Qualcomm's intellectual property and apply it to hardware design forced the company to begin small-scale manufacturing: Qualcomm had to quickly manufacture commercial-sized prototypes for the CAP 1 trials, which would have otherwise been impossible. Everyone in Qualcomm knew that an outside manufacturer couldn't produce commercial-sized handsets in time. And not many at Qualcomm were comfortable with the idea of letting an outside manufacturer do the job, either.

Even after the CAP I trials, when several manufacturers signed license agreements for CDMA, none were eager to divert their efforts from other digital technologies: The incentive to incorporate CDMA into products rapidly was just not yet there. The senior officers at Qualcomm decided that they would have to continue down the path of becoming a large-scale manufacturer for two reasons: first, to get CDMA to the commercial market quickly, and second, to instill a little competitive fear in manufacturers. Qualcomm essentially had to bootstrap its own industry, hoping that at some point in the future, partners or joint ventures would relieve it of this necessity.

Other networks being developed in the 1991–1992 time frame were also plagued by the lack of operational handsets for use in testing. While infrastructure equipment could be developed and assembled quickly, getting portable units manufactured and tested took much longer. Qualcomm saw handset development as the Achilles heel of systems design, so it worked with its partners to focus special attention on this area. Qualcomm certainly intended to continue to develop the specialized chips (ASICs) for use in handsets, but who would incorporate these into phones? None of the major phone manufacturers, such as Motorola and Nokia, to which Qualcomm had licensed CDMA were showing signs of support for large-scale manufacturing of code-based wireless phones. So, in May 1993, Qualcomm extended its agreement with US West to include supplying a minimum of 36,000 cellular phones itself, as it became evident no other manufacturer would be able to meet this early need.

Knowing that they would have to design and manufacture at least some of the early phones, Qualcomm's senior staff explored the issues of building code-based wireless phones in high volume. The company did not have the volume capability to command lower prices on components, so its phones would initially be expensive. In addition, Qualcomm had no brand appeal to consumers, and operators would balk at offering no-name phones in place of known brands like Motorola and Nokia. Qualcomm had no experience in large-scale manufacturing, nor did it have the facilities to house such an effort. But with the PCS markets looking more and more lucrative, it was imperative that the company develop the capability to supply CDMA handsets.

Qualcomm's continuous coaxing of manufacturers to share its vision of code-based wireless phones by the million was going nowhere. By the time CDMA was ratified as an alternative standard in 1993, talks with vendor licensees were not bearing commercial-grade fruit. Some vendors were caught up in manufacturing TDMA and GSM phones, which were already ramping up to significant volumes, and others just plain didn't have enough experience in CDMA to get up to speed quickly. Having no resolution in this area, Qualcomm once again took advantage of the healthy public markets for funding in July 1993 to pull in $151 million from an overallotted secondary share offering. Even though it still had $34.4 million in the bank from the 1991 IPO, taking advantage of a bullish market would allow Qualcomm to expand its CDMA activities further in several areas of mobile communications. But the new funds still would not be anywhere near sufficient to allow the company to embark on a full-scale manufacturing endeavor.

Of all the global manufacturers around the world, though, it turned out that Qualcomm's best chance at a manufacturing joint venture was virtually right down the street from the company in San Diego. Late in 1993, Qualcomm opened discussions with the U.S. offices of Sony Corporation for a joint venture (Sony had already signed a CDMA support agreement with Qualcomm). A mainstay in San Diego since the 1970s, Sony looked like a perfect fit for a partnership in the manufacturing of code-based wireless equipment. The Japanese giant was a top consumer electronics manufacturer with a strong brand name, and it just so happened that it lacked, but desired, competence in code-based wireless communications. Sony had huge facilities in San Diego and nearby Tijuana, Mexico, to manufacture televisions and other consumer electronics, so it could design and build products locally, a major advantage for getting products to market quickly.

As it so happened, Sony was looking to make a major push into advanced communications as well. Its U.S. business was brisk in several areas, and its style of cutting-edge design was a natural fit for Qualcomm's revolutionary code-based wireless technology. After extensive negotiations about roles and duties, the partnership came together in a joint venture in February 1994: Qualcomm Personal Electronics (QPE) was created, with 49 percent ownership by Sony and 51 percent by Qualcomm. The two companies committed to investing up to $25 million combined in equity in the venture, as well as committing divisions within their companies that would form the new subsidiary. Qualcomm and Sony also guaranteed $36 million in loans to QPE to help the venture reach production capabilities by the first half of 1995.

With a firm order already on the books from US West, QPE started rapidly acquiring the necessary equipment, people, and facilities to begin production. Qualcomm started by supplying millions in loans to the venture, choosing to wait to contribute the equity portion until a later time. The partnership began the process of transferring technology, hiring thousands of employees, and opening an advanced manufacturing facility in San Diego.

As an important part of a strategy to be a leader in wireless communication, in 1995 Sony dispatched Yutaka Sato, the prodigy behind the Walkman's success, to lead the venture.

With the backing of Sony, the production of handsets was assured, and Qualcomm's negotiations with network operators eased dramatically. The assurance of competent handset supply went a long way toward strengthening Qualcomm's position in the minds of fast-growing network operators. Once again, time was now critical: It would take months to ramp up production facilities to high volume. The complex task of integrating the two companies' efforts was a serious undertaking for the fast-growing Qualcomm.

With the handset portion of the code-based wireless system now in the capable hands of the QPE partnership, Qualcomm began to focus more on the delivery of the other side of the system—the network infrastructure, which included base stations and landline switching centers. While wireless handsets were tricky to master and produce reliably, network infrastructure components had their own set of challenges. Qualcomm had learned a lot about implementing CDMA in a base transceiver station over the last few years, but it was only in test systems, and there was still much to learn. In addition, none of its equipment licensees were very far along in developing their own product lines, so they needed serious help from Qualcomm if commercial products were to be launched as expected. Just as with handsets, the licensees' lack of motivation to turn away from the already lucrative TDMA products often kept their CDMA efforts on the back burner. But Qualcomm had to find a way to move code-based wireless onto the front burner.

By 1993, Qualcomm already had three major North American licensees for infrastructure—AT&T, Motorola, and Northern Telecom. In addition, the Korean development agreement had been progressing nicely, so Qualcomm was able to sign several Korean manufacturers as licensees in 1993 as well. As with its handset partners, Qualcomm wanted to move to commercial equipment much faster than its partners had planned for, but it soon saw that it couldn't navigate the infrastructure market on its own. To be a major player in the market would require huge investments, and Qualcomm did not have the advantage of participating in any other area of the telecom industry where relationships were forged.

Qualcomm had to find a willing partner to help manufacture the needed infrastructure, so it once again looked at the players in the industry to find the one that would be most able to benefit from the advances of CDMA. Of the North American vendors, AT&T and Motorola were probably the biggest and had a lot invested in TDMA. They had already started to develop code-based wireless, albeit at a slower pace than Qualcomm had hoped. Northern Telecom, however, had not yet progressed far with a CDMA program, although it had signed a license agreement and committed to supply equipment to US West.

Qualcomm saw the potential of a powerful partnership with Northern Telecom, an established player in the industry that needed a technology infusion to be a serious contender in CDMA. A series of discussions in 1994 culminated in an agreement in December, in which Qualcomm and Northern Telecom committed to the joint manufacture of infrastructure equipment for the code-based wireless market. Qualcomm would transfer the technology base as well as the chipsets, test equipment, and software necessary to manufacture CDMA equipment for use in a network. Northern Telecom would supply its industry connections, facilities, staff, and manufacturing capabilities to produce the equipment for sale. Together, the two companies could sell a complete CDMA network solution on a par with the biggest of the TDMA and GSM manufacturers.

With the Northern Telecom agreement in place, senior management at Qualcomm breathed a sigh of relief. They had now surmounted the two major obstacles—production of both handsets and infrastructure—to the delivery of commercial CDMA, staying well within the abilities of their current operations. They were extending Qualcomm far beyond where anyone had imagined it would go, but the potential benefits made it a natural choice. By the end of 1994, Qualcomm had mushroomed to nearly two thousand employees, and by the looks of business prospects in the U.S. cellular market alone, the hiring binge would continue. The integration of manufacturing operations with partners Sony and Northern Telecom would take time, of course, but as usual Qualcomm was confident of the rapid development of the process. It turned out that they were a little too confident.

CHAPTER 11

Wireless Holy Wars

Trials by Fire, 1994–1995

Looking back over the years, the commercialization of code-based wireless (CDMA) technology progressed in waves. Once CDMA was made an alternative industry standard, IS-95, in 1993, Qualcomm enjoyed significant success in wooing carriers, partially as a result of the early stumbling by time-based wireless (TDMA) systems. But now it was Qualcomm's turn on the chopping block. As equipment began to move out of its partners' facilities into trial networks, the industry encountered problems with the operation of CDMA networks. Now the shoe was on the other foot, and the backers of TDMA technology were elated to see their earlier arguments about technical maturity confirmed. Many of the initial problems of time-based wireless networks had been resolved, and these networks were beginning to deliver performance that was much closer to expectations. CDMA, on the other hand, was early in its curve of problems.

Early in 1995, Qualcomm was forced to deal with a whole host of implementation issues. In the early trials and demonstrations, Qualcomm engineers had worked with a small number of suppliers and partners to make the equipment work together nicely. Now they had equipment manufactured by third parties to a new standard document based upon a technology that many manufacturers still did not fully understand—at least not at the level that Qualcomm did. And even the engineers at Qualcomm themselves were running into surprises as more equipment was proliferating in test networks around the globe.

One particularly brutal problem occurred when CDMA mobile units picked up too much noise from nearby AMPS signals generated by rival base stations or even by the same base station. Under certain conditions, the handsets would be disturbed by noise generated by the neighboring analog signals, and the code-based wireless phone would drop a call in progress. In certain tests, the dropped call rate was exceedingly high—so high that some thought the numbers were recorded in error. Qualcomm knew that the network just needed tuning, but advocates of TDMA quickly pointed out that one of their long-running arguments about the capabilities of CDMA was now being borne out. It was an opportunity to turn the tables on Qualcomm and code-based wireless, and the publicity departments of companies that had invested heavily in time-based wireless let it all fly.

BATTLING CRITICISM

With teething problems occurring during implementation, the CDMA Development Group was busy deflecting criticism of the performance of the new technology. Whether a problem was caused by faulty equipment, human error, improper manufacturing by a vendor, or even a rat chewing through a wire, critics were quick to lay the blame on Qualcomm's technology. Certainly the aggressive San Diego company had had more than its fair share of critics since the first presentations of code-based wireless technology in 1988, but more critics than ever now seemed to be coming out to attack CDMA and the engineers who promoted it. While most of the early criticism of the technology had remained within the confines of the telecom industry, it was increasingly moving out into the mainstream media as well.

In the early 1990s, technology guru George Gilder was one of the earliest and most prolific supporters of CDMA technology. In articles for *Forbes* and his own newsletter, Gilder had waxed poetic about the natural ability of code-based wireless to resolve the current bottlenecks in an emerging world of unlimited bandwidth. At the time of his earliest prognostications, code-based wireless technology in the cellular area was still theoretical—test networks were only beginning to be developed and implemented. But the concepts behind CDMA epitomized the "wide and weak" philosophy of communications described by Claude Shannon—one that Gilder wholeheartedly believed in.

In his study of communications theory, Shannon saw two basic ways to utilize a medium: either send a strong signal over a very narrow channel or send a weak one over a wide channel. Strong signals didn't allow much room for other signals in the area they occupied (the frequency channel), but weak ones did. In theory, then, the wide and weak method was far better at allowing multiple entities to use the same medium to communicate independently and at the same time. By Gilder's account, that put TDMA in a less-desirable category, while CDMA embodied the solution to bandwidth constraints.

Gilder's promotion of Qualcomm's efforts in code-based wireless in investing circles was a strong endorsement of the new technology that helped give it credence in its early days. But it also invited heated criticism from many people who contended that code-based wireless was a complete fraud with the subversive intention of mulcting billions of dollars from unsuspecting investors. As arguments about the merits of the technology and its role in mobile communications raged, what became known as "the Holy Wars of wireless" commenced. Public relations and investor relations efforts took shape on several fronts—in the industry, in popular media, in investor journals, and via other technical forums. It seemed that almost everybody had something to say about CDMA and the promises made by Irwin Jacobs.

In much of the popular media, few people at the time actually sided with Qualcomm and supported its story from a technical perspective. Public relations efforts by many European and American supporters of time-based wireless had successfully painted CDMA as questionable at best. With full-blown commercial trials only now commencing, it seemed as though the critics had far more technical ammunition at their disposal. In several forums, two Stanford professors, Bruce Lusignan and Don Cox, took CDMA to task and concluded that the system essentially would not work as planned. Many intelligent and well-educated pundits went so far as to say that code-based wireless would never work on a wide scale.

> "All the capacity claims came down to power management. If that wasn't nailed, the whole thing fell apart."
> —BILL FREZZA,
> PRESIDENT OF WIRELESS COMPUTING

At the top of the list of issues, critics contended that CDMA would not meet the capacity numbers promised when it was actually implemented in a real network. It might all look good on paper, but it just wouldn't add up in the real world. They argued that Jacobs and Viterbi were theoretical mathematicians who could not account for all the variables that can affect an actual wireless network's performance. Since RF was considered more art than science, most people in the industry conceded that wireless techniques could never be deemed successful until they were actually implemented and proven in real settings.

> "For some reason people were unusually intense in opposition to CDMA technology. Bruce Lusignan, a brilliant professor of electrical engineering at Stanford, said that CDMA, as Qualcomm described it, violates the laws of physics."[1]
> —GEORGE GILDER

Particular doubt still lingered about Qualcomm's ability, given the computing technology that was currently available, to tame the problems with power control and handoffs effectively in an actual spread-spectrum system, even though Qualcomm had demonstrated its solutions extensively in field tests. CDMA was very complex compared to the standard approach to communications using frequency-based wireless (FDMA) techniques, and while some people conceded the theoretical potential of code-based wireless, commercial implementation was another story altogether. The most favorable critics at the time believed that CDMA was at least a generation or possibly a decade away from practical use.

The arguments against code-based wireless throughout this teething stage were almost unbelievably heated and emotional. Every industry event included forums discussing the competing technologies, and the rooms were always packed with participants. Panels that normally provided dry, technical engineering discussions were suddenly transformed into tense debates interrupted by pandemonium. For competitive reasons, many critics of the technology seemed to be adamant about denying that CDMA had any chance of success. Some even went so far as to declare that the methods that Qualcomm described and the conclusions it reached violated the laws of physics.

"They [Qualcomm] were very willing to admit when a criticism about CDMA had validity."[2]
—IRA BRODSKY,
PRESIDENT OF DATACOMM RESEARCH

Gradually, as prototype systems showed that CDMA could actually work, the criticism shifted to attacks on the performance claims made by Qualcomm: The capacity mark was missed. The voice quality was poorer than promised. Cell tuning was more complex. Costs were too high. It was still years away from commercial operation. The popular story then became that Qualcomm had overpromised and overhyped the technology. Further, it was argued, Qualcomm's aggressive tactics in promoting code-based wireless as the future of cellular communications had touted products well ahead of their commercial viability.

Out of the public glare, Qualcomm readily responded to valid criticisms of CDMA. In fact, the company frequently came out and modified its claims and gave forthright explanations of performance—good and bad. Qualcomm's engineers readily admitted the problems and issues they were having with certain aspects of operating a code-based wireless network. But they never caved in and said that these issues couldn't be overcome. They simply acknowledged the problems and got to work fixing them. The spin in some popular media, however, made it appear that CDMA was fatally flawed.

The advent of the Internet as a popular source of information in 1994–1995 extended the wireless technology debates across the world. One of the earliest forums that analyzed Qualcomm's claims for code-based wireless was CMP Media's *Network Computing* online magazine. Hosting forums to determine the truth behind the claims for both TDMA and CDMA, Bill Frezza had more than enough critics of CDMA to fill a stadium, while supporters of code-based wireless—outside of Qualcomm—were hard to come by. One of the few independent observers who was willing to hold ground with Qualcomm was Ira Brodsky, an industry research consultant. Brodsky had heard Viterbi argue the merits of CDMA years before and had decided to dig in and research the pitch. He decided that Qualcomm's approach had real merit, and he had enough confidence to defend his stance in numerous debates within the industry.

As the debates on technology moved beyond the industry, one unfortunate consequence was deterioration in the accuracy and substance of the discussions. While there were many debates about CDMA and Qualcomm's proposed solutions to its problems in good technical forums that provided sensible feedback, many other debates degenerated into shouting matches over unsubstantiated and secondhand information. Many people got whipped up over the billions of dollars that were at stake in the global communications markets—and the profits to be made in the stock market. Any time a company comes along and disrupts a good business model for many established players, sparks are bound to fly. To this day, impassioned debate about CDMA's ability to deliver on its initial promises still lingers, although most now concede its superior technical aspects.

Regardless of how the industry was moving, the public information and misinformation surrounding CDMA had to be managed. With the U.S. industry now rapidly moving into new mobile applications in the PCS (personal communications services) spectrum, more was on the line than ever, and perception was a powerful motivator. Through all its efforts and those of its partners in the CDMA Development Group (CDG), Qualcomm had the endorsement of eight of the major cellular operators in the United States. But the stakes in PCS networks were much higher than Qualcomm had first thought—if CDMA didn't secure a large base in PCS networks, it might die out in the cellular area as well. Many operators had even indicated that their PCS network technology choice would eventually drive their cellular upgrades, so CDMA had to make a strong showing in these other networks as well.

WINNING HEARTS AND MINDS . . . AND POCKETBOOKS

With the auctions of PCS spectrum now underway, the trade shows in 1995 were massive endeavors. Companies poured millions of dollars into a presence at the trade show of the Cellular Telecommunications Industry Association (CTIA) in New Orleans in February, where they pitched their products to vendors and operators who were looking to gain an advantage in the upcoming digital age. The battle of information had truly come to the wireless industry, with emphasis being placed on providing the most compelling analysis that favored your own company's product.

Like all the other vendors present, Qualcomm had plenty of information to pass on to anyone who was willing to listen. Thick guides were circulated that compared CDMA to other protocols on several fronts, including cost, capacity, and coverage. The white papers (which looked a lot more like full-sized books) were packed with statistics, graphs, equations, and citations of independent studies on various measures of quality. Some of the booklets were geared toward a technical audience, while others argued from an economic perspective—aimed at the less technically fluent marketers and financiers.

At the CTIA conference, Qualcomm presented a white paper titled "CDMA vs. GSM," pitting the various metrics of CDMA against those of GSM and legacy AMPS. Utilizing everything it had learned from trials and system tests to date, Qualcomm set its solution side by side with competing protocols. The first two dozen pages went through all the major questions concerning the coverage and capacity of code-based wireless, as well as the projected system costs and deployment advantages. Through detailed calculations and graphs supported by in-house and independent data, Qualcomm laid out its case for the vastly superior CDMA standard.

But the best information was saved for the appendices, where Qualcomm took Ericsson to task on a previous publication that had reduced CDMA to little more than an also-ran. Ericsson's "IS-95 and PCS 1900 Capacity and Coverage Comparison," released six months earlier, had concluded that CDMA (the IS-95 protocol) and GSM (PCS 1900) would have roughly the same capacity and voice quality. Qualcomm took great pains to point out all the flaws in these claims, restating everything that had been demonstrated during numerous field trials. Almost unbelievably, the two companies were at odds over capacity claims by at least a factor of five.

In retrospect, it's amazing that two companies could come to such vastly different conclusions about various technologies. The casual observer might find it interesting that an area of technology that was defined rigorously by science and mathematics would leave so much wiggle room for performance claims. But reality was quite different, and many assumptions about the actual performance of different systems were still being made.

The war of the white papers had hit full stride. Companies laid out claims at a furious rate, selectively publishing information that favored their products while bypassing criticisms. The war also took on an ugly tone, with vendors painting competing offerings in unsavory fashion, highlighting failures in trials and beating up executives for unmet targets. Qualcomm's "CDMA vs. GSM" paper dedicated nearly half the booklet to third-party articles on the health risks associated with GSM and other competing technologies. The threat of GSM phones to hearing aids and problems with GSM deployments were prominently discussed. The notion that a TDMA-based cellphone could stop a pacemaker wasn't a particularly subtle message either.

But despite all the energy dedicated to sparring through white papers, Qualcomm knew that above all else it had to win the battle on another front—on economics. As with cellular performance, the technical advantages of code-based wireless had to be translated into real dollars for the network operators who were thinking about deploying or migrating to CDMA. In the new era of competition for PCS networks, the old rules of a regulated duopoly had been trashed completely, and vicious competition had ensued. Qualcomm had to capitalize on this disruptive change in the competitive climate with an equally disruptive economic solution.

Spelling out the economic advantages of CDMA, Qualcomm keyed in on the rapid price erosion predicted for cellular and PCS services. No operator would be spared in the new wireless world; all would have to streamline their operations dramatically in order to be competitive. Those operators with the lowest costs would crush the competition in a price war, so Qualcomm made a point of making sure that operators felt more than a little uneasy about this scenario.

In touting a technology that had not yet even seen full commercial implementation on a wide scale, Qualcomm did a very thorough job of addressing all possible network configurations for the variety of operators in the United States. The financial model for networks depended on the scale of the network (regional or national), the density (urban or rural), and the license portfolio of the operators, so Qualcomm wanted to make sure that it had a solution for everyone. Its publications painted a rosy financial picture of the benefits of code-based wireless. Even though the cost of CDMA equipment was higher, the reduced number of towers required for comparable coverage and capacity efficiency would make up for this cost and put CDMA well ahead of GSM in the new PCS bands.

Qualcomm even went so far as to model how much operators could bid for spectrum licenses and still count on a satisfactory return on their investment. Its modeling put an operator deploying a CDMA network at a net present value of $34 per POP (potential customer in a licensed region), whereas a DCS-1900 (GSM) network operator would enjoy only a $9.19 net present value per POP. While it was admitted that the scenarios put forth were based upon many assumptions, the situation facing U.S. operators was plainly depicted. While this marketing tactic proved successful in many cases, it became a lightning rod for criticism of Qualcomm for years to come. Some people in the industry believed that the "pie in the sky" valuations from technology vendors caused many operators to launch outrageous bids for the PCS spectrum.

The intense focus on the cost of operating a mobile network continued to build throughout 1995. For years now, the industry at large had been salivating over the prospects of PCS services. Whoever walked away with licenses in this era was almost guaranteed immense profits—or so many people thought. The problem was that this outlook was widely held, leading to tremendous demand in the spectrum auctions. The real players were quickly separated out in such an arena—those who were not willing to shoulder tremendous risk would have to sit on the sidelines for another decade. This was just the type of environment that battle-hardened Qualcomm thrived in, though, so it took every opportunity to make itself heard and to point out that CDMA was the only way to guarantee success in such a brutal wireless market.

CHAPTER 12

Make or Break in Personal Communications Services

The Tide Turns at Last, 1995

The PCS (personal communications services) auctions presented both an opportunity and a challenge to Qualcomm and code-based wireless (CDMA). CDMA had a tremendous opportunity to dominate the U.S. wireless market if it could get a significant number of the big players to adopt the new technology for their PCS networks. It was becoming obvious that in whatever direction the PCS operators moved, the cellular players would soon follow. PCS represented the future, and, for Qualcomm, that future had to be code-based wireless. If CDMA was adopted only by smaller, niche PCS operators, it would be dead.

At the dawn of the first generation of cellular networks in 1983, capacity at first did not place any limits on the ability of network operators to sign up thousands of anxious wireless consumers. But this luxury evaporated within months, and additional spectrum was necessary just to keep up with demand. The industry repeatedly appealed to the FCC for more allocations throughout the 1980s. As the 1990s opened and the cellular operators were moving to digital technologies, the FCC and U.S. regulatory agencies were developing a master plan for telecom deregulation that came to light in the 1996 Telecommunications Act. This multifaceted approach was designed to breed new competition and growth in the communications industry, which up until this point was still bound by its monopolistic underpinnings.

The U.S. government's attempt to spark a new era of deregulated competition in telecommunications had started well before President Bill Clinton signed the new act into law, though. In 1992, the FCC was already moving ahead with the idea of auctioning new areas of spectrum for mobile wireless companies, referring to them as a new breed of services—personal communications services, or PCS. Seeing another opportunity for CDMA early on, Qualcomm had started a PCS division in 1992 to adapt CDMA to operate at the new frequencies. It had applied for an experimental license early in 1992 and worked with PacTel on a test in San Diego in November 1992.

Cellular services in the United States, even with their mobility advantages, were still substandard compared to landline service. In general, consumers saw the first cellular services as expensive and poor in quality, with dropped calls and interruptions being the norm rather than the exception. The industry wanted to open the digital era with a differentiated product, one that clearly offered improved features and quality. Arguably, the strategy wasn't very effective—many consumers today still call their mobiles "cellular phones," even though they are the latest vintage of digital wonders.

In the past, spectrum had been allocated to network operators. But the idea of auctioning spectrum to the highest bidder appealed to the federal government because the auction would provide a windfall of billions of dollars for the U.S. Treasury, giving the government the opportunity to capitalize on a booming industry as other countries were doing. In August 1993, President Clinton signed the Omnibus Budget Reconciliation Act, which permitted the FCC to proceed with PCS spectrum auctions in the 1.9-GHz band and award licenses to the highest bidder. This move to a free market–based auction was also motivated by a desire to correct the ills of the past—previous allocations of the cellular spectrum had simply been given away to incumbent wireline operators or randomly dispensed through lotteries. Years of hand-wringing and litigation over the "proper" criteria for allocating spectrum had contributed greatly to the decades-long delay in launching cellular services.

With the intention of making the auctions fair and balanced, in the interest of both incumbent players and start-ups, the FCC split the PCS spectrum into blocks. The A and B blocks were to go to established cellular companies, but the C block was reserved for what were called "designated entities" or "entrepreneurial ventures." The C-block auction would be held separately in order to give minorities, women, rural carriers, and small businesses the opportunity to compete in a newly deregulated environment. The FCC also set favorable payment terms for these smaller entities, giving them what was supposed to be a level playing field against deep-pocketed corporations.

Splitting the spectrum into blocks accomplished two things: It guaranteed that the spectrum would be put to use quickly by cash-rich incumbents, and at the same time it allowed aggressive competition from smaller players operating on favorable terms. The reasoning made sense: New competition from young, nimble companies would force prices down across the industry. The auctions for what was termed broadband PCS carried no specifications of network technology; they required only that the core methods be digital. This meant that new operators coming into the industry could start from a purely digital network base, with no analog legacy.

Enthusiasm for the PCS auctions ran high among small companies that were hoping to jump into an industry that was in the midst of what was akin to a great gold rush. The government was offering great incentives to stake a claim in the ownership of a valuable resource, something that one day could turn the owners into very wealthy individuals. But the anticipation and eagerness soon wore down as problems with the structure of the auctions appeared.

THE PCS AUCTION FIASCO

The first mistake pointed out to the FCC by network operators was the decree that the auctions of the A and B blocks would go first, ahead of the auction of the C block intended for the little guys. (The C-block auction was slated to start seventy-five days after the A and B blocks closed in March 1995.) Several companies complained that the incumbents would be given a great advantage by having their spectrum needs filled prior to the C-block auction. Many small entities hoped to strike up partnerships with the big boys who weren't certain that they could get all the spectrum they needed in the first auction. If the A- and B-block auctions concluded first, the established players would be more certain about their capital expenditures and would have undue leverage in partnering with smaller players.

Issuing A- and B-block licenses first also gave the major players time to develop their networks and start services. The FCC believed that live, operating PCS networks would demonstrate the profit potential of PCS services to Wall Street and banks, and would encourage them to back the smaller entities. But others contended that this would backfire, and that the separation in time would give the incumbents a huge head start on their smaller competitors. To make matters worse, the C-block auction was stalled in litigation for months, with lawsuits filed as soon as the A- and B-block bidding was completed.

Several companies filed suit, claiming, among other things, that the race- and gender-based criteria for designated entities violated their constitutional rights. The FCC delayed the auction and eventually changed the description of designated entities to include any small business. The C-block auctions finally began in December 1995, and did not conclude until the following May.

The combination of effects from offering the A and B blocks to established cellular players led to frenzied bidding for C-block licenses. From the very start, bids shot through the roof, surpassing the value placed on similar licenses in the A and B blocks. Bidders in the C-block auction paid an average of about $40 per potential user, or POP, while the A- and B-block average was around $15 per POP. As a result, the winners of the C-block bids were at an enormous economic disadvantage, while the established players largely enjoyed lower capital costs.

While many complex events contributed to the C-block fiasco, the impact on Qualcomm and its push for CDMA was simple—the cost of doing business in mobile telephony was going up, way up. In one way, this worked to the advantage of code-based wireless advocates, since they had been claiming all along that CDMA networks were more efficient and cheaper to install and maintain (once they had achieved economies of scale). But the high cost of spectrum pushed the stakes much higher than most people in the industry or on Wall Street had imagined, putting more pressure on the equipment vendors to help the network operators lower the cost of building a network. This scenario of an overwhelming debt load on operators led to much more aggressive moves by vendors to finance the purchase of their equipment, offering the operators the option of paying for the equipment in installments once their network was running and cash was flowing.

Qualcomm was not immune to the need for vendor financing of network operators. As an original equipment manufacturer, Qualcomm was an integral part of discussions with equipment manufacturers and a key factor in any operator contract involving CDMA. For example, Qualcomm committed $200 million in financing to Sprint PCS through a vendor contract with Northern Telecom. The commitment obligated Nortel to purchase a certain percentage of its equipment and services from Qualcomm. In this way, Qualcomm was shouldering some of the operator's risk in choosing code-based wireless.

Many vendors also pressed Qualcomm for performance commitments on its CDMA infrastructure and subscriber equipment. Disenchanted by delays and technical problems in some cellular trials, operators wanted drop-dead dates for delivery of products and stipulated various performance criteria as a requirement for contracts with Qualcomm. The relationships among the partners in the industry now became critical for success—since the risk had to be distributed, the commitment of everyone in the supply chain was crucial. Many companies, especially more conservative organizations, balked at the idea of shouldering debt or an undue share of their customers' risk.

Another unknown that heightened the risk in the PCS licensing process was whether a single company or partnership would be able to cobble together enough licenses to make a national wireless network. The assumption of many of the smaller players was that the conflict between incompatible technologies would make it extremely difficult for any one consortium to garner the needed licenses to launch a nationwide PCS network. The decision on which technology to use depended upon whom you wanted to attract as a partner. Bidders remained tight-lipped about their stance on CDMA and TDMA until they saw how the landscape was shaping up.

AND THE WINNER IS . . .

Depending upon which paper or journal you read in the spring of 1995, you would have gotten a very different image of Qualcomm: Either it was dying on the vine, with no chance of overcoming the momentum of time-based wireless, or it was well positioned to make code-based wireless the primary standard in U.S. wireless networks. Pessimistic sources cited the networks based on TDMA, including the GSM standard, that were already in widescale operation in the United States and Europe. While the TDMA standard in the United States still had some problems, it was stabilizing quickly and proving that advanced features and services were attractive to consumers. The GSM standard was hitting critical mass, moving beyond a European base into Asian and African networks and already serving millions of subscribers. Proponents still argued that code-based wireless would outperform these new digital networks, but they had no basis for comparisons to back up their argument—Qualcomm still lacked a fully commercial network with a significant number of subscribers.

The time-to-market issue was catching up with Qualcomm fast, and its inability to show a commercial network in operation anywhere was a huge drag on its efforts to keep up enthusiasm for CDMA. As the days grew longer and the summer of 1995 approached, the days grew darker for Qualcomm—many outside the company saw Jacobs's years of work slipping away. Even a few of the strongest media supporters of code-based wireless were beginning to question whether Qualcomm had missed its opportunity, wondering aloud whether the small San Diego technical powerhouse could come through.

"PacTel had serious capacity issues in its L.A. network, and they realized TDMA wouldn't cut it."
—PERRY LaFORGE,
EXECUTIVE DIRECTOR OF THE CDG
(CDMA DEVELOPMENT GROUP)

But the tide of pessimism turned quickly in June 1995 when PCS PrimeCo—a consortium of Baby Bells (Nynex, Bell Atlantic, and US West) and AirTouch Communications—announced that it had chosen to deploy CDMA technology for its digital networks. A long-time supporter of CDMA, AirTouch was still struggling to meet performance requirements in its Los Angeles network, leading some people to believe that the senior officers of the PCS PrimeCo venture would shut out code-based wireless. There had been too many delays in implementing CDMA to date, and some began to question once again whether it was ever going to work in a commercial network. So PCS PrimeCo's decision surprised and shocked many.

Qualcomm's stock surged on the day of the announcement—it was up almost $5 per share on almost ten times the normal volume. The market value of Qualcomm increased by over 30 percent in that week alone, as investors and industry pundits began to reevaluate the possibilities of the small upstart company. While PCS PrimeCo was not the largest PCS venture, it was a significant one, and its choice of CDMA could sway others. The leader of the partnership, George Schmitt, had been pushing PCS PrimeCo to deploy a version of TDMA, and the decision in favor of CDMA eventually led to his departure to another network operator, Omnipoint.

Emboldened by its success with PCS PrimeCo, Qualcomm pressed hard with the other ventures that were still undecided on technology. Allen Salmasi, Irwin Jacobs, and dozens of other Qualcomm senior executives buttonholed anyone who would listen. The CDMA Development Group (CDG) and proponents of code-based wireless capitalized on the initial success, depicting the momentum of CDMA as a train leaving the station—something that everyone should get on board quickly.

The push paid off, and the watershed event for Qualcomm occurred when Sprint Technology Ventures (STV) settled on CDMA as its technology of choice in July 1995. The company saw code-based wireless as the future of digital wireless communications and wanted a core technology that would set it apart from a crowded field. The STV consortium had cobbled together the most comprehensive span of spectrum licenses, setting it up as the largest PCS network operator in the United States. With this new endorsement, others who were still straddling the technology fence soon followed in choosing CDMA. With continued marketing by CDMA backers, by 1997 more than half of the PCS licensees had implemented CDMA technology based upon the prospect of large numbers of roaming subscribers.

Sprint Technology Ventures's choice of CDMA was seen as the key breakthrough event for Qualcomm and CDMA. Up until this point, the progress in developing code-based wireless and its adoption by cellular operators had been very strong, but a lack of endorsement in the PCS area would have set it back and done irreparable harm to its progress. With the largest PCS operator on board, though, code-based wireless would indeed have a strong presence in the first generation of digital networks.

LOOKING FOR THE NEXT WAVE

The events surrounding the PCS auctions and the eventual build-out of networks were the stuff that movies are made about. Larger-than-life characters going head to head with the government and the FCC, arguing and litigating over billions of dollars in market potential, made past industry dramas look like Sunday school. Particularly during the C-block PCS auctions, the gloves came off and all the major players fought furiously to protect their interests by expanding their businesses. From the perspective of many at the time, there was no other choice—players that did not participate would miss the next wave of economic opportunity and be left far behind.

While most people in the industry knew of Allen Salmasi for his role in helping to establish CDMA in cellular, his role in the C-block auctions will forever dominate his legacy. Salmasi left Qualcomm with the director of PCS marketing, James Madsen, in July 1995 to start NextWave Telecom, a company that meant to capitalize on the PCS auctions by garnering enough licenses to achieve nationwide coverage. The company was not set up to offer services itself, however; it was more interested in wholesaling its network capacity to other carriers that were looking to fill holes in their coverage. NextWave would be a "carrier's carrier."

To confound NextWave's efforts, other companies attempted to point out that Salmasi was still intimately connected with Qualcomm and had actually incorporated NextWave while still employed at the company. The two companies were also tied in several other ways: Qualcomm had initially funded NextWave, and some NextWave senior executives were staunch advocates of CDMA technology. A member of Qualcomm's board, Janice Obuchowski, joined NextWave with Salmasi while she still held her Qualcomm board seat. Also, competitors argued, NextWave violated the FCC's foreign ownership rules because Korean and other Asian entities held more than one-fourth of the company's ownership.

NextWave made a huge showing in the C-block auctions, bidding furiously to snap up dozens of valuable licenses. After walking away from the auction owing nearly $5 billion to the U.S. Treasury, NextWave made only the initial down payment, then declared bankruptcy when funding from investors didn't materialize. On top of numerous complaints and litigation from competitors, NextWave had to battle the FCC for years over ownership of the C-block licenses, which the FCC was attempting to reposses. After a prolonged legal battle, the Supreme Court ultimately ruled for NextWave in January 2003, allowing the company to keep the licenses that the FCC had attempted to re-auction two years earlier.

The major issue in the struggle over NextWave's licenses boiled down to the FCC's dual role as both regulator and creditor. In an effort to motivate smaller companies to join the original C-block auction, the FCC had granted eased payment terms for auction winners. But when NextWave and other auction winners failed to meet the payment terms and filed for bankruptcy, the FCC made several errors in trying to reclaim the licenses. The licenses were considered assets under the protection of the bankruptcy laws, and ultimately the FCC was told that it couldn't avoid these laws under the guise of being a regulator working in the public interest.

The C-block auction is a fascinating study of the results of haphazardly mixing free-market systems with regulatory bodies. An entire book could be dedicated to the study of the U.S. auctions, let alone the problems associated with the auctions of 3G (third-generation) wireless licenses around the globe (mainly in Europe) around the end of the millennium. While not directly involved, Qualcomm was nonetheless greatly affected by the direction and outcome of these events, impelling it to respond and adapt quickly.

Throughout the C-block licensing debacle, Qualcomm continued to focus on the proliferation of CDMA in digital networks. If NextWave had gone on to build out its network based upon code-based wireless, it would have been a huge boon for Qualcomm. (NextWave never built a nationwide network, but it eventually struck a deal with the FCC in early 2004 to return some of the licenses and auction others to repay its debt.) It would have given other network operators—especially those with scarce capacity—a big incentive to migrate to CDMA as their basis for services. The setback with NextWave certainly hurt Qualcomm's chances, but the coup of signing some of the major players in the industry overcame this temporary setback.

THE NEED FOR SPEED—AND MORE MONEY

With a strong endorsement of CDMA in the PCS spectrum bands, Qualcomm was now hard pressed to deliver products. The partnerships that Qualcomm had formed with Sony and Northern Telecom were now vital to the competitive interests of its customers—and the performance guarantees upped the ante for Qualcomm. The next few years were an era of tremendous growth and investment in expansion for Qualcomm. To meet its commitments to CDMA network operators around the world, it had to scale up the production of its CDMA chipsets (ASICs), infrastructure, and handset products dramatically.

> "A late product could have killed it because time was critical."
> —IRWIN JACOBS,
>   QUALCOMM COFOUNDER AND CEO

This next level of expansion was once again far above Qualcomm's current capabilities. Meeting the global needs of CDMA would require hundreds of millions of dollars in equipment and facilities. With all the excitement about the future of mobile communication services, the public markets were once again looking for opportunities in the area, so a public offering was again used. Qualcomm was successful in selling 11.5 million shares of the company to the public in August 1995, raking in $486 million. The money was put to work immediately, and the spending binge continued unabated.

As 1995 came to a close, a few operators were preparing for commercial launches of CDMA, but not in the United States. The first commercial network launch of digital CDMA took place in Hong Kong with Hutchison Telephone in October 1995. Soon after, Korea Mobile Telecom and Shinsegi Telecomm launched their commercial CDMA services to the South Korean population in early 1996. Supporting hundreds of thousands of users in the next few months had Qualcomm's various manufacturing lines buzzing even before they were completed. Its facilities more than quintupled, from a mere 70,000 square feet in 1994 to over 380,000 in 1995.

The chipset design team had developed a new generation of the ASICs that included an x86 processor core, giving them a chance to utilize Intel and IBM semiconductor foundries. In preparation for launches in Asia, the team had booked production with the two companies and NCR, but the ramp-up in volume was only a guess at that point. With the rapid takeoff of CDMA in Asia, the team had to frantically scramble in 1996 to find additional sources of production. The sudden volume demands throughout the year had the team flying all over the world trying to book semiconductor orders with Texas Instruments, Siemens, Philips, and TSMC. In fiscal 1996, the company produced more than 2 million ASICs for code-based wireless.

The handset production venture and infrastructure partnership were being subjected to extreme growing pains as well. While still profitable, Qualcomm had to forgo growth in earnings through 1996 because of the huge costs for the expansion of manufacturing capabilities. It was hiring and training employees by the thousands, and capital equipment costs were soaring. Additional orders to support various PCS launches in the United States were pouring in throughout the year as well, causing Qualcomm to recalculate its projections on a nearly continuous basis. Just when Qualcomm's engineers thought they had figured how to handle additional production, a new order came in that forced them to scrap the old plan.

Qualcomm's rapid expansion to handle the volumes of CDMA equipment was forcing the company further down a road it wasn't sure it wanted to be on—manufacturing hardware itself. But the company had little choice—it had to fill in the gaps that existed with other vendors in the industry. While AT&T, Northern Telecom, Motorola, and many other vendors were building CDMA equipment, its quality still wasn't up to that of Qualcomm's products. With performance guarantees built into many contracts, Qualcomm continued to be a major manufacturer of CDMA products for several years. Despite all the drawbacks, Jacobs felt that the investment and the temporary hit to earnings was worth it. And he wasn't alone in that feeling.

By the end of 1995, a decade after its founding, Qualcomm was entering a new phase of its history. Code-based wireless (CDMA) had attained acceptance as a standard, and commercial launches of the technology were now underway around the world. The journey from theory on paper—including Claude Shannon's mathematical descriptions of information transmission and Hedy Lamarr's foreshadowing of spread spectrum—to commercial realization had largely been completed. It may be inaccurate to say that from this point on, the rest was history, but it is probably correct to say that Qulacomm was now established as the world's foremost developer and provider of CDMA technology. To explore further how the company shored up and enlarged its gains, we change gears in Part 2, switching from a mostly chronological story to a mostly conceptual discussion of the business concepts and practices underpinning Qualcomm's incredible success.

PART TWO

The Intellectual Property Business

"You may have heard people repeat what I have said, 'Genius is one percent inspiration and ninety-nine percent perspiration.' Yes, sir, it's mostly hard work.*"*

—Thomas Alva Edison (1847–1931), inventor, founder of first industrial research laboratory in Menlo Park, New Jersey

CHAPTER 13

Defining the Core Business

–··–··–··–··–··–··–··–··–··–··–··–··–··–··–··–··–→

Equipment Manufacturer or Technology Developer?

With the widespread acceptance of code-based wireless (CDMA) by PCS operators—most notably Sprint Technology Ventures and PCS PrimeCo—Qualcomm knew that its future was more than just bright. CDMA would not be an also-ran, it would be a dominant technology. The hard-fought battles to win the trust of operators and vendors bore fruit in 1995, one decade after Qualcomm's founding and six years after it first proposed code-based wireless as an alternative for mobile wireless systems. The company's efforts now took a dramatic turn: Instead of knocking on doors and asking for trust, it was now mainly trying to keep up with demand. While Qualcomm had been almost exclusively concentrating on external change in the industry during the first five years of the 1990s, in the next five it would be focusing on internal transformation and spectacular growth.

Widespread acceptance as a competitive digital technology in the United States was a huge boost for CDMA in the global wireless industry. Since the United States was one of the more lucrative markets, global vendors now flocked to CDMA technology. Increased competition continued to bring prices down and drive adoption. Indeed, many operators around the globe were rushing to launch commercial networks in 1995. Hong Kong

> –··–··–··–··–··–··–··–··–··–
> "You can argue about how fast our market will grow, but not that it will grow."
> —IRWIN JACOBS,
> QUALCOMM COFOUNDER AND CEO[1]
> –··–··–··–··–··–··–··–··–··–

and South Korea were the first two locations offering commercial CDMA services, with operators in the United States, Canada, and Latin America following soon after. Several countries, including India, China, and Brazil, were also looking at CDMA for use in wireless local loop (WLL) systems, and the Globalstar consortium was picking up additional partners and funding. On top of this, Qualcomm's first commercial product line, OmniTRACS, was experiencing record growth.

The transition from a tightly woven engineering company to a diversified corporate giant with global reach in several product lines was intensive and painful for the company. Through the mid-1990s, Qualcomm's employee base grew at a rate in excess of 50 percent per annum as the company raced to fill positions on manufacturing lines and in supporting functions. The manufacturing that the company was taking on required increasing the operations portion of the company substantially. With nearly $500 million in its bank account after the August 1995 public stock offering, Qualcomm also began acquiring real estate at a rapid pace. The company had occupied only 70,000 square feet of manufacturing space in 1994, but that grew to a whopping 380,000 square feet in only a year. By September 1995, Qualcomm occupied 1.47 million square feet of corporate space, only to increase by nearly 50 percent again the next year.

DESIGNED FOR SPEED AND CAPACITY

The market for mobile communications gear in the mid-1990s was all about time to market and sheer volume. With newly auctioned frequencies that had been paid for and were waiting to be used in the United States, vendors were frantically churning out commercial gear and testing it in networks. What made or broke companies at this time was their operational capabilities in delivering a product that worked for network operators, who were struggling to keep up with subscriber demand for mobile services.

> "I assured our first vice president of engineering we would never go beyond 150 engineers ... now we are over 2,000. Each year I would tell everybody the growth will slow down. I don't try to make those predictions anymore. The opportunities are large and we still have enthusiasm for going out and winning our share."
> —IRWIN JACOBS,
> QUALCOMM COFOUNDER AND CEO[2]

With the idea of code-based wireless mobile networks now firmly established, Qualcomm saw the importance of delivering handsets, infrastructure, and test equipment quickly. Any delays in the delivery of critical network components would give rival technologies time-based wireless (TDMA) and the European version (GSM) more opportunity to steal subscribers. Qualcomm's joint ventures with Sony and Nortel (Northern Telecom) were allocated huge amounts of the company's resources, with key employees being shifted to the new divisions to keep them moving at the fastest pace possible to realize commercial products.

To win the acceptance of CDMA in the early 1990s, Qualcomm absolutely had to guarantee that equipment would be available to operators. With other vendors dragging their feet over the development of code-based wireless equipment, Qualcomm had to commit itself to early production and convince operators that other vendors would be on board soon. Qualcomm's continued push into manufacturing CDMA gear provided several benefits to its customers, and in turn to the company itself. Even though manufacturing was not Qualcomm's core competency and it was operating at a disadvantage to larger vendors, the decision spurred growth in CDMA for three main reasons.

First, it offered commercial code-based wireless products to operators quickly. Having the most detailed and complete knowledge of CDMA allowed Qualcomm to turn out phones and infrastructure faster than anyone else could, helping operators beat their rivals to market with digital services. Getting products into the hands of network operators was almost always the limiting factor in launching a new network service and, in turn, generating revenue for phone suppliers.

> "We had to take market share from the big guys to get them to adopt it."
> —KLEIN GILHOUSEN,
> EARLY LINKABIT EMPLOYEE;
> QUALCOMM COFOUNDER AND
> SENIOR VP OF TECHNOLOGY

Second, by literally offering the entire CDMA package (phones, infrastructure, and tests), Qualcomm made the market more attractive to other vendors. The major manufacturers were watching as Qualcomm won orders for hundreds of thousands of phones for network deployments in the United States and abroad. The successful delivery of commercial products convinced vendors that a lucrative code-based wireless value chain was indeed real and not just a remote possibility. This viable market in CDMA became one that other vendors were eager to tap into, especially second-tier players that were looking to gain ground on giants such as Ericsson.

Finally, building commercial products fed back valuable knowledge to the development portion of Qualcomm's business. When Viterbi, Gilhousen, and others were designing code-based wireless on paper, the company had had virtually no experience in setting up cellular networks. Beginning with the educational meetings with PacTel engineers that led up to the initial demonstration in 1989, Qualcomm gained valuable systems integration experience by building its own prototypes. Designing phones and infrastructure helped add a lot of practical, hands-on knowledge to the company's development efforts. The manufacture of end products was also an especially important piece for continued improvement of the dedicated chip (ASIC) designs. Direct feedback from internal customers is much easier to come by than feedback from third parties.

Like OmniTRACS, the code-based wireless business won in the marketplace because Qualcomm offered a complete solution. When customers hedged on deploying CDMA or adopting a development program, Qualcomm made it easier for them by shouldering the development and production work. In a sense, Qualcomm became a value-added supplier, something that greatly differentiated it from other technology companies. The company didn't simply sell its patents and license its know-how, it set things in motion and helped with the hands-on dirty work. Because of the complexity of code-based wireless and the struggles to get it working right initially, Qualcomm was essentially forced to take on this role—turning a blind eye to struggling vendors would surely have led those vendors to abandon CDMA in favor of the European-based technology (GSM) or time-based wireless (TDMA), which were better understood.

SEEDING MARKETS

Early on in the proliferation of cellular networks, developing markets, especially in areas where no landline telecommunications infrastructure existed, were seen as a primary opportunity for wireless services—including mobile telephony, fixed wireless, and limited-mobility networks. Almost everyone in the telecommunications industry realized that it would be profoundly cheaper to connect homes and people with wireless networks than to string wires on poles the old-fashioned way. Since many of the developed nations were already served by telecom giants, many second-tier organizations exclusively targeted developing nations where populations were large and the field was green.

Qualcomm's evangelizing of CDMA took it to many emerging markets as well. In fact, in the early 1990s, wireless local loop (WLL) systems were seen as the panacea for isolated populations in remote, rural, or simply undeveloped areas. The widely spread populations in countries like China and India could never be connected economically with wire—the tremendous cost of laying millions of miles of cable was simply overwhelming. But billions of people in these nations could be connected with wireless phones—and what better way to have them connected than with a CDMA wireless phone?

Many governments around the world were recognizing the potential of wireless technologies to provide basic telephony services to their populations, and they began to reorganize and deregulate their telecommunications infrastructure to encourage participation from wireless companies. Several nations allocated spectrum for WLL services, but in many cases the amount of spectrum was limited. This played well into Qualcomm's hand, as it pitched code-based wireless as by far the most efficient wireless technology. In countries with huge populations and limited spectrum, CDMA provided the highest capacity of any technology, along with a host of other benefits such as high-quality voice and data capabilities. To many, it seemed as if code-based wireless had actually been made for WLL, as it fit so well.

With images of billions of people buying its products, Qualcomm made a strong push into emerging markets as early as 1992, before digital cellular was even widely commercialized. In 1993, Qualcomm had entered into memoranda of understanding with government and private entities in several emerging markets, including China, India, Russia, and Chile. Within a year, Qualcomm was marketing and demonstrating its QCTel line of WLL infrastructure and handsets around the world. By 1995, several developing countries were testing Qualcomm's WLL solutions in the field, while nations with already developed telecommunications networks were testing cellular and PCS products at the same time.

Of course, Qualcomm was not alone in the WLL market. Many regional players and international heavyweights were vying for installations as well, increasing competitive pressure. As when selling to the operators participating in the PCS auctions in the Unites States, equipment vendors were being required more and more to provide financing and guarantees in exchange for purchase orders. In developing nations, local telecommunication companies were often underfunded and ill prepared to launch huge wireless networks. In order to encourage more operators to adopt CDMA as the technology base for developing cellular, PCS, and WLL systems, Qualcomm began to seed emerging markets by sinking millions into joint ventures and equity investments—on top of committing to significant levels of equipment financing.

In 1997–1998, flush with cash from the fast-growing cellular and PCS CDMA market, Qualcomm entered into several joint ventures with international companies to promote the adoption of code-based wireless around the globe. The business of seeding markets—contributing cash and intellectual resources to facilitate the promulgation of CDMA networks—was a key part of Qualcomm's strategy to drive code-based wireless to be the de facto world standard for wireless communications. GSM network deployments were already spreading rapidly and had much farther reach than CDMA. To stave off further proliferation of GSM, Qualcomm put its cash to work in assisting key operators around the world to launch code-based wireless networks.

Some of Qualcomm's most significant investments occurred in the Americas. In 1997, the company purchased a 50 percent interest in Chilesat PCS in Chile for $42 million, and invested $4 million in Chase Telecommunication in the United States. In 1998, the company committed $110 million to operators Pegaso Telecommunications (Mexico), OzPhone Pty. Ltd. (Australia), Metrosvyaz Limited (Russia), and Orrengrove Investments Limited (Russia). Along with dozens of other ventures in early-stage international companies,

Qualcomm also committed to extending secured loans and providing equipment to get CDMA into markets quickly, ahead of rival technologies.

TAKING A LEAP

The strategy of seeding code-based wireless worked to a large degree, but conflicts soon began to arise in areas where Qualcomm had committed funding to operators. The company realized that its equity investments polarized some markets: If Qualcomm backed a network operator in a given region, this discouraged others from signing up to adopt code-based wireless for their networks. Operators questioned how Qualcomm could fairly support two companies that were in direct competition with each other, especially when they had an equity stake in one but not the other. Increasingly, then, Qualcomm began to see that its investment activities conflicted with its production goals. Moreover, many of the early-stage investments were not panning out, and the expenses were a drag on Qualcomm's rocketing earnings.

Qualcomm found a way to effectively mute the conflicts of interest with operators around the globe: spinning off its investment interests. In May 1998, Qualcomm announced its intention to spin off certain assets and investments in wireless operators. The company argued that this was in the best interests of shareholders, since the company's balance sheet was suffering because of the start-up costs of these joint ventures, and equipment sales to them were not recognized. In September 1998, Qualcomm completed the spin-off of Leap Wireless, which was to be run by one of the original founders, Harvey White, who was its acting president.

Along with the spin-off of assets into a public company went numerous employees and commitments from Qualcomm in the form of loan guarantees. To initiate the new company's operations, $10 million in cash was transferred to the entity, and Leap Wireless International began trading on the NASDAQ market under the LWIN ticker symbol on September 24, 1998. To support its continued operation and the expansion of its investment activities, Qualcomm supplied a $250 million secured credit facility and transferred a substantial portion of indebtedness from the operators to Leap Wireless.

Now that this subsidiary was broken off from Qualcomm, and the boards and management of the companies were separated, each could effectively pursue the expansion of code-based wireless networks without conflicts of interest.

THE ART OF SPINNING

The spin-off of Leap Wireless was only the first shoe to drop at Qualcomm. As CDMA rapidly proliferated around the world and vendors picked up the pace of supplying equipment, production strategies that had been developed only a few years earlier now seemed antiquated. With the furious growth of digital wireless networks in the United States beginning in 1996, Qualcomm was reviewing its direction, strategy, and operations in great detail. As a major manufacturer of cellular and PCS equipment, Qualcomm had to respond quickly to the dynamics of global markets. To deal with turbulent markets and seasonal demands, Qualcomm hired thousands of temporary personnel rather than full-time employees. Any time demand soured, such as during the Asian financial crisis in 1997, Qualcomm could quickly adjust its head count. In 1998, when South Korean demand for phones dropped like a rock, Qualcomm let 700 temporary employees go.

At an engineering company like Qualcomm, dramatic fluctuations in business were the norm. The senior executive team was used to rapid development on fixed budgets (usually from government contracts), giving it an ingrained project-driven approach to the business. When a contract was cancelled, so was all the work, and resources were quickly shifted. As its roots were more in engineering expertise than in manufacturing, Qualcomm tended to react to market conditions much faster than its entrenched peers.

But overall, this approach did not work well in high-volume manufacturing. While Qualcomm remained flexible and fluid in its approach to the production of equipment, the economic and operational realities hit home with the company quarter after quarter. The infrastructure (equipment for radio towers and switching centers, for example) and handset businesses were both booming, expanding at rapid rates with revenues soaring in the high double digits. But the costs were soaring, too. Even though Qualcomm was selling millions of phones and thousands of base stations in 1998, the company was still well under the volume thresholds necessary for profitability. Finnish giant Nokia and U.S. mainstay Motorola were the dominant handset suppliers at the time, selling nearly 70 million phones in 1998; and infrastructure companies such as AT&T (Lucent) and Ericsson were ten times the size of little Qualcomm.

While Qualcomm was enjoying a boom in demand for its technology, the quantities still paled in comparison to the sales of GSM and TDMA equipment. Manufacturers that had jumped into GSM were enjoying a huge demand for their products and were thus able to achieve lower cost points for the equipment through high volume. CDMA was still difficult to implement and was more expensive to manufacture and develop, leading to higher equipment costs for network operators. Even after reaching many production milestones that people had questioned whether it could make, Qualcomm realized that it still had a long way to go if it was to put CDMA on a par with the volume and economics of GSM.

Another disadvantage of being an end-product supplier to operators was that Qualcomm was losing sales of chipsets to other vendors. Again, a conflict of interest was being pointed out by other vendors who wanted to use Qualcomm's chipsets in their designs: If Qualcomm built competing handsets or base stations, how could a third party compete? Many companies even suggested that Qualcomm, in order to keep a competitive advantage, reserved its latest and most cost-effective ASIC designs for its own products, leaving the leftovers for other parties. To rub salt in the wound, the chipset business was moving at a much higher volume and was proving to be very profitable, so the loss of business in this division in order to support a money-losing venture was a hard pill to swallow.

By late 1998, it was clear to Qualcomm executives that the company was spinning its wheels supporting manufacturing operations. As each quarter went by, management watched tremendous profits from several divisions get burned away in others. The infrastructure division required huge levels of capital and purchase commitments that weighed on the books. The handset division required the same, and it seemed as if each quarter presented new problems and placed new pressures on the division. Margins were very thin in both product divisions, and Qualcomm was still a small fish in a big pool of sharks.

As Qualcomm's peers were also enjoying the fruits of digital wireless telephony around the world, public markets rewarded the fast-growing companies. Nokia was making a big push into digital handsets, taking over Motorola's number one spot in market share in 1998. As the Finnish giant showed its skill in efficiently navigating the global handset market, investors rewarded the company by bidding its stock up more than fivefold over the 1997–1999 period. In contrast, Qualcomm's share price remained essentially flat over the same period as analysts continued to harp on the company's meager bottom-line growth. Pointing to the record top-line growth and the infant nature of the CDMA market did nothing to assuage Qualcomm's Wall Street critics—especially with the dot-com mania brewing.

Continued drubbings by investors over shareholder value in Qualcomm's business compelled a major review of company operations in late 1998 and early 1999. As the market for digital wireless equipment and services was rapidly running away, Jacobs and his operational staff wanted to review once again where Qualcomm best fit into this picture. The meetings led to one certainty: The company would have to do some belt tightening to respond to stockholders' wishes and remain competitive. In February 1999, the company instituted another major reorganization, eliminating another seven hundred positions. This time, permanent employees, most of them from the infrastructure division, were also dropped. The company continued to struggle to gain traction against the larger players in the market.

But out of the review came another key conclusion: that Qualcomm was indeed starting to lose the CDMA product business. As this reality became painfully clear on Qualcomm's bottom line, the management realized that this was a key signal: Qualcomm was no longer the key supporter of CDMA products. Other companies, such as Lucent, Motorola, and Samsung, were now devoting serious resources to the development and deployment of code-based wireless products. In addition, more than a dozen top manufacturers were turning out new handsets for various markets. While the Asian region (mostly South Korea) was by far the dominant base for code-based wireless subscribers, the technology was beginning to show similar growth in many other countries, including the United States. This key insight pushed the team to finally shift away from the thought of taking the infrastructure division any higher and further, and instead to pursue a joint venture or divesture of its manufacturing operations.

FOR SALE, BY OWNER

While Qualcomm had always been open to the idea of remaining in the manufacturing business for the long haul, the signals in late 1998 made management aware that this would no longer be necessary. The infrastructure division was now clearly on the block in many ongoing negotiations Qualcomm had with its partners. But the division proved to be most valuable not to one of Qualcomm's joint venture partners, but rather to one of its most bitter rivals, Ericsson.

As part of the settlement in March 1999 of the respective patent lawsuits between the two companies (discussed in Chapter 18), Qualcomm agreed to sell its infrastructure products division to Ericsson. With one of Qualcomm's key patent claims having been reaffirmed by the U.S. Patent Office, Ericsson also realized that fighting Qualcomm's CDMA momentum was no longer beneficial, but that acquiring Qualcomm's product expertise quickly was an attractive opportunity. Qualcomm ended up taking $240 million in charges for the company's reorganization in 1999, including the transfer of approximately 1,200 employees to Ericsson, along with equipment, facilities, open contracts, and the writedown of other assets.

The news of the Ericsson settlement and the spin-off of the infrastructure division sent Qualcomm's stock soaring. Already up over 25 percent in the month since the announcement of the strategy to improve competitiveness, the stock leaped another 50 percent in a week. Qualcomm had killed two birds with one stone—it had eliminated the doubt that was overshadowing its intellectual property rights, and it had offloaded a money shredder. The event turned Qualcomm back to its main core competency in CDMA engineering and design save for one more division—the handset manufacturing business.

The Qualcomm Personal Electronics (QPE) venture between Sony and Qualcomm that had started in 1994 had its own string of problems. Up until the first part of 1997, the QPE partnership was the only company producing commercial code-based wireless handsets for the U.S. market. But in the latter part of 1997 and early 1998, several other manufacturers, including Nokia, Motorola, and Samsung, began offering commercial CDMA units. As the market for cellular phones zoomed ahead in 1997 and 1998, component shortages became the norm, and the small-volume Qualcomm was having trouble keeping its assembly lines going with material. As Qualcomm struggled to produce sleek and compact designs similar to popular GSM and TDMA models, development and manufacturing costs were cutting into the bottom line. With many international players with much lower labor costs now producing CDMA phones, Qualcomm was struggling to remain competitive, given the salaries of its U.S. labor force.

In addition to day-to-day operational issues, Qualcomm was also hit with a lawsuit from Motorola over the design of the Q Phone, a compact clamshell model that Motorola claimed violated the patent on its popular StarTac model. Qualcomm was also being whipsawed by the dramatic seasonal cycles for phone orders, laying off and rehiring hundreds of workers over short periods. Since the QPE venture was still small compared to its competitors, it could not easily absorb the seasonal variation, and the market dynamics affected the profitability of the business. As with the infrastructure equipment business, Qualcomm kept rapidly expanding the phone manufacturing lines to meet demand, all the while hoping that the business would soon grow large enough to compete effectively and show a profit.

The Sony side of the QPE partnership was not faring well either (both companies developed and launched products independently as well as jointly through QPE, using the partnership mostly for manufacturing but also for co-development). Sony's products were generally slow to market, with launches being delayed by component shortages and quality problems. Once commercially released, the product lines were then out of step with current market demands for style and features. In one particularly painful instance, Sony had to recall approximately 60,000 phones in December 1998 when they were shown to violate FCC emissions guidelines.

A harbinger of what was to come occurred in July 1999, when Sony announced that it was pulling out of the North American market for CDMA handsets and canceling the launch of several announced products. Beleaguered by its setbacks in the production of phone models, Sony decided to exit the market and regroup operations under its Japanese parent. The company remained committed to the QPE joint venture and turned over its manufacturing lines to Qualcomm, which was still looking to increase deliveries at the time. While this boosted Qualcomm's production capacity in the short term, it was a clear signal that the handset business was taking its toll on the company. If a consumer electronics powerhouse like Sony couldn't succeed in the handset business, how could Qualcomm expect to last?

In September 1999, Qualcomm announced that it was considering all strategic options related to its phone development and manufacturing business. With commercial CDMA in full swing, the phone division was struggling to remain competitive, even as it shipped its fifteen-millionth phone. Costs were rising dramatically, and Qualcomm did not have the purchasing leverage enjoyed by the likes of Motorola, Ericsson, and Nokia, who controlled over 50 percent of the market. Learning to scale the manufacture of millions of products a month with minimal cost in a fiercely competitive market was the forte of consumer products companies, not a hard-core technology innovator like Qualcomm: The company's technical elite was used to pouring money into developing ideas, not squeezing pennies out of parts, materials, and labor.

The obvious choice among the available strategic options was to sell the division altogether. By 1999, dozens of handset manufacturers were producing CDMA phones in volume, so the factors that had provided the initial impetus for Qualcomm's foray into handset production no longer existed. Later in the fall, Qualcomm announced that it had had several preliminary offers for the handset division. With the entire wireless industry roaring ahead, it was an opportune time to sell the business, as widespread optimism would add to its value. Many analysts and industry watchers expected one of the big three handset manufacturers—Nokia, Ericsson, or Motorola—to pick up the division. Selling the division to any one of these companies, which would have better capabilities to proliferate CDMA phones around the globe, would be a boon to Qualcomm. Qualcomm's stock was already hitting the stratosphere in late 1999, and Wall Street waited anxiously for the deal that would cement Qualcomm's lucrative future as a technology provider.

In December 1999, the announcement was made that the handset manufacturing division would be sold to Kyocera of Japan. While not a major player in handsets and without a presence in the U.S. market, Kyocera was nonetheless a promising CDMA entrant in Japan. A major shareholder in DDI (Daini-Denden Planning Company), Kyocera had announced only a week earlier that it planned to merge its operations with those of two other major Japanese telecom companies—KDD (Kokusai Denshin Dewa) and IDO (Nippon Idou Tsushin)—to form a tough challenger for Japanese market leader Nippon Telephone and Telegraph (NTT). The new company, called

KDDI, would consolidate mobile networks operating under CDMA, and would capitalize on the enhanced wireless data features that code-based wireless afforded thanks to Qualcomm's continued development of advanced chipsets.

While many analysts were disappointed that a bigger name was not part of the deal, there were some generous perks associated with the transaction. As part of the agreement, Kyocera agreed to purchase a majority of its chipset requirements and system software from Qualcomm for the ensuing five years. A previous CDMA license agreement between the two companies remained intact, with Kyocera maintaining royalty payments to Qualcomm. Kyocera would also take over much of the manufacturing equipment and facilities used by Qualcomm, and would also retain many of the employees in the personal electronics division for three years. The deal would also create a larger presence for CDMA in Japan, with Qualcomm's direct involvement providing beneficial market share against other technologies.

The announcement of the deal capped a tumultuous year for Qualcomm, coming full circle from its early start in CDMA essentially a decade before. With the sale of all the ancillary production divisions, Qualcomm returned to its core competencies of technology development and chipset design. Qualcomm was still the home of some of the best and brightest minds in communications engineering. The industry was rapidly moving ahead developing wireless Web access—basically enhancing cellular-PCS phones to accommodate the high-speed transmission of data. In this area, Qualcomm was launching significant efforts to build upon the inherent strengths of CDMA for efficient data transmission, including other desirable features such as autolocation capabilities using GPS.

Qualcomm's decade-long effort in building CDMA equipment had finally reached an apex, yielding a self-sustaining industry. With rapid growth ahead of it, and with the world's telecom giants now acknowledging the significance of code-based wireless in the market, Qualcomm returned to what it did best and what made its business so profitable—licensing core CDMA technology and advanced chipset designs to the world.

> "We'll do the innovative part and let others do the manufacturing."
> —IRWIN JACOBS[3]

CHAPTER 14

Developing an Intellectual Property Business

---·—·→

Establishing a Firm Foundation

Qualcomm became successful not simply because it generated revenue from thousands of patents, but because it provided solutions that gave its customers competitive advantages. Qualcomm's patents were the by-products of its capacious level of intellectual activity—a badge of honor, so to speak. While the patents themselves formed the centerpiece of licenses and the object of litigation, a piece of paper containing an idea was only the most visible part of a much larger picture. To successfully build a business based upon licensing intellectual property, the company needed far more than patent ownership.

Qualcomm's talent in code-based wireless (CDMA) has inevitably come to be recognized by the world through its core patents (which adorn the walls of their corporate headquarters, as seen in Figure 14-1). Rather than using patents as a moat to ward off competitors, Qualcomm licensed those patents to hundreds of companies, even today. If Qualcomm were a product manufacturer at its core, a defensive patent strategy would have been in order. But Qualcomm has been first and foremost an innovator, and successful innovators are by nature not defensively minded—they want to see their ideas proliferate.

In 1989, with its plan to license its core patents and expertise in CDMA technology, Qualcomm moved into new territory. The team of engineers at the time had no idea that their CDMA systems would become so pervasive so soon, and they had not given a lot of thought to explicit patent protection of their inventions for purposes of profit. But they knew that they were on to a good thing, and they knew that many other companies in the industry would have to be educated in this "good thing" for it to catch on. Defending its inventions with patents or trade secrets wouldn't help an industry that was largely clueless about code-based wireless—the technology had to be spread diligently and widely without giving it away.

Figure 14-1. *Courtesy Qualcomm Inc.*

THE BEST DEFENSE IS A GREAT OFFENSE

While many people contend that the American system for governing and protecting the rights of intellectual property holders has stifled the rapid proliferation of new technologies, it is no doubt one of the reasons for the country's rapid economic expansion over its relatively short, two-hundred-year life. If nothing else, the system of protecting an inventor's patents has supported the proverbial American dream—supposedly, all it takes to get rich is a good idea. But turning ideas into dollars was never this straightforward, and different periods of innovation throughout American history have alternately fostered and inhibited the capitalization of patented ideas.

When looked at over large spans of time, such as decades, the role that patents and intellectual property have played in the strategies of U.S. corporations has varied dramatically. In particular, the role that patents have played—and the relative strength of their protection from violation—has been instrumental in the development of the U.S. economy on a global scale.

In the mid- to late 1800s, during the unfolding of the abrupt revolution in communications (the development of the electronic telegraph and subsequently the "speaking telegraph," or telephone), patents were a key part of wealth creation. During short periods of time, lawsuits were filed at a furious rate over the control of what many knew to be the key to the future—electronic communications. Alexander Bell himself is said to have successfully withstood more than six hundred legal tests of his intellectual property in the telephone.

The control and ownership of key patents was also fundamentally related to the valuation of a business. The shares of publicly traded corporations gyrated wildly based upon investors' belief, that the courts were leaning one way or the other on the validity of a patent claim. Truly, investors of the nineteenth century saw the primary value in these companies as being the patents themselves, above tangible assets such as equipment and facilities.

With patents a key ingredient in corporate wealth creation, a natural byproduct was the subversive exploitation of this condition for financial gain. The overwhelming volume of innovation that was being poured into new telegraph and telephone communication systems in the nineteenth century generated a wave of frivolous litigation and outright scams. Patents, which many had once seen as a great equalizer between the individual inventor and corporate behemoths, were branded as nothing more than a license to steal. The pooling of patents by many financial magnates at the time set up the conditions for the following century, when both the government and public at large became wary of the use of patents to gain advantage in the course of business.

Beginning in the early 1900s, the use of patents by individuals and companies moved toward a more benign goal. In this period, patents were typically created to shield small and large companies alike from competitive pressures—a sort of legal permission to operate in a moderately protected market. In this sense, patents were used more as defensive tools—an innovator's intellectual insurance against any unforeseen intruder. Pursuit of financial compensation in the form of a royalty was more commonly seen as being brazen at best and outright extortion at worst.

The legal and business climate of most of the early part of the twentieth century was at least partly due to the government's stance on business competition and its particular intolerance for monopolistic practices. Both the Antitrust Division of the Justice Department and the Federal Trade Commission gave corporate executives reasons to weigh carefully any actions they might take with regard to patents. Initiating too much legal activity to uphold patents could be seen as attempts to stifle competition and could attract the eye of government regulators. Throughout much of the early part of the twentieth century, few companies would go heavily into the practice of obligating payment for the use of core innovations shored up by patents.

But the rapid innovation in the nascent computer industry that began in the 1970s helped reawaken the importance of intellectual property and patent protection for an industry that thrived on common product interfaces. In the new high-tech era, many computer and software technologies also became more portable, which favored companies that licensed intellectual property (IP) rather than developing it in-house. When all the plans for a product could be handed over on a single disk—or beamed in milliseconds over the Web—the speed-to-market aspect began to counterbalance the reasonable cost of licensing IP. Back in the days when a patent merely gave a diagram and instructions for a mechanical apparatus, there was less incentive to license rather than develop an improved version independently.

The patent strategies of many U.S. corporations began to change quickly in the 1980s. Several changes in the legal system and government regulatory agencies—such as the creation of the specialized federal circuit court for patent appeals—again created a climate that supported the protection of innovation through patents. In the telecommunications industry, the breakup of AT&T in 1982 and the subsequent efforts by the government to deregulate other industries helped encourage companies to once again invest in protection of their IP with the intent of licensing it to others. A new competitive environment forced time-to-market pressures on a telecommunications industry that was more accustomed to squeezing profit from legacy architecture than to innovation.

Qualcomm got its start right in the midst of this transition to a nationwide fostering of innovation rather than regulation. Now that the Cold War was over and the U.S. space program was scaling up its shuttle launches, the prevailing idea was that the breakthrough technologies that were coming out of universities and research labs could be applied to commercial endeavors, if the government would just get out of the way. With a huge pool of intellectual talent on both the East and West coasts (and everywhere in between), the United States stood poised to improve its global competitiveness. Companies began to see patents as greater assets than they had previously thought, and they soon began to see possibilities in licensing their intellectual property.

> "The rest of the industry was going in another direction. One small company from San Diego couldn't do it all."
> —STEVE ALTMAN,
> EXECUTIVE VP AND PRESIDENT,
> QUALCOMM TECHNOLOGY LICENSING

MAKING A BUSINESS OUT OF CDMA

In the latter part of 1988, when the Qualcomm staff met to assess their prospects for bringing CDMA to commercial viability, they realized that they would quickly have to make a decision about which business model to employ. Jacobs and the rest of the technical team were excited about the prospects that lay ahead of them: Their internal simulations had shown that their unique spread-spectrum approach would provide tremendous performance in mobile networks. The cellular industry was their best opportunity to see code-based wireless realized, but many roadblocks stood in the way. While still relatively young, the wireless industry had little room for small newcomers; new entrants typically needed big friends with deep pockets if they wanted to succeed.

Two competing lines of thought boiled to the surface in these discussions of Qualcomm's business strategy for CDMA: become a technology licensor or become a product manufacturer. Simply developing and patenting technology and licensing it to corporations was appealing to many, because the financial model was very attractive—the R&D overhead would be relatively low and easily manageable. There would be no inventory concerns to worry about and no heated competition on razor-thin margins. The licensing model, if successfully employed, had virtually no drawbacks. But successful employment was a big if—companies wouldn't just line up to license technology; there had to be compelling value offered.

Alternatively, developing Qualcomm into a product manufacturer was attractive because no one else would be likely to be able to match the performance of its equipment as a result of its proprietary knowledge of code-based wireless. If the business could be scaled up sufficiently to be competitive, it could probably hold its own with superior products. This model offered Qualcomm the best chance to dominate the business of CDMA, basically taking control of all aspects of design and manufacture. The manufacturing model had several hurdles, though, the most significant being the huge up-front investment required for scaling up a top-notch manufacturing enterprise.

Neither choice seemed to provide the optimum chance for success in the cellular industry, especially with the industry already migrating toward time-based wireless (TDMA) at the time. As Jacobs and the team mulled over their future path on several occasions, the story of the Betamax failure was often brought up: The VHS standard for videotape players ultimately won out in the market, even though it was considered technically inferior to Betamax. Some contended that Qualcomm's code-based wireless could fall victim to the same fate—the best technology doesn't always win out. But Jacobs realized that there were several reasons for the success of VHS, one of which was the widespread licensing of the technology early on. If CDMA could be quickly and efficiently licensed to a wide base in the industry, it could outpace the alternatives. Even so, the team kept coming back to the question of what would motivate carriers and vendors to license IP from a small, unfamiliar company like Qualcomm. After all, Qualcomm had few connections in the cellular industry, and no one in the company had much experience in licensing technology.

But the alternative of being a product manufacturer was equally vexing. Qualcomm was far too small to compete outright against the likes of AT&T, OKI, and Motorola in the full-scale manufacturing of cellular equipment. Qualcomm had enough trouble building a few thousand OmniTRACS units every year. So how would it fit into the manufacturing puzzle without overextending itself beyond its areas of competency? The manufacture of cellular phones was beyond the comprehension of the San Diego technology incubator; it would require huge investments in manufacturing lines and processes to turn out millions of products a year. It would also be extremely difficult to transform a team of Ph.D.s who loved to tinker into process managers and operational controllers.

> "We debated what was a reasonable business plan if we were successful, and certainly one could think about trying to take one's arms around it and do the manufacturing yourself. Fairly early we decided that we would try to license the technology, but we needed to get the major manufacturers involved."
> —DR. IRWIN MARK JACOBS, QUALCOMM FOUNDER AND CEO

The answer to this dilemma had profound implications for the future of the company, so it was important that various scenarios be fleshed out. In every scenario, though, the team kept coming back to the reality that for CDMA to be taken seriously and progress at a rapid pace, they had to build something besides ideas on paper. The industry was already moving toward a time-based wireless solution for the second generation of cellular systems (2G). If Qualcomm was to have any hope of capturing a decent piece of the market, it needed as much leverage as possible to encourage the major equipment manufacturers to adopt code-based wireless.

It soon became obvious that Qualcomm would have to blend the two models to have the best chance of success. Just licensing intellectual property—no matter how compelling as a business model—didn't seem strong enough to guarantee success. Without anything to offer beyond paper knowledge and experience, it would be very difficult for Qualcomm to reach critical mass and make a sustainable business from just licensing. But widespread licensing was important in order to get a major portion of the industry on board rapidly, so it had to be a significant component.

In addition to licensing, then, the team realized they would have to develop some low-level competency in manufacturing CDMA components and products to help stimulate the adoption of CDMA by the industry—especially by manufacturers. The most natural fit for Qualcomm's intellectual talent and specialized products was in the development of dedicated chipsets (ASICs) and integrated circuits. The team had highly developed knowledge of chip-building techniques, and their designs could be manufactured on any scale by outside foundries (making Qualcomm a fabless semiconductor company). Whether they wanted to stamp out ten chips a month or ten million a year, semiconductor fabricators in the United States, Europe, and Asia could accommodate this.

Even with lingering disagreement about the details of the approach, Jacobs and the senior staff settled on this business approach to best foster CDMA's adoption in mobile networks. The company would first develop and license the core technology for mobile code-based wireless. Test hardware and software would be built to demonstrate performance, and this experience would later be converted to processes for building commercial hardware. The core implementation of code-based wireless signal processing would be captured in proprietary ASIC designs that could be sold to product manufacturers, maintaining Qualcomm's leverage over CDMA system design.

Jacobs felt that code-based wireless would be compelling enough to encourage investment by some network operators if they were assured that equipment could be produced rapidly. Cellular technologies had historically been limited by the availability of equipment for testing designs, so the early buy-in of manufacturers would be vital. But if vendors could not be initially convinced to build equipment, Qualcomm would have to build the equipment itself. At some point, after hardware and software were sufficiently developed, vendors could either purchase Qualcomm's product designs or license the underlying technology to design and manufacture their own. This approach kept CDMA on the fast track for adoption while still preserving Qualcomm's key role in its development. The key to pulling it all off was developing win-win relationships with the major carriers and vendors in the industry. But first, Qualcomm had to develop a strong technical base for its proposed CDMA solution.

BUILDING AN IP BASE

For Jacobs, Viterbi, and the other engineers in Qualcomm, novel solutions to complex communication problems were a regular occurrence. Even during their days at Linkabit, Jacobs and the senior team were renowned for creative thinking in numerous areas that showed opportunity—basically throwing a variety of solutions up against the wall to see what stuck. The core development team would regularly revisit bottlenecks in current communication architectures and look for ways around them, looking at all angles to see if there were solutions that most people had missed. If they could not find a feasible solution for any particular problem at the time, that problem would be dropped, but it was rarely forgotten. If any commercial viability could be seen in the company's research, the whole team would jump in to flesh out a workable design. Thanks to their extensive experience with government contracts, Jacobs and the team were diligent in protecting their solutions with extensive internal documentation.

Applying CDMA to mobile communications required a high level of innovation from the company in order to produce a viable product in the commercial marketplace. An extensive array of proprietary solutions was involved in solving the major drawbacks of spread spectrum's use in multiple-access systems, so from the outset Qualcomm was diligent in preparing its ideas for patent application. Whether the company decided to pursue the manufacture of products itself or through joint ventures, the team needed to protect their ideas. Since no one else was experimenting in the area of CDMA for mobile communications in the late 1980s and early 1990s, they knew they were ahead of the curve in their research. But putting that research on dated documentation would be important in proving that they were well ahead of anyone else at the time, no matter what direction the business ended up taking.

Qualcomm's major differentiator from its nearest competitors was its novel approach to solving a few key problems in applying CDMA to cellular networks, such as the issues of power control and call handoffs. These and other problems with code-based wireless were well known in academia, but no simple solutions had yet been developed. But it was typical of Jacobs, Viterbi, and the others in Qualcomm's core that these problems were slowly chiseled away at until complete solutions were found. Looking back from the technology mindset of today, the solutions were not that much of a stretch. But for an era in which digital electronics was still in its infancy, they were extremely sophisticated.

By the time the Cellular Telecommunications Industry Assotiation (CTIA) adopted CDMA as a North American standard in 1993, Qualcomm had already developed a substantial base of intellectual property in the methods of implementing the technology in mobile networks. Unlike many other standards efforts, in which multiple companies are committing substantial resources to developing different aspects of a protocol, Qualcomm was essentially alone in bringing the core methods of CDMA into a standard in the early 1990s. With most of the rest of the industry forging ahead in the area of TDMA and GSM— where they saw a more stable, lucrative field—Qualcomm continued along a do-or-die path to get CDMA adopted for commercial use. It was a big bet—one that eventually paid off, but not without Herculean efforts to make it happen.

Qualcomm's huge proportion of intellectual contributions to the standard left it in a powerful position to dictate licensing terms and royalties once

CDMA reached a minimal level of acceptance. Since Qualcomm had shouldered more risk than any other company at the time, it essentially controlled the royalties on the first generation of CDMA. Standards like GSM, on the other hand, had dozens of companies contributing essential IP to the standard, distributing the royalty leverage across a wide base. Companies implementing GSM technologies therefore tended to cross-license different patent portfolios in order to be able to enter markets. Qualcomm had everything it needed to implement CDMA, so it simply asked for up-front license fees and ongoing royalties in order to develop the technology further.

When Qualcomm signed its very first CDMA development agreements with network operators such as PacTel Cellular, it did not yet have a single patent covering CDMA in a cellular implementation. It had done extensive testing and simulation, and had submitted one patent already for the system concept. But the continued work in developing code-based wireless systems led to a handful of patents that embodied the basic functions of CDMA in mobile wireless networks.

FUNDAMENTAL CDMA PATENTS

What gave Qualcomm such a clear competitive edge in developing CDMA for mobile telephony was its command of the fundamental methods necessary to make it actually work in practice. Several corporations around the world, the U.S. military, and research bodies had extensive patents and other IP in CDMA and spread spectrum, but no one had implemented techniques that would make it possible in a multiple-access mobile system. Qualcomm's unique expertise in code-based wireless centered around a few novel concepts spelled out in a handful of early patents. Most of these patents were filed just a few days after the 1989 demonstration in San Diego, but the first came much sooner.

The earliest patent Qualcomm had filed in the area of mobile CDMA, U.S. Patent No. 4,901,307, was filed in October 1986 under the names of Klein Gilhousen, Irwin Jacobs, and Butch Weaver. Based upon the engineers' current experience with the Hughes Aircraft satellite communications project, this patent laid out the basic concepts for implementing CDMA in a satellite or terrestrial application. The patent explained why most prior art (concepts and drawings filed with previous patents) had considered CDMA inferior to FDMA and TDMA in its capacity to handle multiple users—that previous analyses had always assumed that signals from code-based wireless users were fixed at a high power. This new patent explained ways to drop the power transmitted by each user in proportion to that user's level of information activity, vastly increasing the capacity of a CDMA system. It offered a method for controlling power in mobile units, and it identified methods for overcoming the other problems that plagued CDMA's use in a mobile environment. Granted to Qualcomm on February 13, 1990, this single patent would become the basis for many others to come, and would be referenced by hundreds of future patents from Qualcomm and others in the industry.

> "Once we completed that [the Schneider OmniTRACS] contract, then it was possible to switch our attention over to CDMA."
>
> —IRWIN JACOBS,
>   QUALCOMM COFOUNDER AND CEO

After the filing of this early patent, though, the engineers at Qualcomm had their attention diverted to their OmniTRACS business; and further work in mobile CDMA did not pick again up until after the Schneider contract in October 1988. After a year of work, on November 7, 1989, three more patents were filed, covering Qualcomm's novel inventions for CDMA in finer detail. One in particular, U.S. Patent No. 5,056,109, laid out their elegant scheme for managing the power level in a mobile cellular phone. The other two patents presented novel methods for soft handoffs and improved receiver design. All three patents were intimately tied as components of a cellular code-based wireless system, and each was submitted under the names of Klein Gilhousen, Roberto Padovani, and Chuck Wheatley. In these four initial patents, Qualcomm captured the fundamental technical concepts necessary to implement CDMA in a fully functional, commercial cellular system. Hundreds of patents that further defined and optimized these techniques ultimately followed, but this relatively small core of ideas was the foundation of cellular CDMA.

A primary strength in these early patents (as in all of Qualcomm's patents) was the extensive knowledge of prior art by inventors. Qualcomm's engineers had extensive knowledge going back decades in the area of CDMA and spread spectrum, so they were intimately familiar with the prior art on the subject. Many inventors fall victim to inadequate research of prior art in their patents, and this mistake often leads to the undoing of their ownership of proprietary methods. But the principal engineers at Qualcomm didn't have to research prior art—they lived it. They were familiar with most peer researchers on a first-name basis, and they were often consulted for a review of concepts themselves, so they didn't have to look far to see what was already being done. With detailed knowledge of what had already been invented and was being invented, Qualcomm was able to develop much stronger patents that would withstand legal challenges.

The core strength and fundamental nature of these few early patents were the underpinnings of Qualcomm's competitive advantage in CDMA. Its ability to license its IP was anchored in its ownership of these concepts, but patents were only a first step. Qualcomm's full value as a technology provider stemmed from its experience in implementing these concepts and hundreds of finer points necessary to optimize a CDMA system. This latent knowledge ultimately gave Qualcomm's customers a competitive edge. Companies that simply worked from Qualcomm's patents to develop CDMA learned that there's a lot more to making the technology work than was made public. The millions of hours their technical staff dedicated to making CDMA robust equated to extensive trade secrets held closely by Qualcomm.

While these fundamental patents were not issued until the 1991–1992 period, Qualcomm nonetheless used this proprietary knowledge to advance CDMA well into its commercial development cycle. The company's internal expertise had to be disseminated throughout the industry in a prudent way so as not to simply give away the keys to CDMA. As it turns out, CDMA was so difficult for most companies to get a handle on at the time that Qualcomm had little to worry about early on. What this meant, though, was that an extensive amount of hand holding with manufacturers and network operators was needed to educate them on the finer points of making code-based wireless work.

To help accelerate the growth and adoption of CDMA, many of Qualcomm's early license agreements contained support provisions—development assistance was, after all, in the best interest of promoting the technology. Every licensee was offered the collective knowledge of Qualcomm's engineers on top of the legal license to use the techniques covered in the issued or pending patents. Those who chose to make ample use of Qualcomm's resources were much more successful in launching their new products or services. Especially in the very first implementations of code-based wireless in trial networks in the early 1990s, Qualcomm was learning the details of cellular CDMA as well, so on-site support worked well for all parties.

But in order to offer a high level of technical support for the development of CDMA, Qualcomm had to be compensated for it. As interest grew in 1989, Qualcomm's key engineers were in great demand, and they were quickly burning through every dollar that was coming in from the OmniTRACS business. Balancing the need to keep the doors open with the concurrent goal of spreading CDMA far and wide in the industry required a delicate balance in negotiating partnerships with network operators.

MONEY FOR IDEAS

Midway through 1989, when Irwin Jacobs and the rest of the Qualcomm team were working furiously to prepare for their first demonstration of CDMA, they realized that they needed legal expertise for establishing and negotiating the relationships with the carriers that they were attempting to woo to the technology. In their search for an appropriate counsel, they tapped their established employee base to come in contact with Steven Altman, then an attorney at Gray, Cary, Ware & Freidenrich in San Diego. Altman's wife was already working for Qualcomm in the legal department, handling contracts for Omni-TRACS. Altman's experience with intellectual property and international joint ventures made him an ideal candidate for the job of negotiating development partnerships. He was hired in October 1989, a month before the initial CDMA demonstration.

> "License fees early on were extremely important because we needed money to survive. We also felt that if a company paid an upfront fee, they would be more committed to realize their investment."
> —STEVE ALTMAN,
> EXECUTIVE VP AND PRESIDENT,
> QUALCOMM TECHNOLOGY LICENSING

Altman was primarily responsible for structuring and negotiating development agreements and licensing terms for CDMA in mobile communications with network operators and equipment vendors. For the next several years, Altman was the primary negotiator and counselor on all of Qualcomm's license and joint venture agreements. The task was onerous—to determine a framework for agreements that would provide complementary benefits for Qualcomm and its licensees in bringing CDMA to commercial fruition. The licenses had to balance the need to rapidly divulge the details of CDMA to the world with the need to retain control over the technology—two aspects that were diametrically opposed to each other. And, by the way, the agreements had to bring in enough cash to pay the bills.

In these early days of defining Qualcomm's cellular CDMA effort as a serious business (not just a radical idea from a small San Diego start-up that no one had ever heard of), three things were paramount:

1. *Time was critical.* CDMA had to be deployed as rapidly as possible if it was to be competitive. With the industry already rapidly moving toward TDMA technologies, each day lost was a leg up for the incumbent technology's momentum. Qualcomm had to not only quickly communicate CDMA to operators and equipment vendors, but speed them to commercial realization of the technology as well.

2. *Broad acceptance was necessary.* CDMA needed the support of as many equipment vendors and carriers as possible. The cellular market is driven by consensus and standards, so wholehearted adoption by a strong con-

tingent of leading network operators and suppliers was necessary. Luke-warm interest from tier two organizations would spell certain death.

3. *Funding was the lifeblood.* The financial resources necessary to develop the technology were immense, and the cash flow from OmniTRACS wouldn't be enough to pay salaries, let alone capital equipment costs. Since they had a vested interest in the outcome, the network operators were the best potential source of funds for developing CDMA prototype systems, so joint ventures had to encompass a reasonable level of cash infusion to enable the company to survive.

Balancing all three of these factors in developing partnerships with other companies proved very difficult, but Altman worked with Allen Salmasi and others to develop a consistent pitch that they felt would be compelling to the various players in the industry. They also developed several strategies to leverage existing relationships between competitors to turn them in favor of CDMA. They already had their first partner, PacTel, willing to support early development with critical funding. The trial that PacTel paid for in November 1989 started a whole new phase of advancing CDMA into the industry.

Once the first trial had been completed and the promises of CDMA had been demonstrated to be real to the industry at large, Qualcomm knew that it would have to start seriously courting the major cellular equipment manufacturers in addition to signing up a critical mass of network operators. PacTel and the other U.S. carriers that showed interest in CDMA made it clear that the technology had to have a strong base of support—they wouldn't rely on a small, fledgling newcomer like Qualcomm, no matter how well CDMA performed. Qualcomm had also repeatedly been hit with the requirement that CDMA become an adopted standard of the major industry body, the Telecommunications Industry Association (TIA), not just a proprietary technology. And it took until 1993 to achieve this.

CHAPTER 15

Fitting Into the Value Chain

---·➡

Disseminating Proprietary Technology

The timing of Qualcomm's introduction of its dark-horse technology made it a do-or-die proposition. Qualcomm would either have niche acceptance in the market or be the dominant supplier—there was no in between. This key aspect is at the heart of the company's success in disrupting the status quo: A technology that had been given more time to mature under the eyes of many companies would have certainly been diluted until it had a less than revolutionary impact. And the impact on Qualcomm's bottom line would have been equally diluted.

Yet from the outset, Qualcomm learned that no carrier in the world would invest in—let alone adopt outright—a technology that could be provided only by a single source. PacTel and the other network operators made it clear that widespread adoption of code-based wireless (CDMA) by multiple manufacturers was a prerequisite for their acceptance of the technology. So the company faced a dilemma in the dichotomy between expanding knowledge and expertise of CDMA outside Qualcomm and protecting the company's proprietary innovations through patents. Qualcomm had to create a brand image of a value-added technology supplier that would afford adopters a critical advantage over their competition.

Qualcomm had to find its niche in the cellular value chain and focus on the core competencies that were necessary to excel in that role. By the early 1990s, the company had several businesses operating—OmniTRACS, government contracts, satellite telemetry, HDTV signal processing—with no assurance that its efforts in cellular code-based wireless would pay off. So, Qualcomm had to use its resources wisely. The natural place to start offering CDMA products was in an area of strength for Qualcomm—integrated circuits, extending up into the higher levels of cellular products and systems. The move to develop breadboard and prototype systems was well within Qualcomm's capabilities and could help facilitate the adoption of the technology by other manufacturers.

Courting equipment manufacturers and encouraging them to dedicate resources to CDMA development was a tricky endeavor, however. Since in the early 1990s the industry had already decided to move to time-based wireless (TDMA) in the United States and GSM in Europe, major equipment manufacturers such as AT&T, Motorola, and Ericsson had a strong vested interest in seeing their investments in these other technologies come to fruition. Adopting the competing code-based wireless technology would be counterproductive for them, unless there were extremely compelling reasons for them to do so. For the most part, compelling reasons usually came in the form of purchase orders from network operators. Qualcomm therefore realized that the strongest leverage lay with the carriers—Qualcomm would push the new technology while the carriers pulled. Having one without the other wouldn't accomplish anything.

Qualcomm's push came in the form of intense lobbying to encourage vendors to get a jump on their competition by building expertise in the future of communications immediately. Qualcomm presented itself as holding the keys to the future, which were there for the taking: Code-based wireless was characterized as a wise investment in the future of communications. But this message alone was not enough to dissipate the momentum that time-based wireless already had with vendors. The stakes had to be raised so that vendors would no longer feel completely safe with TDMA alone—it was too easy to dismiss the risky CDMA route and stay on a promising and stable time-based wireless path, where returns seemed more certain. What Qualcomm did to break this momentum was pure genius.

PROVIDING INCENTIVES TO SPEED ADOPTION

Qualcomm realized that there was no single argument that would make vendors jump into code-based wireless. It had to weave several compelling drivers together and leverage the demands of the carriers for increased capacity down the supply chain. It had to turn the perceived weaknesses of code-based wireless into strengths, and every disadvantage had to be turned around and presented as a chance to jump ahead of the competition. Qualcomm's basic message for equipment vendors came down to four elements:

1. CDMA was the future, and investing in it now will give you an advantage in time to market.

2. We'll offer a "try before you buy" agreement, where you can test-drive CDMA.

3. We will add value to your business by providing technical support.

4. And finally, we are fully prepared to build and sell CDMA equipment ourselves.

Qualcomm's only hope of surviving in this market was to demonstrate that its capabilities were extremely valuable to equipment manufacturers. If equipment manufacturers were convinced that their customers (carriers) would soon be ordering code-based wireless equipment, they would need a partner to provide this, and Qualcomm was the natural (and only) partner. Offering vendors a low-risk, low-cost method of entering into CDMA backed up this argument, making at least looking into the new technology almost a no-brainer for vendors. In the meantime, while equipment providers were developing CDMA products, Qualcomm could rally more network operators to put further pressure on vendors to make the big leap and commit the resources needed to commercialize code-based wireless products. The added threat of Qualcomm itself becoming a manufacturer of equipment would spur vendors on and keep them interested in CDMA.

The performance of CDMA was obviously key to the success of the whole effort here, and it was almost assumed that the ideas of Jacobs, Viterbi, and the rest of the team would work out. If the concepts didn't work, and work well, no amount of marketing could sell the industry on code-based wireless. Hence demonstration trials were the key to driving interest. Once code-based wireless had demonstrated its tremendous capacity in field trials, forward-looking network operators would begin to demand the technology from their vendors.

As it turned out, this approach to proliferating CDMA worked rather well, though it was a hard-fought battle. Qualcomm was quickly successful in getting a few major network operators to consider code-based wireless as opposed to an uncertain future with time-based systems. The company used support from network operators like PacTel to successfully court AT&T and Motorola to sign licenses with Qualcomm for the manufacture of gear. With a handful of key players on board early, Qualcomm had much more leverage to negotiate more licenses with other suppliers and operators.

But signing a license agreement did not in itself motivate equipment companies to develop CDMA with the same fervor that Qualcomm did. Early on, when Qualcomm was still ironing out its innovative CDMA design, the senior engineering staff realized that it would be very difficult for equipment vendors to take what the engineers had learned and implement it right. CDMA was new and complex compared to current methods, and any outside vendor wishing to develop competency in this area would need lots of hand-holding.

That few companies took CDMA seriously to begin with actually turned out to be a major advantage for Qualcomm, once the technology started to take off with network operators. With the major equipment vendors absorbed in developing time-based wireless solutions, Qualcomm went virtually unchallenged in pursuing CDMA. This is not to say that other companies did not challenge Qualcomm technically—many organizations were actively developing code-based wireless and claimed that their innovations were essential to successful operation of the technology. But most competitors envisioned CDMA as an immature technology, something not yet worthy of commercial consideration.

Given the complex nature of relationships in the cellular industry, combined with the acceptance of time-based wireless as an accepted path forward, vendors moved very slowly in considering CDMA. Equipment manufacturers such as Motorola were inclined to take their time in evaluating the merits of code-based wireless, seeing it as a "back burner" item that should be watched while they pushed ahead with their own preferred solution (N-AMPS, in Motorola's case). To bring code-based wireless to the forefront, Qualcomm had to sweeten the deal to get vendors to take a close look.

To further entice equipment manufacturers, Altman and the senior staff developed a support agreement as an option to a full license of the technology. The support agreement was basically a "try before you buy" plan, in which the vendor would pay only a portion of the full license fee to gain access to all the designs of code-based wireless, along with development support from Qualcomm. The licensee would then have an agreed-upon period during which it could either consent to a full license plan or terminate the existing agreement, with all rights reverting to Qualcomm.

> "After a period of time they had to decide to pay the whole license fee or forgo the information and development help. Just about every company ended up signing the full license."
>
> —STEVE ALTMAN,
>   EXECUTIVE VP AND PRESIDENT,
>   QUALCOMM TECHNOLOGY LICENSING

In this arrangement, the licensee's risk was reduced, and it could make a more informed decision about CDMA. Even if the licensee backed out of the full agreement, which very few actually did, it would gain firsthand information about the true potential of code-based wireless. The risk to Qualcomm was that a vendor now "had the goods" on the technology and could refocus its efforts on improving TDMA. But Jacobs and the technical team were confident that code-based wireless had no holes and that, if vendors could see the two approaches in detail on a level field, the benefits of CDMA would be overwhelmingly obvious. At a minimum, it might shake a vendor's confidence in time-based wireless as the best solution to capacity problems.

The support agreements went a long way to encourage early buy-in from several manufacturers in the industry. In August 1990, Qualcomm negotiated a breakthrough with AT&T, NYNEX, and Ameritech in the form of a multimillion-dollar deal to develop and provide equipment for mobile telephone networks based upon CDMA. Many more agreements would follow this one, with equipment manufacturers brought to the table by network operators that were eager to investigate the potential of code-based wireless.

PRODUCT ROYALTY

Qualcomm's licensing business had two main goals: one, to keep the company and its development of CDMA going and, two, to compensate the company over the long run. Up-front development fees were included in license deals (and continue to be to this day) because Qualcomm needed money to pay its engineers and other staff. Also, partnering companies tended to commit more strongly to ongoing development if they had already invested cash in Qualcomm's CDMA. So licensing and development fees were the primary points of negotiation in all of Qualcomm's early joint ventures. But the management was wise to always stipulate a royalty provision that kicked in when products became commercialized at some point in the future.

> "From the beginning we structured in development funding and ongoing royalty into license agreements."
> —STEVE ALTMAN

The ongoing royalty that CDMA licensees would pay to manufacture and sell products based on CDMA was a percentage based upon the average selling price of a product over a given time period. This would make it easy for manufacturers to factor royalties into their forecasts of product costs for high-end or low-end devices. Since commercialization of code-based wireless was seen as a long way off in the early 1990s, few manufacturers were overly concerned about ongoing royalty payments. But with the eventual commercialization of CDMA, the royalties on CDMA equipment became more of a focus for equipment manufacturers, especially those making handsets. With intense competition in maturing wireless markets, royalty payments became a bigger concern for many licensees.

OFFERING VALUE IN PROPRIETARY TECHNOLOGY

Breaking into telecommunications in the early 1990s, Qualcomm was uniquely positioned to capitalize on its cutting-edge intellectual talent and growing list of issued patents. With the wind of deregulation at its back and a fertile "niche" of digital wireless telecommunications blossoming into a multibillion-dollar industry, Qualcomm had a welcome environment for the assertion of intellectual property rights (IPR) in the international wireless market. The company was not alone in advancing the rediscovered value of patents in the technology sector, but outside of companies like Microsoft in the area of computer operating systems, few had so effectively cornered the market on a technology and cobbled together the necessary financial backing to pursue its development. Because Qualcomm had carried out all the principal development and testing of the technology's most fundamental aspects, it was considered the CDMA kingpin.

> "We began to negotiate with AT&T, Motorola, and Nokia as well as others. The give and take of that began to set the terms and conditions of how we would license. None of us had any experience in licensing before this, so that was kind of educational as well."
>
> —IRWIN JACOBS,
> QUALCOMM COFOUNDER AND CEO

When Qualcomm was first considering a licensing business for code-based wireless, one major drawback that Irwin Jacobs saw was that neither he nor anyone else in the company had significant experience in creating license agreements. They had relied on an intuitive approach to structuring win-win relationships with their partners and customers. Fortunately, this was the most important element, but they still had to develop the legal expertise to make their licensing program into a legitimate and effective business on a global scale. After learning a great deal about licensing as they progressed through multiple agreements in the first few years, Qualcomm effectively set a base structure for license agreements to compensate them for their work in making CDMA work in mobile systems. Once the licensing business had reached critical mass with a small number of key suppliers, additional licensees were much easier to bring on board.

Licensing IP was rarely as simple as patenting an idea and then getting someone to send regular royalty checks for its use in a product or service. Companies like Qualcomm that have made an effort to monetize their intellectual property have quickly realized that the work does not end when the patent is issued and the deal is signed. If a company wanted to retain and actually grow the value of its licensed IP, a high level of ongoing maintenance was necessary. Basically, IP licensing was far from being a "get rich quick" scheme, as some have described patent windfalls—it required a sustained level of hard work from an exceptional and seasoned team.

The ongoing work that Qualcomm carried out to inject a high level of value into its intellectual property was multifaceted and complex. For starters, licensing its IP was not the company's sole business. Licensing was intimately tied to its core competency in developing chipsets, and was significantly augmented by Qualcomm's early efforts to build products through partnerships in network infrastructure and handsets. The practical implementation experience the company possessed proved invaluable not only in developing the key intellectual property behind CDMA, but also in helping licensees get up to speed fast on the technology and quickly introduce it to the market.

Another major factor that dictated whether a company's IP had any value was the industry consensus on standards. Since the wireless industry was driven in the direction of approved standards, intellectual property that was not embodied in the elected standards had little chance of providing any value to manufacturers and hence no hope of providing income to its owner. In this case, Qualcomm's nearly complete dominance of code-based wireless IP almost shut it out of a standard, since the major industry bodies—the FCC, CTIA, and TIA—were uneasy about adopting an effectively proprietary standard. As discussed in Chapter 9, "Becoming a Wireless Standard," in order to establish a foothold, Qualcomm had to navigate deftly through the politically charged process of standard setting. Success in developing the first CDMA standard (IS-95), while a significant victory, did not guarantee similar successes outside the United States or in the development of future generations of standards.

At the time of Qualcomm's entry into cellular, the approach to setting wireless standards varied greatly across continents. Global harmonization was on everybody's mind, but getting there was a task that few could visualize in the early stages of the market. While the cellular markets of various nations had developed largely independently of each other because of the newness of the technology, the succeeding generations of wireless communication would become more global in scope, and interests would increasingly cross borders. In addition, the digital communications generation would add a new level of growth and complexity to an industry that was only beginning to define itself.

A SHORT BACKGROUND IN WIRELESS STANDARDS

Standards have been vital to the global wireless industry for a number of reasons. Because of the extensive array of systems involved in wireless telecommunications, no single company produced all of the various pieces of equipment used in any one network. One company might produce wireless phones, another the base stations that those phones communicate with, and yet another the network gear that routes the call along the PSTN (public switched telephone network). Several levels of equipment must "talk" to each other with a high level of reliability, making common and well understood protocols absolutely essential.

The standards that define the various protocols used in wireless communication usually have been developed by independent technical bodies that aim to produce a diverse representation of all the companies that are developing products for that portion of the market. The standard itself will specify the necessary attributes and functions, such as operating frequencies, power levels, or other parameters. Full consensus on these operating parameters must be reached, and a significant level of due diligence on the part of companies must occur to prove out the merits of selecting any particular element of the protocol's design.

Standards development organizations (SDOs) have been set up within countries to control the development and deployment of equipment within those countries' borders. But wireless communications added the complexity of mobility—roaming across borders made it necessary for SDOs to interact with each other on a global level. In the late 1980s, for instance, the U.S. cellular industry was taking cues from wireless protocol advances in both Europe and Asia, weighing the merits of the various protocols. Joint groups were developed to unify a number of SDOs into consortiums with a regional outlook. These partnerships took the various regional interests of standards bodies and worked to unify the various standards or combine them into communications systems that were interoperable at some level.

In Europe, the formation and direction of the European Union acted as the ultimate driver in the standard-setting process for telecommunications and wireless in particular. The economies and populations of the countries in Western Europe are more intimately linked than those of countries in other regions of the world, necessitating a level of collaboration and unification that may not be appropriate elsewhere. Consolidated economic and political policies in the European Union started to formally take shape in the early 1990s and unified the member states in a number of significant ways. A common currency, common regulatory measures, and common approaches to critical services for member societies, including communications, now all fall under the same umbrella. Of course, the EU could not effectively institute common policies without unified communications. This policy of common communication protocols in the EU led to the development of the GSM standard—currently the most widely used mobile protocol in the world.

As the EU was moving to regulate a common technical standard for European countries, the United States was taking the completely opposite approach: technology neutrality. Some cite simple geography as the primary basis for the two styles—the European nations were tightly interwoven, and travel across countries was common. The United States was largely isolated from other industrial powers by two large bodies of water. These geographic differences tended to support either a collaborative or an isolationist philosophy toward consensus on technical standards.

But the United States also made a very strong push to deregulate the former communications monopolies. With the view that technical innovation will ultimately lead to a telecommunications infrastructure that will better serve all areas of the American economy, the U.S. government put in effect consistent policies to open up markets to competition. The leanings of U.S. regulators toward a market-driven approach to standards were an absolute prerequisite for Qualcomm's success in bringing CDMA to the commercial cellular market. By contrast, the EU policies favoring a single common interface explain why CDMA still has a limited presence in Europe.

The Asian nations have taken a mixed approach to wireless standards over the last few decades. Japan has mostly taken the technically advanced track with little consideration of global consensus, pushing the most cutting-edge technology and services to the island's consumers. This approach has isolated the Japanese from European markets in much the same way as it has the United States. Other nations throughout Asia have adopted a mix of wireless standards in their second-generation systems, with many even deploying competing standards side by side like the United States.

Standards for both the first-generation analog networks and the second-generation digital networks were characterized by regional collaboration and global fragmentation. At the close of the millennium however, many nations around the world saw the third generation as an opportunity for true global consensus under the umbrella of the International Telecommunications Union (ITU). Heartened by the growing regional success of GSM, many saw the possibility of uniting mobile communications and Internet technology and developing worldwide standards that would usher a new era of communications into the world.

Headquartered in Geneva, Switzerland, the ITU was originally established in 1865 as the International Telegraph Union. The role of the ITU at its formation was to facilitate efficient international communications by establishing consistent standards among member nations. Just as in its early days, the ITU continues to be a consensus-driven body whose membership is made up of the various regional groups. In the interest of propelling the industry through interoperability, the ITU members have sought to find the best middle ground for all member companies. The various consortiums from individual nations have proposed various standards or families of protocols to the body for review and eventual selection.

In the particular case of wireless communications standards, not only must signaling protocols be synchronized, but the frequencies that carry signals over the air must be coordinated as well. Various countries have a variety of services—such as television and radio broadcasting, satellite communications, or public safety services—locked into different areas of the frequency map. This has made the job of coordinating spectrum use for mobile services especially difficult. Most countries have collaborated globally in moving cellular services into the bands at 800–900 MHz and 1,800–1,900 MHz. Future mobile wireless services in areas such as 1,700 MHz and 2,100 MHz have also been coordinated by the ITU. Driving global consensus in the designation of frequency bands for mobile communications has been a major function of the ITU.

Participation in the ITU and other multinational standard organizations, however, has obviously been voluntary. Because in many nations around the world the telecommunications industry is still either owned outright or heavily influenced by government entities, the selection of technological standards for the evolution of communication services can be complex. In different regions of the world, governments have had long-standing arrangements for managing communications infrastructure that play an important role in political and social relations with neighboring nations. The different directions that countries have taken in developing standards have therefore been strongly tied to their foreign trade policies. This variety of policies on technology adoption and incorporation into standards has also provided an array of opportunities for multinational countries exporting wireless equipment and services.

An Open-and-Shut Case

Even with all the consensus that has been achieved in standards groups, though, the member companies' underlying motivation for deploying wireless systems has been to profit through the sale of their products. Perhaps more than any other company, Qualcomm has succeeded in profiting immensely from the standardization of its proprietary technology. This is the point at which the happy visual of everybody holding hands and singing in unison crumbles into disarray. While consensus in standards can open up markets and offer opportunity to equipment manufacturers and technology developers, it can just as easily kill a company's chance to profit if the standards chosen don't include the systems that the company has developed. For this reason, standards development has been an extremely competitive and complex endeavor that has required more than just technical competence— the ability to lobby for corporate interests has weighed in heavily.

Since standards have been largely made up of individual contributions from commercial ventures, there must be a structure in place to deal with the rights of the inventors of proprietary technology. Each standards group has had to have a policy for dealing with the often-unbalanced contribution of various companies and the degree to which this occurs. Most standards bodies have had methods to determine which members have contributed intellectual property that is essential to the functioning of the system architecture described in the standard. This essential IP is often counted as a contribution worthy of some form of compensation, usually a licensing royalty from product manufacturers. Firms contributing essential IP to a standard, however, most often have had to agree to license this IP on a fair and nondiscriminatory basis.

In the case of the initial North American CDMA standard (IS-95) published in 1993, Qualcomm was the holder of nearly all the essential IP in the radio interface portion of the standard, and it agreed to license the technology through independent agreements with equipment manufacturers. The control of the standard was not wrested from Qualcomm and the marketplace, though, because no other companies could contribute effectively to the initial CDMA standard to any great degree. So Qualcomm's success early on was based on its ability to convince companies that CDMA's merits outweighed its royalty cost. But concern remained that Qualcomm was the sole source of knowledge about the details of CDMA. Even though several manufactures had signed up to develop equipment, the standard code-based wireless design was still under the sole control of Qualcomm.

An industrywide standard that is made up largely of technology protected by one or a few companies is considered a closed standard—one that cannot be easily used or built upon by outside companies. In contrast, an open standard is collaborative across a wide base of members and has many "free use" rules in place for continued refinement and evolution of the system architecture. Open standards have been well publicized and highly modular, while closed architectures tended to be limited to the methods of a single implementation—usually in proprietary applications under the control of a single company.

Much has been made of the concept of open vs. proprietary architectures in a variety of high-technology markets. As the various approaches to developing and maintaining common interfaces in an increasingly networked world have grown in importance, strategies for capitalizing on them have proliferated. Open architectures tend to spread more rapidly than closed platforms, but innovation has often been sacrificed in exchange: As architectures become openly diluted across many contributors, the ability to advance or enhance a technology is generally diminished. A company founded upon a base of technical excellence, Qualcomm has always favored the adoption of superior technology, albeit proprietary, over a "good enough" consensus around a more open standard.

The single largest reason that Qualcomm has been both victim and perpetrator of some of the most turbulent controversy in the wireless industry over the past fifteen years has come from the company's espousal of a closed standard—and the resultant bickering over these two divergent approaches to standards. Many companies fought against the implementation of CDMA, arguing that Qualcomm's monopoly of the technology was an unworthy basis for global markets. Especially in Europe, where the more open standard GSM spread like wildfire, a particular distaste existed (and still does) for standards that give too much control to a single company (particularly an American one). Qualcomm's dominance of CDMA technology from the beginning certainly made it more difficult for the company to rally standards groups around CDMA and to encourage companies to adopt its technology in cellular networks.

A common criticism from Qualcomm's competitors was that the company was forcing closed and proprietary standards into the market, fragmenting the industry and slowing the momentum in the adoption of digital technologies. The amount of truth in this argument remains open to debate (as many see the opposite to be true), but the resulting fragmentation in the worldwide industry has had little to do with CDMA's being a closed standard. Another criticism has been that Qualcomm has profited unduly from a closed standard, and that CDMA's success came at the expense of other, more open standards such as TDMA and GSM.

While the closed nature of the initial CDMA standard was probably inevitable, the succeeding generations of code-based wireless standards have proved to be more open and collaborative. After the initial standard was documented and implemented by dozens of companies, subsequent standards have seen significant contributions from other companies that have invested in CDMA development. This evolution from a closed standard to a more open one affected Qualcomm's royalty income, since others had over the years contributed to a CDMA standard to some degree. This issue is discussed in more detail in the next chapter.

In truth, Qualcomm really didn't need a sophisticated strategy in working with the standards groups—the

> "A dozen years ago CDMA was all Qualcomm, but now other companies have substantial input in standards, and there's lots of contribution."
>
> —ED TIEDEMANN,
> SENIOR VP OF ENGINEERING,
> QUALCOMM

company simply had to show up and claim its intellectual contribution to CDMA. Since it held the overwhelming majority of code-based wireless IP early on, Qualcomm's strategy was simply to not allow the standard to become diluted and drift too far from its tested system design, ostensibly because that would slow down the implementation. Since Qualcomm was able to achieve acceptance of IS-95, and its ownership of the intellectual property was well established, succeeding generations of CDMA standards extended this control, protected further through licensing agreements. Qualcomm established critical business strategies through these agreements, the success of which hinged on the company's ongoing relationships with a growing family of licensees.

CHAPTER 16

Tax Collector or Vital Partner?

Disseminating and Protecting Essential IP

One of the most delicate balances that Qualcomm had to maintain—literally on a daily basis—involved the partnerships and customer relationships that it developed over the years. As a company that was based on the technical excellence of an elite team of engineers, Qualcomm was not ideally suited to forging corporate partnerships. By their nature, companies that are focused on innovation ahead of everything else can make difficult partners. Indeed, both Jacobs and Qualcomm as a whole came across as being brash and even arrogant in their relations with their peers in the industry. While this view was somewhat misguided and colored by the position of the other party, it spoke to a level of tense reverence between Qualcomm and its partners and competitors alike.

Qualcomm's business model was another source of difficulty with its partners. Contract negotiations can be, as some aptly put it, like two porcupines making love. License discussions were a delicate matter and involved many interpersonal traits, such as conceit, ego, and—in the case of the global wireless market—ardent nationalism. That Qualcomm sometimes partnered with its direct or indirect competitors made the equation all the more complex. But even with its technical corporate grooming, Qualcomm has done exceptionally well in developing and maintaining healthy relationships with its licensees.

One trait of Qualcomm, like many other companies that base a large portion of their livelihood on intellectual property (IP) licensing, was a love-hate relationship with its licensees. In one respect, a company offering IP to a manufacturer can be a boon to that manufacturer's product development—the development time for a product can be brought down by orders of magnitude. As the relationship matures, though, the licensee often has a change of heart, seeing royalty fees as a drag on its business—forgetting that it was the original offer of IP that got it there in the first place.

The rapid evolution in technology and regulatory structure also strained Qualcomm's relationships with licensees. Disputes often arose over the terms of the license, usually when the market entered a new phase of development that was ambiguously covered or unanticipated by the agreement. Qualcomm encountered one such case with one of its strongest and earliest allies in developing CDMA—the South Korean Electronic & Telecommunications Research Institute (ETRI).

SIBLING RIVALRY

In an effort to encourage ETRI to adopt code-based wireless and share the cost of its development in Korea, in its 1992 agreement Qualcomm had promised to return to ETRI 20 percent of the royalties it collected from Korean manufacturers. This provision was intended to close the loop of a self-supporting technology ecosystem, in which the success of a certain technology platform directly fed the research into even better solutions. In 1998, ETRI formally complained to Qualcomm that a portion of the royalty fees that it believed were supposed to be given back to the organization were not being paid.

The point of contention came down to the wording of the original agreement. It was clear to both parties that Qualcomm would feed back 20 percent of the royalties it collected from Korean equipment manufacturers making CDMA products. But Qualcomm argued that PCS equipment was not covered by this provision, since it was not specifically provided for in the agreement—only cellular equipment was covered. ETRI contended that the agreement covered all forms of CDMA equipment—whether technically cellular or PCS—over the life of the agreement, which was fifteen years.

Negotiations between the organizations failed to yield a suitable result, so both parties entered into arbitration as specified by the agreement. In late 2000, the International Court of Arbitration ruled that Qualcomm did indeed owe the disputed royalties to the ETRI organization. The award covered royalty payments retroactively to 1992, and Qualcomm cheerlessly took an $80 million charge to its accounts, in addition to future quarterly payments of $4 million.

While unhappy with the result, Qualcomm well understood the importance of this decision. Not everyone in Korea was happy about paying royalties to Qualcomm. The *Korea Herald* and *Korea Times* increasingly published articles citing the huge amount of won that was going to Qualcomm each year (it would eventually climb to US$329 million in 2002), while ignoring the larger benefits to the local economy. Korea's largest wireless equipment manufacturer, Samsung, had sent many public signals that it wanted to improve its leverage over CDMA technology and made efforts to reduce its dependence on Qualcomm.

With hundreds of millions of royalty dollars and a significant percentage of its business coming from Korea each year, it was obviously in Qualcomm's best interest to maintain an amicable relationship with the Koreans. From this perspective, even the $100+ million judgment was insignificant in the larger picture. But in recent years Qualcomm has continued to have to grapple with increasing Korean discontent, which has largely been dwarfed by a more general displeasure with U.S. socioeconomic policy on a grand scale. Indeed, recently the Korean industry has pushed to move toward a home-grown data application provisioning system and away from Qualcomm's BREW (binary run-time environment for wireless, an open-source programming platform developed by Qualcomm), for which one mobile operator has already paid Qualcomm millions in royalties. Continuing to build on its South Korean partnerships as the market matures, as opposed to letting the relationships deteriorate, has remained one of Qualcomm's bigger challenges.

Another recent test of Qualcomm's—particularly Jacobs's—diplomacy skills occurred during one of the highest points of Qualcomm's long struggle for acceptance of CDMA in China. In the final meetings between Jacobs and Chinese officials, CDMA was approved for use by China Unicom only after royalty rates on domestic units were reduced to a reported 2.65 percent. Once news of this lower royalty rate came out, many companies in Korea began to complain that their preferred rate was no longer valid, and that the lower domestic rate in China—essentially a prohibitive tariff—had effectively locked them out of that lucrative market.

On August 21, 2001, Qualcomm received a letter from Representative Hyong-O Kim, chairman of the Science, Technology, Information and Telecommunication Committee of the National Assembly of South Korea, formalizing many of the sentiments that had been expressed by various Korean manufacturers—mainly that the reduced royalty rate being given to Chinese manufacturers violated the terms of Korea's "most favored" royalty terms. Because of their importance in developing CDMA early on, Korean manufacturers were supposed to receive the best royalty rates, under a most favorable royalty rate (MFRR) agreement, and these rates were reported to be 5.25 percent of the average selling price (ASP) for domestic sales, and 5.75 percent for exports.

> " 'Any time you are negotiating, you have to come up with something that is acceptable on both sides,' says Mr. Jacobs, conceding that China received favorable terms. 'They offer a very large market, so there is a possibility of Chinese manufacturers having a lower royalty rate than other places.' "
> —IRWIN JACOBS,
> QUALCOMM COFOUNDER AND CEO[1]

While the formal discussions between the companies and the foreign ministries remained subdued, public opinion in South Korea was not as subtle. Korean companies had already been rattling ETRI with complaints about ongoing royalty payments to Qualcomm and the apparent lack of recognition of their own role in developing CDMA into a commercially viable technology. As ETRI echoed these concerns to Qualcomm and U.S. regulatory bodies, the leaked details of the China agreement fueled this fire even more.

Jacobs and the Qualcomm team were once again forced to walk a fine line. Much of the media would have investors and industry followers believe that Qualcomm's licensing practices were heavy-handed, discriminatory, and even arbitrary—basically designed to exploit the company's licensees for maximum potential profit. But the truth was quite the opposite: Qualcomm had designed a balanced and intricate set of license agreement terms that could be integrated and combined in various forms and adapted to different situations.

Qualcomm did not have a boilerplate license agreement for its licensees to sign—instead, it had developed a set of optional terms combined in a balanced way to provide both Qualcomm and the licensee with what Jacobs routinely called a "win-win proposition." Terms that were more favorable to the licensee could be selected in some areas of the agreement, but these terms would be balanced by other benefits for the supplier, Qualcomm.

In the case of China, the lower domestic royalty rate was balanced by the requirement that chipsets and equipment be purchased directly from Qualcomm and a much higher export royalty rate—reported to be 7 percent. This requirement was not included in the Korean agreements, which included more standard royalty rates without the other terms that were more favorable to Qualcomm. The increased size of the Chinese market and the willingness of the government to facilitate the launch of CDMA networks rapidly were also factored into the contract.

The problem was not so much the actual fairness of the agreements, but the perception of fairness, which was obscured by the confidential nature of the terms. In the medium of public opinion, human nature also came into play. In secretive discussions, the juiciest pieces of information are often the first to leak out, out of context of the entire story. Many Korean manufacturers, media, and other organizations were whipping up controversy, partially caused by their limited knowledge of the entire license agreements. Many news sources portrayed China as being given a better deal than South Korea, when in actuality the Chinese deal was much more balanced than was perceived. Nonetheless, this was the public perception battle that Qualcomm has had to continually fight.

Jacobs had to set the story straight, and he did so with a letter back to Representative Hyong-O Kim. In the letter, Jacobs explained the rationale behind the Chinese licensing terms, and stated that all of the Korean licensees would be offered the same set of terms if they elected to alter their existing agreements. He granted that the Chinese manufacturers had been given a lower rate because of their plans to deploy extensive CDMA networks rapidly, but that the Chinese had agreed to numerous other terms—such as chipset purchase guarantees—in exchange for this lower rate. Jacobs believed that the launching of CDMA in China was a very positive event for Korean manufacturers as well. He believed the framework of the agreements between Qualcomm and the Chinese remained competitive with that between Qualcomm and the Koreans and did not favor any manufacturers.

While arduous and exhausting, the continued discussions with Korean and Chinese licensees to date have succeeded in avoiding the type of catastrophe that many viewed as imminent for Qualcomm. These incidents highlighted the necessity of up-front and constant communication with partners, especially after deals have been done. This is the work in IPR licensing—the constant communication and delineation of the terms and the ensuing benefits for both parties. Many of those outside of the business view IP licensing as entailing a lot of work until the agreement is signed—then the only work is cashing the royalty check. Nothing could be further from the truth.

Many still contend, however, that there is bad blood between Qualcomm and some of its licensees, and that it's only a matter of time before the legal web of agreements starts to fall apart like a house of cards. To date, though, none of this has happened. Qualcomm has been able to perform this delicate dance over and over again to relieve any tensions that have come to a head with licensees. A key to its long-term success is that Qualcomm has in fact defined the standard for the business of licensing intellectual property. More tests are undoubtedly ahead as the technology ages and becomes more widespread, but Qualcomm's legal team can be expected to have an equally elegant approach to changes in the dynamics of global IPR licensing.

CONFIDENTIALITY IN LICENSE AGREEMENTS

By almost all measures, Qualcomm is still years ahead of other companies in the development and implementation of CDMA systems in mobile networks. Most of its technical breakthroughs and key designs have become public knowledge through the very patents that restrict their widespread use. Nevertheless, a multitude of details in the design, engineering, and operation of CDMA systems are not commonly known outside the company. These important details stay with the Qualcomm engineers and scientists, who rarely leave for positions with competitors. Thus a significant portion of the company's technical IP has remained closely held, allowing Qualcomm to continually provide value to customers and licensees ahead of its competitors.

Confidentiality thus becomes a key aspect of all licensing agreements covering intellectual property, primarily because much of the information that is being shared through the agreement is not public knowledge. Often, the price paid by a licensee and the terms of the agreement reflect the fact that the public knowledge is only a small piece of the value—as indeed has been the case for the myriad of agreements Qualcomm has signed with its licensees.

Qualcomm's situation has been unique in terms of the sheer number of its licensees and other partners. While all its licensees have been interested in producing CDMA products, each has had a variety of ambitions in terms of markets, product types, and volume. Qualcomm's ongoing effort to maintain a consistent level of ownership in CDMA has made its task in partnering with hundreds of companies around the globe all the more difficult. Qualcomm has had to be vigilant in negotiating balanced agreements with different companies, as each potential licensee comes to the table with a different set of circumstances and potential return.

The Korean and Chinese situations cited in the previous section exemplified the difficulty Qualcomm has had in managing its licensees. Disputes over the level of royalties and their fairness in view of other license deals have frequently arisen with licensees. The crucial element of all these agreements, though, was the required secrecy concerning the details of any agreement. If licensees were not legally gagged concerning the terms of their licenses, Qualcomm's leverage with new licensees would be reduced and negotiations would be much more difficult.

For this reason, the legal team at Qualcomm has been adamant about the confidentiality of the company's license terms, especially in the case of royalty points and financial terms. But even with strict agreements limiting any discussion on license financials, no one has been surprised when this important information leaks out to the media, analysts, and other companies. From the beginning, Qualcomm was prepared to deal with breaches of contracts, planning strategies that could be put in place if certain confidential information became public. While no serious problems occurred early in CDMA licensing activities, a recent case involved Qualcomm's license agreement with Texas Instruments (TI) in 2000. Qualcomm and TI agreed to cross-license current and future patents and IP used to make several types of wireless semiconductors.

A serious problem occurred in May 2003, though, when TI executives were quoted as stating publicly that their agreement with Qualcomm stipulated that no royalty would be paid to Qualcomm on the sale of TI's CDMA chips. Qualcomm notified TI that the statements were in breach of its contract, constituting public dissemination of confidential terms of the agreement. TI did not acknowledge the breach, so Qualcomm filed a lawsuit in July 2003, seeking damages and termination of TI's rights under the agreement.

Obviously, this breach could seriously undermine Qualcomm's ability to negotiate future license deals with other parties. As in the Korea-China case, future licensees may be privy to only one aspect of a prior confidential license agreement, taken out of context of the entire agreement. The licensee may then take issue with that single point, using it to move the deal more in its favor, to Qualcomm's detriment. With confidentiality still in place, Qualcomm would not even legally be able to explain the context of the agreement in order to justify its position, as that in itself would be a breach of the contract. Qualcomm's only choice has been to ruthlessly adhere to the confidentiality of its agreements and to make sure that licensees do the same. The courts have ruled that Qualcomm could seek damages from TI for a nonmaterial breach of contract, but that Qualcomm could not terminate the original contract based on this finding. With the door still open for Qualcomm to seek millions in damages from TI, the company instead opted to drop the suit in August of 2004 rather than divulge details of the confidential contract in court. While the company passed on a potential cash settlement, Qualcomm achieved the important goal of ensuring that licensees are more cautious when speaking publicly about confidential agreements with the company.

LITIGATION

Of course, as a large portion of Qualcomm's ongoing revenue has come through license contracts, litigation and arbitration have been a normal part of the company's business. Not all relationships remain amicable, and not all disputes can be settled outside of the courts. Qualcomm's first significant legal tests over CDMA started in 1993 as the TIA committee was developing a standard largely based on Qualcomm's intellectual property, contained in Qualcomm's common air interface specification. Ericsson and InterDigital both challenged Qualcomm on its essential monopoly of CDMA's cellular implementation. InterDigital threw down the gauntlet first, filing a lawsuit in April 1993, on the final day of the vote on the CDMA standard.

InterDigital also had a significant stake in intellectual property and sought licensing revenues for its patents, but its business and history have been markedly different from those of Qualcomm. Starting as International Mobile Machines (IMM) in 1972, InterDigital focused on commercializing digital wireless technologies. For more than a decade the company concentrated on bringing advanced military technologies into the commercial sector, and it was successful in developing one of the first digital mobile phones with very limited mobility, called the Ultraphone, using time-based wireless (TDMA) technology. Ironically, to develop this product, the company contracted with none other than Irwin Jacobs's first company, Linkabit.

As InterDigital progressed in developing and refining its TDMA expertise, it was getting increased revenue from sales of digital phones but was having mixed success in licensing its patents. Because many other deep-pocketed companies—such as Ericsson and Motorola—were also developing TDMA-based technologies, the smaller InterDigital was struggling to hold its ground in a market dominated by giants. Late in 1992, InterDigital moved into the CDMA market with the acquisition of SCS Mobile, which also gave it ownership of several dozen patents in various implementations of CDMA. As ratification of the first CDMA standard approached in early 1993, InterDigital moved to defend its claims on various patents that it thought were being used but not recognized in the IS-95 standard.

On April 16, 1993, InterDigital filed suit against Qualcomm and OKI for infringing on some of its CDMA and TDMA intellectual property that was protected under patents. The claim against Qualcomm was for declaratory relief, since InterDigital believed that the implementation of IS-95 would infringe upon its patent 5,179,571 (issued in January 1993), which specified the handoff methods incorporated in CDMA. Qualcomm quickly enlisted outside counsel Brown, Martin, Haller and McClain to file a suit of its own less than a week later. On April 22, 1993, Qualcomm sued InterDigital for declaratory relief on two other patents, U.S. Patents 5,081,643 and 5,093,840, that InterDigital threatened to assert to stop the production of CDMA equipment. Qualcomm argued that the IS-95 implementation of CDMA did not infringe on the InterDigital '643 and '840 patents, and also asked that these patents be ruled invalid. Qualcomm pointed out that its patents in the same area of receiver design and power control were filed a year earlier than the comparable InterDigital patents.

Prior to the InterDigital lawsuit, Qualcomm's internal legal department had basically consisted of one individual, Steve Altman, so this initial suit forced Qualcomm to begin developing legal counsel within the company. As the InterDigital case wore on, Qualcomm tapped the talent of an external firm, Cooley, Godward, Castro, Huddleson and Tatum (a local San Diego firm that also helped take Qualcomm public in 1989), to take the lead in its defense. An expert in intellectual property litigation, Louis Loupin, was working at the firm and took the lead role in the case. He worked with Altman and the Qualcomm team to develop a defense against the InterDigital filing and to more thoroughly investigate the various CDMA patents held by both Qualcomm and InterDigital.

Qualcomm continued to fight with InterDigital for more than eighteen months over the rights to certain inventions, racking up millions in legal bills. Late in 1994, after extensive filings and ten days in court, Qualcomm agreed to settle the lawsuit by paying InterDigital $5.5 million for release of all claims in the future. While Jacobs continued to contend that Qualcomm did not infringe on the patents in question, the settlement was nonetheless perceived as a better alternative than prolonged and costly litigation. Qualcomm wrote off an additional $7.5 million in legal costs for the case. InterDigital reportedly spent $4.5 million.

Leading up to the settlement, Qualcomm was concerned about setting a precedent by "giving in" to InterDigital. Even though the legality of the claims was never settled, that was not the perception, and Qualcomm was concerned that any number of other competitors could step forward to file similar suits in hopes of reaching a lucrative settlement or forcing Qualcomm out of the CDMA business altogether. Fortunately, the cost of such a legal undertaking deterred frivolous suits against Qualcomm, and the settlement proved to be a wise move. At the completion of the case, Qualcomm hired Louis Loupin, who remains a senior vice president and the company's general counsel.

Qualcomm's first big IP litigation case showed that much of the constant work involved in making a business out of licensing IP would be in legal proceedings. The legal cost of maintaining the validity and market value of IP could easily soar into the millions. Another wireless company that was recently embroiled in many legal battles over intellectual property, Research in Motion (RIM), took a $7.5 million charge for litigation in the first quarter of 2003 alone, casting a dark cloud over an otherwise stellar quarterly performance. RIM was sued for patent infringement by NTP Inc., which stated that RIM's products utilized five patents that NTP owned. In the prior year, RIM spent nearly $40 million on patent litigation—more than 12 percent of its revenue for the year (though RIM still hopes to overturn the rulings and recover these costs).

While the total cost of defending intellectual property rights can be staggering, what's more intriguing is how normal such costs are now considered. Many organizations that dedicate millions to litigation, such as RIM, InterDigital, and Rambus, routinely state their earnings both with and without legal costs included, so that investors can determine the impact of litigation on their normal business operations. Litigation has become a normal part of business for these and other IP companies, including Qualcomm (which does not normally break out its litigation costs).

Another view treats the legal costs of IP licensing companies as simply ongoing expenses that are connected to R&D. It's only natural that companies that derive revenue from intellectual property also must shoulder a "cost"—not only for developing the IP, but also for maintaining its viability in the marketplace. Once the salaries and patent fees to establish a property have been paid, fees to preserve its benefits should be expected. After all, patents and IP don't license themselves—their value must be demonstrated, which requires putting a lot of time into crafting legal agreements to bind the licensing. The only hang-up, especially for investors, is that the level of these fees can unexpectedly vary dramatically from year to year (even from quarter to quarter).

After more than a decade of promoting CDMA, Qualcomm was definitely no stranger to litigation, and it now maintains a deep team of legal experts. The company spends millions every quarter to maintain its rights to its intellectual property. In comparison to other IP licensing companies, Qualcomm does exceptionally well at managing the ongoing costs of litigation. With few significant exceptions, the company consistently reports licensing income margins of 90 percent or more of licensing revenue.

After perhaps its largest legal challenge to date—the third-generation (3G) patent disputes in 1999 (discussed in Chapter 18)—Qualcomm's next major hurdle may be the expiration of its fundamental CDMA patents. These initial patents are so central to CDMA that many critics of Qualcomm contend that their eventual expiration will spell the end of Qualcomm's control of CDMA. Of course, Qualcomm disputes this contention, as its licensees pay to have access to the company's entire patent base of over a thousand issued U.S. patents. Qualcomm has been diligent in building off these core patents (currently an additional 1,700 U.S. patents are pending) to ensure that it retains its role as the primary provider of code-based wireless technology for decades to come (see Figure 16-1).

> "I'm sure there will be some more IP disputes in the future, especially as we move toward multimode chips."
> —IRWIN JACOBS,
> QUALCOMM COFOUNDER AND CEO[2]

To this day, though, Irwin Jacobs and the other Qualcomm founders still contend that they never envisioned the level of success Qualcomm would achieve through the licensing of their intellectual property in CDMA. Fortunately, Jacobs and the rest of the senior engineering staff invested in an equally competent legal team of intellectual property experts.

Qualcomm's Growing U.S. Patent Base

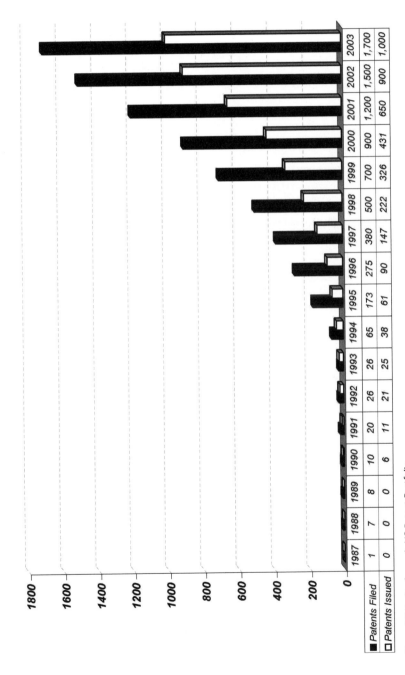

	1987	1988	1989	1990	1991	1992	1993	1994	1995	1996	1997	1998	1999	2000	2001	2002	2003
■ Patents Filed	1	7	8	10	20	26	26	65	173	275	380	500	700	900	1,200	1,500	1,700
□ Patents Issued	0	0	0	6	11	21	25	38	61	90	147	222	326	431	650	900	1,000

Figure 16-1: Qualcomm's US Patent Portfolio

Source: SEC Filings and Company Documents

CHAPTER 17

Breaking Through Bureaucratic Barriers

‒ ‒→

Regulatory Politics and Practices at Home and Abroad

Since the end of World War II, the telecommunications industry has arguably experienced the most turbulent history of any industry in the United States. Around the globe, basic telecommunications services began to take on primary importance to developing nations in the age of information. Progressive-thinking governments around the world moved toward a deregulated telecommunications structure to spur growth and invite private investment. This process of deregulation was long and painful, and wireless communications in particular had the added difficulties of government management of spectrum as well.

During the explosive growth of personal communications in the last few decades, the policies of various national governments to encourage the development of mobile services were critical. The actions taken by regulatory agencies during this period, as well as the policies established during previous decades, set the tone for competitiveness on a global scale for individual nations. In the United States, the Federal Communications Commission (FCC) wrestled with spectrum management problems largely caused by the success of other industries, such as television broadcasting. The distribution of spectrum resources favoring industries like broadcasting continues to handicap the growth in the U.S. wireless industry to this day.

For Qualcomm, though, the fact that in the late eighties and early nineties, the premier superpower was struggling to boost domestic development and regain dominance in the global marketplace for consumer electronics turned out to be a blessing in disguise. Had Qualcomm been pitching code-based wireless (CDMA) to a nation that was already enjoying global success in mobile telephony, fewer customers would have been compelled to consider the risky alternative. But the United States was falling behind other nations in wireless development, and this played into Qualcomm's hands.

AN AILING INDUSTRY CAN BE YOUR STRONGEST ALLY

Many analysts around the globe have traditionally considered the wireless industry in the United States to be at least a few years behind the rest of the world. European and Asian nations have enjoyed wireless penetration rates far above those of the United States, and the adoption of other multimedia services via wireless devices remains mostly an international experience. While Europeans were sending billions of text messages a month (via SMS, or short messaging services), most Americans still didn't even own phones that were capable of the service. If they did, they were severely limited in whom they could send a message to, because of incompatible networks. The wireless Internet experience was commonplace for a majority of Japanese and Koreans in the late 1990s—not just a technically savvy minority of early adopters. At that time, even technology freaks in the United States were frustrated with the quality of similar domestic services.

In any corporate success story, sheer luck and good timing can be as important as shrewd business management and execution. Rarely did Qualcomm blindly trip over opportunities, but it certainly benefited from being in the right place at the right time. In many ways, its founding in 1985—during the nascent stage of personal communications—was perfectly timed to permit the company's disruptive emergence into the cellular industry only a few years later. In its assault on the global marketplace, Qualcomm was also the beneficiary of a period of American backsliding in the burgeoning global cellular industry, amid fresh trepidation concerning global competitive threats—leaving the door open for Qualcomm to boldly pursue global alliances.

Prior to the late 1980s, many U.S. government officials continued to view mobile telephony as only a niche sector of telecommunications. But as the 1990s approached and subscriber rates soared, many of them quickly realized that the wireless industry would play a key role in global trade. A dramatic surge in the Japanese economy during this period—and productivity gains in technology in particular—caused widespread concern about U.S. competitiveness. In the early 1990s, the Japanese economy was viewed as an unstoppable global juggernaut. An insatiable U.S. consumer market was swallowing more and more products designed, manufactured, and imported from Asian and European nations. A heated backlash to this situation even led to a strong "Made in the USA" consumer campaign in the early 1990s that was emotionally tied to patriotism.

Starting with the breakup of AT&T into the Baby Bells in 1984, the United States initiated a path of privatization and open competition in the telecommunications industry in order to spur growth. In the first generation of cellular networks, a duopoly was created, in which two companies were licensed to serve any one market. For the next-generation networks, the FCC saw that the European Union's requirement for GSM technology offered few American companies other than Motorola any significant benefits. Adopting GSM or placing similar requirements on technology choice in the United States was not seen as a very effective way to serve the American public or help U.S. companies compete abroad.

To help stimulate American technology, the United States rushed to counter the European approach of a mandated GSM standard with a high level of competition accompanied by an open policy on technology. Network operators in the United States could use whatever technology or transmission protocol they preferred, as long as it stayed within the boundaries of their spectrum license. Regulators put policies in place to open up markets for several competitors—at least six companies could be licensed for wireless service in any given region. This was all controlled primarily through the licensing of spectrum—without approval for spectrum use within certain areas, a company could not legally operate a wireless network. This approach to regulation was designed to spur the development of advanced technology that would be more attractive and competitive in the global marketplace.

The period of transition in the late 1980s from the first-generation (1G) cellular networks to second-generation (2G) networks was either the best or the worst time to launch a communications revolution in the United States, depending on your perspective. While the United States had long enjoyed the distinction of being one of the most technically advanced nations, churning out the latest and greatest advances in technology, translating this advantage into a flourishing wireless consumer and business culture was not happening. Reversing the early successes in the 1980s in developing unified analog networks, the open technology policy led to a whole host of incompatible networks being developed and deployed alongside each other—with a jungle of acronyms like TDMA, GSM, CDMA, and iDEN—resulting in a fragmented industry characterized more by incongruity than by progress. Meanwhile, by the mid-1990s the European GSM standard was blowing down barriers and taking the entire world by storm, even outside of Western Europe and the EU.

Domestic and export equipment volumes for wireless product makers such as Nokia and Ericsson were skyrocketing, while U.S. companies were struggling to achieve similar economies of scale. Even with the growth in GSM, the Clinton administration was still confident that the U.S. approach would pay off and prevent a technology that was largely controlled overseas from overrunning American companies.

Those who feared that the United States could again lose its dominant influence in global markets could take comfort in Qualcomm's CDMA as a purely American technology that was attractive both for use domestically and for export around the world.

Depending upon whom you talk to, Qualcomm deserves either the primary blame or considerable commendation for the state of the U.S. domestic wireless industry today. A strong majority of the industry was formally coalescing under TDMA just weeks before Qualcomm proposed the idea of CDMA in 1989, and a large contingent of industry professionals still contend that unified TDMA networks would have set the United States on a more equal footing with its global peers. Certainly, Qualcomm had a large role in splitting the industry along technology lines. But an equally large contingent of the industry claims that this bifurcation was exactly what the United States needed to spur development away from TDMA technologies that were largely controlled by companies outside the United States. Adopting a less than stellar technology like TDMA would have relegated the United States to being an also-ran in the global wireless race. Many in the industry feel strongly that, having embraced and propagated CDMA, the United States is now poised to distance itself from other nations as we move into third-generation (3G) technology and beyond.

The debate over the state of the U.S. wireless industry in comparison to those in Europe and Asia still rages today. The disruption caused by changes in U.S. regulatory policies and Qualcomm's early push for advanced technology have certainly upended what used to be an old-school, conformist telecommunications industry. The traditional rules have been completely rewritten, although many still yearn for the predictability of the former structure. What is certain is that the importance of the U.S. contribution to wireless markets around the world has inflamed both love and hatred of Qualcomm.

MAKING THE MOST OF RESOURCES

Whichever view people hold of Qualcomm's impact on the direction of the U.S. wireless industry (and most people hold one view or the other, rarely anything in between), in truth several other factors influenced the progress of the domestic market for wireless equipment and services. Of all the forces driving the industry, perhaps none was as important as the allocation of spectrum by the FCC. The inefficient allocation and delayed licensing of spectrum over the last several decades has often been cited as the primary reasons for the slow development of wireless networks. Since the electromagnetic spectrum is the essential medium for all wireless services, effective allocation and control of this frequency space has been vital to a strong, competitive industry.

Part of the problem with spectrum allocation for mobile wireless services comes from the FCC's obligation to cater to multiple interests, as its original charter specified that the agency was put in place to work for the best interest of all Americans—the public at large. This is a simple goal in theory, but the realization of this mission has been quite complex, because the public interest includes many conflicting demands—such as national security, education, and the pursuit of happiness. The FCC must allocate sections of the radio spectrum for military use, public safety agencies (police and fire), nonprofit and educational institutions, and the private sector, among others. Managing, balancing, and arbitrating among the needs of the various industries within the private sector, such as television, satellite, and mobile communications, has been a mess in itself. But problems with spectrum allocation in the United States started long before the explosive growth in mobile communications in the 1990s.

Early mobile phone systems in the United States, beginning with the noncellular MTS (mobile telephony system) at the end of World War II, were very popular but lacked the capacity to support many users. Up until the 1980s, mobile phone service was something that only the superrich, or the president, could afford. The idea that mobile phone networks could have their architecture radically modified to accommodate hundreds, thousands, and eventually millions of users in a city—rather than just a few dozen—was already being developed by AT&T (Bell Labs) in the late 1940s. This concept, called cellular, took decades to implement commercially—not because the technology was immature, but rather because the FCC took so long to sanction its use in approved frequency bands.

Part of the long delay in licensing new wireless networks arose from the changing policies of U.S. regulatory bodies toward AT&T's longstanding monopoly in wireline telecommunications. While the FCC had originally favored AT&T's extension into cellular telephony, it reversed that stance in the 1980s and favored opening up the market to competition. This change in attitude went right along with that of other government agencies such as the Department of Justice, which eventually pushed for the AT&T breakup in 1984. It was more than thirty years after cellular networks were first conceived before the FCC finally settled on a method of allocating half the apportioned spectrum to an incumbent wireline operator and half to a new wireless entrant.

The apportioning of the spectrum among other industries also contributed to the long delay in bringing cellular networks to market in the United States. The television broadcasting industry in the United States was a huge success in the 1940s and 1950s, and much of the spectrum in the prime areas for mobile services had already been handed over to broadcasters. Since television channels served millions of households, and potentially millions more, it was easier for the FCC to justify the allocation of spectrum for these services than for mobile telephony, which only the elite could benefit from at that time.

As a result of protracted planning, most European nations did not have the spectrum hang-ups that dogged the U.S. industry. Many nations in the European Union vacated well over 200 MHz of spectrum for GSM digital wireless services, while the United States struggled to free up 170 MHz in different bands, many of which still have unused portions in many regions. These constraints on spectrum in the United States provided a huge amount of leverage for Qualcomm and its CDMA message. Because of the manufactured scarcity of spectrum in the United States and the subsequent rising cost of spectrum licensing, network efficiency became of prime importance. For a given wireless technology, spectrum efficiency was king.

This led the Cellular Telecommunications Industry Association (CTIA) in 1988 to call for at least a tenfold improvement in capacity for coming digital standards—underscoring the significance of preparing for millions of new wireless subscribers in the coming years. The rapid adoption of wireless was coming, whether the operators were prepared or not, so those operators that had the capacity to absorb paying customers in droves would be the big winners. While Qualcomm came a little late to the party with its CDMA solution, the company effectively argued that the huge performance gain that code-based wireless offered made it a must to consider for commercial implementation. Qualcomm's CDMA was pitched as the savior for those languishing in spectrum purgatory. Since the FCC couldn't regulate the industry out of the mess, the engineering whizzes at Qualcomm offered their vastly superior technology to do the job.

While the reality may have actually been quite different, the perception of spectrum scarcity and global competitive threats were significant motivators for the adoption of code-based wireless technology in the United States and abroad. Indeed, a primary motivation for South Korea's adoption of CDMA early on was the rapid steps that Japan was already taking to secure its dominance of the wireless future. In a rapidly changing wireless world, Qualcomm was successful at convincing many in the industry that the time for the future was now.

WORKING FROM THE OUTSIDE IN

Perhaps more than any other industry, wireless enterprises have to compete on a global playing field. A corporation that limits itself to regional markets sacrifices many of the opportunities—and benefits—of appealing to a global client base of other companies or consumers. In many cases, wireless start-ups quickly bring in international talent to build connections to other continents and support bridges of important revenue sources.

Bad mojo in international circles can frustrate and even eliminate companies that are attempting to grow or expand beyond their traditional customer base. Microsoft has fallen victim time and time again to lackluster support from international partners when it has tried to break into the wireless market with its operating system. Nationalism in the highest political circles permeates many countries and their regulatory bodies—even those that are not under government control.

Tremendous success in any region of the world also doesn't necessarily transfer across borders and cultures. NTT DoCoMo was hailed as the master of the wireless Internet experience when it launched its i-Mode services in Japan in the late 1990s. DoCoMo signed up users for the service by the millions— even faster than AOL had captured Net-hungry Americans. When the company tried to export i-Mode outside of Japan, though, the service met with what can only be termed a lukewarm reception.

Qualcomm's success has not been a typical story of first dominating the U.S. market, then turning overseas. Much of the company's success—actually, its very livelihood—has been largely attributed to its success overseas, even before it broke into the U.S. wireless industry. By most reports, the first official, fully commercial CDMA cellular network began normal operation in Hong Kong in 1995. Soon after the initial entry into several Asian markets, the technology spread like wildfire through South Korea, now a long-standing bastion for code-based wireless. Only after these initial successes overseas did some companies in the United States have the confidence to step up and deploy the technology in their networks.

Without the support of Korean and other Asian customers, Qualcomm certainly would have had a tougher time building momentum in code-based wireless. With the European market completely closed to it, the importance of other international partners was heightened. Even to this day, the Korean marketplace is looked at as a vision of the wireless future—where the United States and other countries are headed once they implement more advanced versions of mobile technology. Qualcomm's success at exporting a sophisticated mobile communications solution was no easy feat, and it involved a complex set of capabilities in many areas. One of those was obviously political.

In its early efforts to bring CDMA to the world, Qualcomm made few sophisticated efforts on the political front. There were no high-priced lobbyists. There were no Washington attachés. There was simply a group of highly skilled engineers evangelizing the technical opportunities they saw. The extent of politicking in the early 1990s was Irwin Jacobs's persuasive demeanor in high-level meetings with organizations that were looking at the possibilities of code-based wireless technology. But many of Qualcomm's partners and early supporters did have extensive international connections. Its first partner, PacTel, helped with many of the connections to the Korean ETRI research group and government ministries.

But as CDMA and other digital wireless technologies matured, winning overseas customers took increased resources and dedication on the part of Qualcomm—with no real guarantee of success. Many of these gambles did not pay off, and the company has written off many millions in international efforts. But in the global wireless poker match, Qualcomm seemed to be capable of routinely pulling aces out of the hole on the big hands—the ones that really counted. It wasn't luck that led to some of its best international achievements, however.

PLAYING POLITICS ON A GLOBAL FIELD

Irwin Jacobs knew that countries with developing markets and telecommunications infrastructure were a very important market for the new technology. Those countries that had low teledensity rates (the number of telephones per person) were better candidates for wireless infrastructure, because it was a more economical means of communication. Installing wireless towers to give widespread populations basic phone service would cost far less than running cables over wide areas. In addition, people in those countries who had never had a phone eagerly adopted wireless communication—unlike Americans, who often complained about wireless service because the voice quality on landline networks was higher.

Areas of the world such as India and Russia were a particular focus for wireless local loop (WLL) systems

> "We had very positive responses in terms of the technology, but politics came up very early."
> —IRWIN JACOBS,
>   QUALCOMM COFOUNDER AND CEO[1]

based upon code-based wireless. But China in particular had always been one of Jacobs's prime targets for cellular systems. Seeing its huge population and low penetration rate for telecommunications services, he recognized that CDMA technology could in short order literally change the way the country functioned. Jacobs first visited China in 1992, when the world was in flux over adopting next-generation digital technologies. The opportunity to have code-based wireless adopted as the digital standard in China was too good to pass up.

While initial discussions with the Ministry of Information in China went well, the governing body nonetheless decided to implement GSM technology in its developing wireless networks. As in many other regions of the world, code-based wireless had come too late to the party. Time-division systems like GSM had already been proven and were being sold to network operators around the world as the quickest way to capitalize on a booming industry, while the exact progress of code-based wireless in fielded networks was not yet clear. Anyone who was slow to the game would be left behind, the CDMA critics claimed.

But there was much more to the story: the behind-the-scenes political maneuvering concerning China's relations with the United States.

For Qualcomm, it was back to Jacobs's mantra of building a win-win relationship. In his dealings with China, there were several dynamics taking place. While Jacobs was focusing heavily on coming to an agreement on terms for licensing and developing CDMA, the larger picture involved the strategy behind U.S.-China relations at a national level. Jacobs soon realized that the two issues could not be separated, and that one was not likely to happen without success in the other.

> "There seemed to be a correlation between how well things were going in the political realm and how they were going for CDMA."
> —IRWIN JACOBS[2]

To bolster Qualcomm's international efforts, Lt. Gen. Brent Scowcroft, who was once National Security Advisor to presidents Gerald Ford and George H. W. Bush, was named to the company's board of directors in 1994. His company, the Scowcroft Group, also brought a high level of political clout, with advisers who had spent their entire careers in foreign relations and international business intelligence. Many of the people on Scowcroft's team had specialized in relations with China, and Scowcroft himself had built a high level of trust with government officials in the country during a visit to the country's leaders shortly after the 1989 Tiananmen Square massacre. Scowcroft was also well connected to all branches of the U.S. government, providing a powerful lobby for corporate interests.

The Chinese military was the party that was most interested in code-based wireless in the early 1990s when Qualcomm first began to propose its use in a mobile environment. The People's Liberation Army (PLA) was enticed by the secure aspects of CDMA, something it coveted for use in communication with fielded troops. The Chinese army fortunately had ownership of spectrum in the 800-MHz band, the same place that cellular operators had their systems deployed in the United States. The natural fit for code-based wireless in this application helped Qualcomm secure its first break in China, though it was limited in scope; the military went on to develop its own network based upon CDMA.

But soon the PLA realized that it could make use of excess spectrum capacity by opening a commercial network. Profits generated from the commercial network would benefit the military and help it advance its own communications infrastructure. However, the announcement in 1994 of this network expansion set off an internal power struggle within China. The minister of posts and telecommunications, Wu Jichuan, was planning to have the state-owned telecom conglomerate, China Telecommunications, expand wireless networks throughout the country. The military network would do nothing but take earnings away from the state-owned network, so there appeared to be a vested interest in keeping commercial CDMA at bay.

In order to gain control over the army's use of code-based wireless in mobile networks, Wu Jichuan negotiated the formation of a venture between the military and China Telecom and aptly named it Great Wall. The venture was licensed to start code-based wireless services on experimental networks in a few urban areas, with plans to expand the networks upon completion of this phase. The prospect of the growth of CDMA in China enticed several foreign vendors—including Motorola, Nortel, Samsung, and Lucent—and investors to commit resources to the country. Optimism was running high that code-based wireless would grow rapidly once it had developed a foothold in the developing mobile market.

> " 'European governments make a practice of getting heads of states to be active on behalf of their domestic companies, including some of our competitors,' Jacobs said. 'Our main effort was to ensure an even playing field.' "
>
> —IRWIN JACOBS[3]

At the same time that Great Wall was developing its commercial CDMA network, however, China Telecom was quickly deploying its own GSM network nationally in the 900-MHz band. The Ministry of Post and Telecommunications had struck a deal with European companies to deploy their digital technology and make a significant investment in the country. The GSM networks in the mid-1990s went on an expansion binge, while the CDMA networks never grew beyond the initial four trial cities. The reason that code-based wireless sat in limbo was simple—the Ministry of Posts and Telecommunications never granted the venture the licenses it needed to expand. Quite simply, the ministry believed that CDMA was not in China's best interest . . . at the time.

During most of the Clinton administration, Qualcomm and other vendors backing CDMA continued going in circles negotiating with Chinese politicians. As time wore on, U.S. companies grew increasingly frustrated with China, but in 1999 the relations between the two countries took a turn for the better when Chinese Premier Zhu Rongji began to emphasize the need for China's admission to the World Trade Organization (WTO). The United States was the chief opponent of China's admission, and Zhu realized that the country would have to make concessions in order to make WTO entry in the near future possible. Zhu saw CDMA as a great source of leverage in the ensuing negotiations. Not surprisingly, so did the U.S. government.

The American-developed code-based wireless technology thus became a bargaining chip. Although intellectual property rights had historically been a sore spot in U.S. relations with China, both governments recognized the importance of China's upholding licensing rights to CDMA. The perception in U.S. business circles has traditionally been that all too often advanced technologies were simply copied or reverse-engineered and reproduced in Chinese provinces. Microsoft, a central target in Chinese copyright violations, had seen its Windows operating system going for as little as $5 a copy from street merchants when legitimate copies sold around $250. Numerous consultants estimate that more than 90 percent of Chinese software has been pirated. The worst part of the problem, though, may be that the Chinese export huge amounts of pirated software, especially in Asia and in developing countries elsewhere.

The importance of how Chinese companies handled a well-patented U.S. technology like CDMA was impressed upon the Ministry of Information Industry (or MII, the new name for the Ministry of Post and Telecommunications), and some even considered it a test of admittance to the WTO. China could certainly not permit domestic companies to make illegal copies of CDMA and expect a warm reception into the WTO.

This change in the political climate spurred negotiations between Jacobs and the MII at which details of technology transfer and equipment licensing would be worked out. But the negotiations were far from straightforward. The MII balked at paying license fees that it considered to be excessive, whereas Jacobs maintained his demands for terms that he considered competitive with those offered to other licensees. The MII eventually turned the issue over to China Unicom, the country's number two telecom operator, to work out a deal with Qualcomm. The MII also planned to transfer the Great Wall network to China Unicom, giving the company full control of CDMA's destiny in China.

Finally, in January 2000, Qualcomm and China Unicom struck a licensing deal for CDMA that included concessions from both sides of the bargaining table. Qualcomm would accept lower licensing rates on domestic sales of equipment—reported to be 2.65 percent—in exchange for Chinese manufacturers purchasing chipsets exclusively from Qualcomm. What many in the media branded as a giveaway to the Chinese angered some of Qualcomm's other licensees, especially those in Korea (as discussed in Chapter 16), who felt they were no longer getting the best deal.

Once the licensing agreement between Qualcomm and China Unicom was signed and executed, the relationship remained anything but stable. A number of subsequent delays—some of which seemed to have nothing to do with Qualcomm— began to mysteriously affect the timetable for implementing widespread CDMA networks in China. In June 2000, Unicom even stated that it would move ahead with implementing GSM networks rather than CDMA. All the while, the U.S. government was debating the formal entry of China into the WTO.

After many delays and mysterious "quiet periods" in 2000, progress in developing widespread CDMA networks in China began to be made. Billions of dollars in contracts to build out the network were awarded to several companies, even American companies such as Lucent and Motorola. However, questions and concerns resulting from uncertain U.S.-China relations continued to haunt the business of code-based wireless going forward. For instance, the collision between a U.S. plane and a Chinese fighter over purported Chinese airspace in April 2001 gave Wall Street the jitters and cut 20 percent off of Qualcomm's share price in the few days following the incident.

After nearly a decade of on-again, off-again negotiations, Qualcomm had finally broken into the fertile Chinese market. Today, the Unicom CDMA network is rapidly expanding and has even upgraded to the next generation of CDMA, called CDMA2000 1x for added features and capacity. The service now supports over fifteen million high-revenue subscribers in China and for its next stage of growth is looking at prepaid subscribers and customers of the original GSM networks. Qualcomm has also completed trials of its GSM1x product with Unicom that would overlay the CDMA air interface and Unicom's existing GSM network. This solution would essentially allow CDMA to be built and expanded on top of the existing GSM network in the country, preserving the original investment but opening up future growth in CDMA infrastructure and handsets.

As in many areas of business outside of Qualcomm's core technical competency, the company's navigation of the politics attached to the wireless industry has been based on a combination

> "Anytime you select a board, you look for people that are sharp and that will supplement your own background. With his extensive foreign affairs background, Lt. Gen. Scowcroft fit all those categories."
> —IRWIN JACOBS[4]

of good timing, savvy partnerships, and shear persistence. Rather than directly fighting its own political battles, Qualcomm courted appropriate partners to bear the brunt of politically charged negotiations. It selected board members wisely to help in these efforts, and it used partner channels in the industry to work across borders. But above all else, it simply kept at it—the team knew that

CDMA had clear advantages in many applications, and they stayed faithful to the message. Sometimes it didn't work, and decisions were made based on factors other than technical merit. But at other times, having a political heavyweight in their corner—and a stellar technology to back it up—was enough to break through bureaucratic barriers.

CHAPTER 18

Creating the Future of Wireless

Working Toward a Smooth Transition to 3G

Unlike the personal computer and consumer electronics industries, where product cycles turn every six to nine months, the cellular industry takes a comparatively long time to roll out new generations of products with new feature sets. While that new computer you just bought could be outdated soon after you plug it in, as new models that are 30 percent faster become available, it takes several years for a new wireless product with significantly faster data transfer speeds to come out. While there are incremental improvements in the features of wireless handsets all the time, the major leaps in technology and capabilities take roughly a decade to go from the lab to mainstream. The reason it takes so long is that wireless products have to go through various stages—about two to three years in early development, two to three years in standards, and then two to three years for regulatory approval and testing. Advancing wireless products involves the collaboration of several companies and regulatory bodies, and products and services must be tested in both the networks and consumer handsets, which understandably takes a long time.

Qualcomm fought a seven-year battle from 1988 to 1995 to bring code-based wireless (CDMA) to the commercial cellular industry—a time frame that was amazingly short considering the completely undeveloped nature of the technology in 1988. By comparison, the European-based GSM and time-based wireless (TDMA) in the United States took years longer to launch commercially, even though they were much closer to the proven and tested analog technology. Qualcomm was essentially the sole authority on the initial CDMA platform, and it put significant resources into rushing the technology through the standards process. Had more companies in the industry had a vested interest in the technology, it would have undoubtedly taken longer than it did to achieve consensus.

But even while Qualcomm was up to its neck in efforts to get the first code-based wireless products into the hands of consumers, the industry was looking ahead to the next generation. While the various flavors of second-generation (2G) digital technology were coming into widespread commercial use in the mid-1990s, various research bodies and standards groups around the world were already buzzing about third-generation (3G) technology—what it would look like and what it would do for mobile users. The International Telecommunications Union (ITU) had already laid out in 1985 a road map for future wireless services called Future Public Land Mobile Telecommunication Systems (FPLMTS), which would later become IMT-2000 (International Mobile Telecommunications in the year 2000). This new specification had been germinating for more than a decade, and frequency blocks were being set aside for the future technology as early as 1992.

The two biggest distinguishing features of 3G technology would be support for high-speed wireless data and global roaming. The IMT-2000 recommendations called for full multimedia capabilities in wireless devices, using the same spectrum everywhere in the world. With the World Wide Web now tantalizing consumers and businesses, the dot-com era was building steam and the focus on global data connectivity was front stage. The Internet euphoria quickly spilled over into the wireless world, where the vision of handsets with the power and capability of a Net-connected computer—what George Gilder dubbed a "teleputer"—was an oft-mentioned goal.

With millions of GSM phone users making ample use of the minimal data capabilities in the short messaging service (SMS) of their 2G phones, the industry was pleasantly surprised to see consumers using their phones for wireless data services. If consumers were so eager to tap out messages and send them at a paltry 9.6 kbps, they would certainly be blown away by being able to send high-resolution images at high speed, or maybe even hold a videoconference over their mobile phones. With a media revolution in the making in the 1990s thanks to the Internet, 3G wireless technology would have to jump on the broadband bandwagon or be left behind.

ENDOWING GENERATIONS

As commercial CDMA networks were coming on line in 1996, Qualcomm was relishing its success in reaching a point that very few outsiders thought it would get to. But relishing did not mean slowing down—actually, quite the opposite. With a major chapter in Qualcomm's corporate life—breaking into digital cellular with code-based wireless—now behind it, the rapidly growing company's focus returned to the next challenge facing it—ensuring that CDMA would be the choice for 3G wireless networks. Since the focus of the business had been the implementation of CDMA (in the form of IS-95) for so long, Jacobs realized that the company would quickly have to concentrate its efforts on the development of succeeding standards.

In June 1997, Qualcomm's global standards chief, Ed Tiedemann, gave his first presentations on 3G technology activities to Qualcomm's executive staff inside the company. In that same month, the company announced that it was partnering with three code-based wireless equipment suppliers—Lucent (once part of AT&T), Motorola, and Nortel—to jointly develop the next-generation CDMA standard that would meet the requirements of IMT-2000. With many other regions around the world, especially Japan and Europe, moving quickly on standardizing 3G technology, Qualcomm needed to ensure that any future technology would be a simple upgrade for current network operators. And without a doubt, any future technology also had to be code-based wireless.

As the LMNQ (Lucent, Motorola, Nortel, and Qualcomm) consortium set out in concert with the CDG (CDMA Development Group) in 1997 to develop the next standard, they realized that the dream of global ubiquity for 3G would be hard to realize. There was a major problem in the marketplace—given the rapid growth of GSM, the next-generation standard would certainly have to integrate easily in a GSM network. But the GSM and CDMA air interfaces were incompatible. In addition, the way in which the two technologies interfaced with the fixed landline network was completely different. For 3G systems to easily evolve on top of 2G systems, the technical details of the new standard would have to include both interfaces. Given the complexity of both systems, a single, clear solution seemed difficult to achieve.

A major sore point with operators at the time was the huge costs and efforts associated with upgrading networks to newer technologies. Network operators were diligent about minimizing costs when upgrading equipment because of the large amounts of capital required. To address this, the LMNQ consortium set the strategy early on of making all of its CDMA technology fully forward- and backward-compatible. This would ensure that legacy users could still use upgraded networks, so that customers would never be alienated or pressured to upgrade before they were ready. The consortium also focused on making it as easy as possible for the network engineers to overhaul or upgrade base stations and switches with next-generation gear.

MILLENNIUM EDITION

Qualcomm and the LMNQ partnership faced a wireless industry that was a mishmash of network systems, with little attention paid to scalability (how the network technology would evolve into future versions). Qualcomm was determined to make sure that code-based wireless networks were capable of seamless upgrades to future generations of mobile radio access technologies. The company had already gone to great lengths to propose a new release of CDMA—IS-95B—that was fully forward- and backward-compatible with the

IS-95A standard released in 1995. The IS-95B standard (which was eventually ratified in 1999) offered higher data rates by aggregating multiple channels to transfer data, but the higher data rates cut down voice capacity, something that network operators in the United States complained about.

Even with the focus of 3G being on wireless data, Qualcomm soon realized that its next-generation technology would have to balance data needs with improvements in voice capacity. It was clear that even an improved IS-95B specification that was currently being developed would not both live up to the IMT-2000 data standards and provide additional voice capacity. So the LMNQ consortium pored through many of the technical minutiae of CDMA to come up with an IMT-2000 proposal. To capture the excitement of the coming wireless age, the next step into the wireless future was aptly named CDMA2000.

While the basic CDMA architecture remained intact, the CDMA2000 proposal put forth in 1997 entailed almost a complete overhaul. Qualcomm went through all the weak areas of the technology to improve performance and flexibility. The company needed a solution that not only met speed and capacity criteria, but also remained modular enough to be easily integrated into a variety of networks around the world. In particular, it had to fit seamlessly into the current CDMA networks deployed by operators in the United States and Asia.

Qualcomm and its partners continue working toward a smooth evolution of CDMA standards to higher capabilities and features (see Figure 18-1). Each step along the way, the family of technologies maintained compatibility with earlier stages to minimize the operators' investment while increasing features and capabilities. Often, upgrading to the next version of CDMA meant only software upgrades or minimal hardware upgrades in phones and base stations.

THE DOORS CLOSE AGAIN

While Qualcomm was working with its partners and with research bodies in Japan on what would become its CDMA2000 standard, the European bodies were working on their own version of CDMA. The European Commission (EC) had funded the Advanced Communication Technologies and Services (ACTS) group to work through the details of proposals based on each technology. Out of all the versions of wireless air interface specifications floating around, two main technology bases bubbled to the surface—time-based (TDMA) and code-based (CDMA) wireless.

Under ACTS, in 1997 the FRAMES (Future Radio Wideband Multiple Access System) Project organized two groups to address the technology modes for 3G. Qualcomm's success in commercializing CDMA for 2G networks proved that the technology was viable and possibly even preferable for 3G applica-

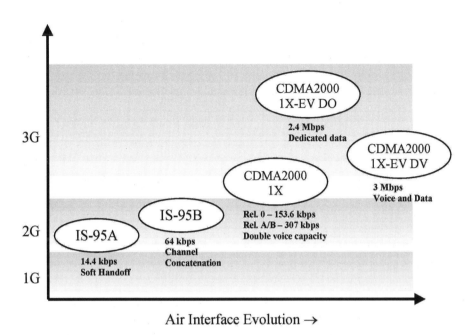

Figure 18-1: Qualcomm's Technology Roadmap

tions, so it was under serious consideration by this and many other groups. But given Qualcomm's IP control of IS-95, many companies wanted Qualcomm to have little to do with a 3G version of CDMA, so that they would be able to compete in the technology themselves.

With parallel efforts to develop next generation code-based wireless standards going on in different regions of the world, Qualcomm attempted to participate in some of the European meetings coordinated through the European Telecommunications Standards Institute (ETSI). But Qualcomm quickly found it rather difficult to participate to any meaningful degree, as ETSI stipulated that only European companies could participate. To get around this exclusion, Qualcomm opened a European subsidiary with the expressed purpose of having a voice in the technology it pioneered and knew so much about. But the voice was a very small one—European revenue determined the number of votes a participant in ETSI was allowed. Since GSM dominated the EU, Qualcomm's European revenue was effectively zero. Having only one vote, Qualcomm held no power compared with other companies such as Ericsson, which had more than sixty-five votes.

Nevertheless, Qualcomm participated in several meetings and submitted several proposals for the group to review. Upon reviewing the Wideband

CDMA (W-CDMA) standard that was being assembled by the body, Qualcomm found not only many flaws, but technical specifications that excluded operation with current-generation code-based wireless networks. The W-CDMA standard being put together in Europe focused exclusively on evolution from GSM, and some aspects of the design seemed to serve absolutely no purpose other than to make it incompatible with other networks in the United States and abroad. What Qualcomm saw, in effect, was an effort to perpetuate the success of GSM, not to open up to foreign competition, as the EU and the United States had politically agreed to do.

Not surprisingly, then, all of the proposals and suggestions that Qualcomm had so far submitted to the body were summarily rejected by the committee chair (who just happened to be from Ericsson). It was obvious that what Qualcomm had been approaching as a technical issue, everyone else was approaching as a business and political issue. The worldwide 3G effort, which had spent several years as a highly technical endeavor, had now become distinctively political.

OPEN COMPETITION IN A GLOBAL MARKET

During the late 1990s, the United States and European Union butted heads on many issues regarding open markets and international competition under the auspices of the World Trade Organization (WTO). But 3G mobile network disputes took on a life of their own, inciting more fury and tirades from high-ranking political officials than anything else. The European Union was understandably against "Americanizing" the continent, as the United States was currently a patchwork of several incompatible technologies. A similar scenario across Europe in the next generation would set the area back to its problematic days of analog networks, when chaos reigned. Moving forward in Europe meant selecting a technology that was closely aligned with GSM and that carried the same incentives for adoption. Anything less would be a smack across the face of European companies.

Their vested interest in propagating the success of GSM also moved European regulators to consider mandating the W-CDMA standard as a condition for granting the spectrum licenses to operate 3G wireless services. Qualcomm's repeated attempts to open up the process in Europe bore no fruit, so the company appealed to the U.S. government. In testimony before the Subcommittee on Trade of the House Committee on Ways and Means in July 1998, Kevin Kelly, Qualcomm's senior VP for external affairs, called the behavior of the ETSI a "flagrant act of protectionism ... creating an artificial monopoly." Objecting to the political nature of the standard setting, Qualcomm issued a letter to the European body stating in unequivocal terms that it would deny the licensing of its intellectual property rights (IPR) in CDMA if ETSI continued with the exclusionary W-CDMA standard.

In every respect, Jacobs genuinely thought that Qualcomm was being more than reasonable in its requests, reiterating to ETSI that Qualcomm would license its IP for a CDMA standard on three conditions:

1. That they work toward a single, converged 3G standard.

2. That the standard be made compatible with both European GSM-MAP and American ANSI-41-based networks

3. That the technical specifications be chosen clearly on the basis of proven superior performance, features, or cost

Qualcomm published its three fairness principles and continued to work with ETSI to resolve differences. But the response to Qualcomm's hardened stance was severe: ETSI countered Qualcomm's claims of unfairness, stating that the process was open and fair to all parties.

Behind the scenes, though, the battle in the standards bodies over versions of CDMA actually mainly involved two companies—Ericsson and Qualcomm—wrangling over ownership. Based on its 1995 claim that it owned essential IPR in IS-95, Ericsson filed a suit against Qualcomm the following year, claiming continued violation of several of Ericsson's patents. Qualcomm vigorously contested the suit, of course, and many suits, motions, and countersuits followed. The companies were locked in a duel over their IPR for years, and this was reflected in the process for developing 3G standards. Still denying Qualcomm's rights in CDMA (and claiming its own), in 1997 Ericsson set out with Nokia and other companies to develop a CDMA standard that was different from Qualcomm's implementation of CDMA in IS-95A and B.

Qualcomm, however, maintained that it held essential intellectual property rights in all versions of CDMA standards being developed that it was aware of. The fundamental nature of Qualcomm's early patents in the area meant that it was impossible to implement CDMA without using the company's patents. With the two companies deadlocked over who really invented CDMA, no progress could be made toward 3G. While this battle continued through the latter part of 1998, the ITU submitted letters to Qualcomm and Ericsson to request assurances that they would license their CDMA IPR for 3G proposals. If such assurance was not forthcoming before the end of the year, the companies risked seeing all CDMA-based proposals removed from the list of candidates for IMT-2000 standards because of the lack of clarity on IP rights.

By December 1998, the touchy situation had reached fever pitch. Qualcomm and the CDG had communicated the events that were transpiring in

ETSI to U.S. government officials and urged them to act. Finally, a letter from U.S. Trade Representative Charlene Barshefsky, Secretary of State Madeleine Albright, Secretary of Commerce William Daley, and FCC Chairman William Kennard notified EC Commissioner Martin Bangemann in stark terms that the United States was strongly opposed to a recent edict apparently stating that EU member nations must adopt whatever 3G standard ETSI decided upon. Bangemann fired back an equally blunt response stating that no such mandate was in place, but rather that countries licensing spectrum for 3G should consider the ETSI concept of W-CDMA as an option.

Bangemann stated that the regulatory body would not act on the disagreements in the standards body. He argued that this was an industry issue, and that it should be resolved by the industry. Essentially, he was stating that Qualcomm and Ericsson would have to settle their disputes. In support of this, the ITU set a new deadline of March 31, 1999, for resolution of the issue. With spectrum license auctions coming soon, the issue had to be taken care of immediately. In the meantime, Qualcomm and Ericsson were gearing up for another big day in court in the United States, where they would present experts and arguments over their respective intellectual property.

SETTLING SCORES

But Qualcomm and Ericsson both had more to gain by promoting CDMA than by opposing each other. Ericsson had already come out and supported Qualcomm's call for a single 3G standard, albeit with some particular technical specifications that Qualcomm disagreed with. But the possibility of CDMA's being set back because of their dispute was not in the best interests of anyone, so the two organizations met continuously to try to find a way to hammer out a deal. At each turn, though, it seemed that the companies were too far apart.

In February 1999, one month before the ITU deadline, Qualcomm and Ericsson were in court in Texas for a five-day hearing arguing the finer points of Ericsson's patents that Qualcomm was reportedly violating. Both sides presented expert witnesses to flesh out proper interpretations of the patents. On the day that the judge was to render his decision, however, both companies asked for a delay so they could continue settlement negotiations.

Ericsson and Qualcomm settled their lawsuits in March 1999, ending their suits against each other over intellectual property rights, but also transferring Qualcomm's CDMA infrastructure division to Ericsson. The companies had actually been discussing the sale of the infrastructure manufacturing unit to Ericsson for some time, but the complications of the IPR disputes made the deal complex and shaky. With a clearer understanding of each other's patent positions through the litigation process, the companies finally felt assured of a win-win deal, and handshakes sealed the end of a battle that had worn down both companies for years.

With the settlement statement and press releases issued by both companies, the industry breathed a collective sigh of relief. Qualcomm and Ericsson together supported a single 3G standard that had three modes of operation—one for each major variety of 2G network around the world. Efforts were already underway in the Operators Harmonization Group (OHG)—an international group set up in 1998 to reconcile proposals made to the ITU—to bring the three modes closer together under a single umbrella standard. With this plan moving forward, no network operators would be alienated or placed at a disadvantage in the 3G world because of their choice of 2G technology. Both companies agreed to license their CDMA IPR on a fair and nondiscriminatory basis.

With the Ericsson-Qualcomm lawsuit settled, the wireless industry was anxious to move ahead with plans for 3G. With the major standards battle behind it and a trade war between the United States and Europe avoided, the industry pushed forward to ratify the 3G proposals and start the auctioning of spectrum. But while resolving the lawsuit and standards battle proved to be a pivotal turning point for Qualcomm, many more struggles lay ahead for the company. Other players in the wireless market were not eager to fall in line behind Qualcomm and move forward—many were still jockeying for a position in the market and attempting to wrestle control away from other players.

Even after Ericsson's settlement with Qualcomm (which included cross-licensing of each other's patents), several companies in Europe with significant GSM business were not keen on paying a royalty to Qualcomm for the coming 3G networks. Nokia in particular continued to haggle with Qualcomm over the payment of royalties. Slowly but surely, though, Qualcomm negotiated deals with all its current licensees—and some new ones—for all flavors of CDMA networks coming in the next generation. But Qualcomm once again revamped its business structure to leverage two of its primary businesses—customized chipsets and IP licensing.

STRADDLING THE FENCE

As the world moved toward 3G in 1999–2000, it became increasingly important for Qualcomm to license the rights to make products based upon GSM-GPRS (general packet radio service) and other time-based protocols. While the company had a huge base of IP in CDMA, it was devoid of rights in the competing protocols and standards. Qualcomm had knowledge of the intricacies of competing standards, but it had never spent resources on developing leverage in those areas. After all, code-based wireless was the future. But now it was becoming important to be technology-agnostic and provide solutions across the board, since many of the 3G modes of operation would be blended together in a single product.

Early in developing the vision for IMT-2000, technical bodies had realized that global roaming would probably come in the form of multimode chipsets in the mobile units. A single standard protocol was unlikely, but with integrated circuit technology rapidly advancing, several operational modes could be integrated inside the units. Most bodies were projecting that more than one billion people worldwide would be using 2G wireless devices before the first 3G network would even be launched. In much the same way that digital networks had to be laid on top of analog ones, 3G devices would have to function on top of 2G networks for several years. While CDMA-AMPS and TDMA-AMPS phones bridging 1G and 2G networks in the United States were fairly straightforward to create, several protocols were being used now throughout the world, making the creation of chipsets to bridge 2G and 3G protocols a much greater challenge.

What this boiled down to was that Qualcomm needed the ability to integrate GSM-GPRS and other protocols into its CDMA chipsets. The company could make all flavors of CDMA chips without problems, but it needed to resolve IPR conflicts with European manufacturers over selling GSM devices. In order to negotiate effective cross-licenses for the technology without diluting its own ability to collect royalties on CDMA licensees, the company developed a plan to separate the chip manufacturing business from the technology licensing group. In July 2000, still lacking the necessary rights to manufacture GSM, Qualcomm announced plans to spin off the dedicated chipset (ASIC) division into a separate company.

The plan would also benefit Qualcomm in case negotiations with several key GSM players on licensing continued to stall. Qualcomm wanted to move into multimode chipsets quickly, so it wanted the IPR issue put to rest early. The ASIC division would be spun off the following year, and shares would be distributed to existing stockholders. To give the company the leverage it needed to negotiate licenses for GSM technology, Qualcomm intended to transfer ownership of a particular set of CDMA patents to use for this purpose. With the lion's share of the essential IP still in Qualcomm's hands, the company's licensing division would be unaffected in their normal collection of royalty from licensees.

Only a year after announcing the restructuring, though, Qualcomm called it off. After announcing the divestiture strategy, Qualcomm secured forty licenses with many of the top companies holding IPR in multiple technologies, the most notable being Nokia. Confident that it had the full rights to produce all the various flavors of TDMA, GSM, and CDMA that it needed,

Qualcomm opted to keep the company intact. To succeed in license negotiations at this stage, Qualcomm had to demonstrate only that it was willing and ready to take this further step to achieve its goals.

Today, Qualcomm is actively shipping and testing its early versions of its multimode chipsets for vendors and network operators around the world. With all versions of wireless networks rapidly coalescing to include CDMA technology, Qualcomm's available market for chipsets is growing substantially. While many critics of Qualcomm and CDMA like to point to the dominance of GSM in the wireless world today, Qualcomm is quick to point out that this condition will soon change. Jacobs likes to remind the world that while GSM may lay claim to the first billion users, CDMA will take the next billion.

CHAPTER 19

Stacking the Deck with the Best Talent

Building Internal and External Teams of Innovators

Qualcomm always has been and always will be a company whose core competitive strength is tied to technical excellence. Deeply rooted in innovation and cutting-edge ideas, the company continues down a path of offering the best and latest designs that are commercially viable. Achieving ongoing success hinges on the company's ability to retain, hire, or partner with the world's best in chip design, systems integration, and network engineering.

The makeup and character of the core employees within Qualcomm have everything to do with its success. In a company that lives or dies by product innovation, the people who drive the ideas are everything. From the founders of Qualcomm through the hundreds of staff members who followed, the core technical employees were hired through a network of referrals. Unknown engineers were never brought in simply to relieve a heavy workload that was encumbering the current staff—the core technical staff of Qualcomm was hand-picked, referred by current employees and other colleagues close to the company. It's also no surprise that many people who were still working at Linkabit in 1985 gradually made their way to Qualcomm in the following years.

Therefore, one of the most significant qualities of Qualcomm's founders, along with their personal technical acumen, was their collective ability to consistently capture the right people for the myriad technical tasks that were necessary to bring products to market. Following right behind this was their ability to inspire this growing base—a quality of leadership that cannot be forced or bought.

START WITH THE BRIGHTEST OF MINDS

When Jacobs, Viterbi, and many of the other core executives left Linkabit to start Qualcomm, the original wind of innovation was taken out of the sails of the company they left and implanted in the new start-up. With them went a reputation for creativity—a mentality that called for groundbreaking ideas first, novel implementation next, and corporate bureaucracy last (if at all).

Above all, Irwin Jacobs stood for the empowerment of creative minds. He held the doors of innovation wide open for those who would pour their heart into radical new ideas that held commercial promise.

Unlike most start-ups, Qualcomm had a world-class team from day one. It literally opened its doors as a mature organization with a talented team that was already hard at work on some of the toughest problems in the field of communications. Since a sizable, veteran team came into Qualcomm together, Jacobs spent little time managing his crew—they all knew one another and their skills. The first several dozen employees that followed the founders were also long-time friends, colleagues, or coworkers at Linkabit. The reputations of Jacobs and Viterbi were a powerful magnet to talent in communications, and many of the brightest minds in the industry were eager to join the Qualcomm team if they could stomach the risk.

Because of the electrifying nature of the industry at the time, many early employees of Qualcomm considered compensation an afterthought—as if it were just something they needed if they were to pay the rent and keep the car in order to make it to the office at any hour. None of the founding members of Qualcomm joined because it paid well. And none of them risked what was, in some cases, their entire career for a benefits package and a title. The founders and future generations of employees joined Qualcomm primarily for one thing—the excitement of being on the cutting edge of product innovation in communications.

Talking to employees at Qualcomm—especially the engineers who formulated the core technologies within the company—almost leaves one with the impression that their work has been more religion than science. They gush with excitement and zeal over their current and past projects. They glow when they describe the barriers they've broken and the problems they've overcome. No discussion goes on for very long without examples of how other companies have fallen short of real breakthroughs in their product innovation. The aura of Qualcomm's technical elite leaves you with a sense that everyone else is struggling just to keep up. Or maybe a sense that engineers at other companies are by and large just working for a paycheck.

Whether or not Qualcomm really has such a huge lead on its competitors is not necessarily as important as its staff's firm belief that this is so. It may be the egocentric nature of a company bent on technological leadership, but the company's morale is extremely strong, and the confidence at its core runs high. With a series of successes at Linkabit and Qualcomm—doing things that many said could not be done—the staff has catalyzed the company's role as a leader in the communications revolution. Failures along the way were seen as practice for something bigger to come, as the work environment has remained open to the exploration of new ideas.

While Andrew Viterbi left the company in 2000 to pursue other interests, Irwin Jacobs has remained as chief executive, ensuring that the technical core of the company still drives the organization. With its focus still heavily on technical innovation, Qualcomm continues to seek out and retain the best minds in communications for its engineering staff. For other corporate roles, Qualcomm seeks to foster knowledge of its core products and technology, believing that this is an essential part of every job in the company. Holding a casual conversation with any employee in the organization—be it a human resource assistant, a member of the legal staff, or a manufacturing associate—leaves one with the impression that the person's primary education was in the technicalities of CDMA and the like.

The emphasis that Qualcomm places on the aptitude of prospective employees is an important factor in maintaining the technical focus of the organization. Finding individuals who are open to self-improvement, education, and learning is a necessary first step if the company is to maintain a high ongoing level of technical and business competency. Therefore, Qualcomm never settles for a body to fill a role—it opts instead to leave a position open until the right person is found to fill it.

This careful process of selecting only the brightest of individuals to fill the company roster lays the foundation for succeeding generations of the company, but it is only the beginning. To guarantee that the organization's core inventions and ideas do not remain and die with a precious few, the company invests heavily in education and staff development. But even these two efforts would probably fail without the glue that binds them together to create the formula of Qualcomm's technical success: the motivation to succeed, both individually and, more importantly, as a team.

On Inspiration

Thomas Alva Edison is credited with the oft-quoted mantra of innovation: "Genius is 1 percent inspiration and 99 percent perspiration." While these words convey the message that inventors have to work hard—very hard—to achieve breakthroughs, one shouldn't minimize the absolute importance and necessity of that first 1 percent. Edison did, in fact, recognize that a great deal of forethought and planning comes before sitting down and digging into any experiments. He is also credited with saying, "Being busy does not always mean real work," wisely understanding that perspiration alone won't suffice.

Edison's comments, though, are often interpreted through the image of a lone inventor—a single man brainstorming a new invention or contraption. Even in Edison's case, nothing could be further from the truth. His Menlo Park laboratory was inhabited by scores of assistants at any hour of the day or night. Many of the staff in his famed idea lab worked directly on his ideas, but many of them also did ancillary tasks such as lab maintenance, bookkeeping, and legal filings—the background work that keeps the doors of any company open. Edison was not a rogue inventor—he was the CEO of a company that was the epitome of an invention machine.

By the evidence of the accomplishments of his laboratory, Edison by no means disparaged the importance of inspiration in the pursuit of invention. His skilled assistants and craftsmen shared his passion for invention and the propagation of new ideas. The starting salaries of his assistants were comparatively low so that, as at Qualcomm, applicants did not have dollar signs dancing in their heads. They were drawn by the magnetism of Edison's character and the chance to be part of something truly great, akin to the spiritual draw of a religious calling.

Edison's ability to inspire his staff set him apart from most great inventors. Similarly, Irwin Jacobs is often given credit in this area—he breeds passion in his work. His own personal dedication to groundbreaking efforts almost automatically creates a following. Many of Jacobs's colleagues have worked with him for their entire professional lives, sharing their careers and their passion for the pursuit of technical excellence.

Where Jacobs's character distinctly departs from that of Edison, though, is in the area of education and formal training. Edison was known to place little emphasis on formal schooling when he was looking for talented people to assist him with his ideas. In the case of Qualcomm, though, the predisposition for highly degreed personnel comes from Jacobs's collaboration with the likes of Viterbi in the elite corners of academia. In 1999, even after years of rapid growth and branching into several manufacturing endeavors, 25 percent of Qualcomm's employees still held one or more graduate degrees.

In Qualcomm's formative years, Jacobs and Viterbi gathered much of their talent from the various halls they walked in prior to its founding. In addition to many people coming directly from Linkabit, many of the core technical staff came from MIT Lincoln Labs, where much of the early work in advanced communications and information theory had been done. With the rapid development of ideas that was going on at MIT, many of Qualcomm's early technical employees came during their postgraduate work or right after its completion. Throughout the following years of rapid growth, Qualcomm continued to recruit heavily from educational institutions in its hometown and abroad. Not surprisingly, once they had relocated in San Diego, many of these employees, who came from places such as Harvard, MIT, and the University of Illinois, continued their education at the University of California, San Diego (UCSD) as well.

Developing the local talent pool in San Diego was also important, as the demand for engineering and other professional talent put a strain on the local job market. A critical aspect of the development of the local knowledge base around Qualcomm's headquarters is the company's tight relationship with UCSD Connect, a program started the same year Qualcomm was founded to help keep the San Diego area tuned in to the needs of the high-tech industry. The goal of the program was to link the regional high-tech and life sciences industries to resources in education, investment banking, law, marketing, and communications. With the framework of collaboration that the program has fostered, hundreds of budding companies in the San Diego area have been catapulted ahead in their respective markets.

Because of Jacobs's early tenure as a professor at UCSD, Qualcomm has maintained an intimate connection with the university and with the Connect program since the company's inception. Many of Qualcomm's business partners and supporters were found through UCSD and the network of professors there. For instance, in 1987, Qualcomm elected Jerome Katzin, a former SEC employee with a diverse background and intimate connection with UCSD, to its board of directors. The insight and relationships brought into Qualcomm by people like Katzin have been critical to its continued success. In an effort to continue to foster this type of collaboration with UCSD, Qualcomm has already fully funded six chairs at the university.

A valuable resource in attracting top talent to feed Qualcomm's voracious appetite for employees, the UCSD Connect program helped Qualcomm ally with several organizations that proved key to its growth. Of course, the success of the Connect program is largely due to contributions from member companies. In 2000, Qualcomm announced a $25 million commitment to fund local educational institutions to bridge the "digital divide" in the areas of mathematics and science. UCSD in particular was earmarked for $15 million of this donation over five years to foster the continued improvement of higher education, particularly in the areas of engineering and international relations.

After many years of pulling students from—and sending employees to—the university, Qualcomm formally sponsored a CDMA engineering certificate with the UCSD extension program in 1998. With this educational curriculum, engineering students would be privy to CDMA expertise that had once been available only within Qualcomm through its private CDMA University program. Qualcomm's CDMA University grew from its early work in educating the wireless industry on the technical details and benefits of code-based wireless. Qualcomm continues this program today to disseminate knowledge of CDMA to current and prospective customers and partners.

When describing the atmosphere within Qualcomm, many employees will say that the work environment is more akin to a university than to a corporation. There is no formal dress code or working hours, and employees focus on projects, with little structure. Development paths within the company are always open to new ideas, and the senior technical staff still ensure that employees continue to exercise their "free thinking" skills. Employees are encouraged to return to school for additional degrees, and accommodations are made for staff members who are studying. This open and flexible environment, coupled with the charisma of the leadership, makes Qualcomm one of the most attractive prospects for skilled job seekers.

THE PLACE WHERE EVERYONE WANTS TO WORK

The focus on education and continued improvement in Qualcomm does not just come from the top of the organization, either—it permeates all levels. Each level of the employee base is inspired to build upon its success and, in turn, Qualcomm's. Certainly, the technical prowess and mentoring of Jacobs and Viterbi have had a profound influence on the company, but their legacy of knowledge and learning did not have to be forced upon succeeding employees. The desire to learn and advance has been bred into the organization by the way it operates on a daily basis, so that continuing education is a reason that people come to the company in the first place.

Prospective employees who were just looking for a paycheck would quickly find that they didn't fit into the academic environment, where much of the reward is in the achievement—not the proceeds. Especially in its first few years, Qualcomm had few financial incentives to give employees. But that didn't matter; many people wanted to be there anyway. In the late 1980s, cofounder and technical lead Franklin Antonio is often remembered for sitting on his uncashed paychecks for months, finally forcing the company's first CFO, Dee Coffman, to institute direct deposits of payroll checks to keep the books clear. While some employees, like Antonio, didn't need the money, even those who couldn't afford to miss a paycheck stayed because they knew that no other employment would be nearly as exciting. No other company was even close to breaking the boundaries that Qualcomm was pushing.

Throughout the 1980s, when it was a relatively small company, Qualcomm had few problems finding appropriate talent to fill its employee base. But as Qualcomm matured and began to pick up staff by the thousands, not everyone in the company was doing the most exciting work. The team atmosphere was still there, but the bond that existed in the small, young start-up was diluted by the sheer size of the corporation. Qualcomm hit its most aggressive growth phase in the mid-1990s, when it hired thousands of employees within a few short years (see Figure 19-1). Most of these employees were picked up to rapidly expand the infrastructure manufacturing division and operations in the handset development and manufacturing group. Someone had to ship

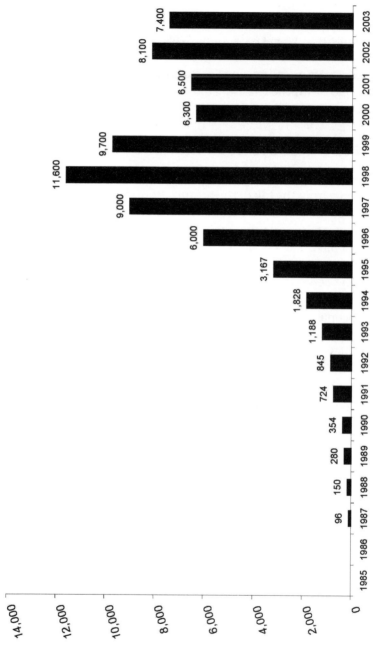

Figure 19-1: Qualcomm's approximate number of employees by year
Source: SEC Filings and Company Documents

the boxes, and someone had to sweep the floors. Not everyone could be on the team that found a breakthrough signaling method to double the capacity of a network.

Like most high-tech companies in the 1990s, Qualcomm offered stock options as an incentive for joining and staying with the company. Many companies admitted at the time that it would be impossible to fill positions without giving options on company shares, because there was just too much euphoria in the market and demand for technical talent. And Qualcomm's hiring binge had left the San Diego area devoid of the specific talents it was seeking. While stock options and company ownership had always been a part of the company, they became a significant focus only during this time period of rapid technical advance and a flourishing job market.

With the NASDAQ breaking new highs on a monthly basis, the wealth promised by stock options jaded the high-tech workforce, so that employees often skipped in and out of positions looking for the sweetest deal. While Qualcomm did offer stock options, it realized that this alone would not keep employees at the company once they were there. In the face of this dilemma, Qualcomm, like many other companies, instituted a myriad of employee benefits to build compensation packages that would allow it to court and retain good staff. In addition to typical health and retirement benefits, Qualcomm also put in place many quality-of-life services, such as on-site day care, gyms, and recreation facilities. Its strong efforts to improve their employees' quality of life has paid off: Qualcomm's voluntary turnover rate is often less than 5 percent—well below that of its peers.

As a testament to its commitment to employee quality and morale, Qualcomm has received numerous corporate awards. In 2001, it was listed in the top fifty training organizations in America. It has been on *Fortune*'s "100 Best Companies to Work For in America" five years running. While the high-growth phase was turbulent and painful in many ways, the company was able to move through the ups and downs of the high-tech "bubble years" and maintain a solid employee base. By and large, Qualcomm is still one of the most sought-after employers in the country.

WELL, MOST OF THE TIME, ANYWAY . . .

Even being repeatedly selected as one of the top companies to work for doesn't make you immune from employee problems. In fact, companies that are ranked favorably on how they treat their employees can have an unusually high level of employee disputes. Great companies such as Qualcomm become so because they put a great deal of effort into resolving mitigating disputes and invest heavily in open and thorough communication through all levels.

But even the best preparation and execution in employee management cannot head off all problems quickly and easily. It's inevitable that a company will fall victim to disagreements over how an employee or employees should be treated. Qualcomm's biggest and most visible dispute with a portion of its employee base is actually ongoing at the time of this writing, with a class action lawsuit still pending. It's also no surprise that the dispute centers on—stock options.

In the late 1990s, with stock prices soaring and no end in sight, companies increasingly relied on generous stock option plans to attract talent, and Qualcomm was no different. By that time the salaries were great, but the choice of a particular company for employment was often bought with stock. With Qualcomm's stock soaring and its unquenchable appetite for staff, some recently hired employees saw stock options as a ticket to a wealthy retirement. While Jacobs did everything he could to maintain the small start-up dynamic of the company, the hypergrowth inevitably brought up compensation and stock allotment issues with the employee base.

When Qualcomm sold its infrastructure division to Ericsson in 1999 as part of its legal settlement, more than one thousand employees were encouraged to stay with the group and become Ericsson employees. The employees were offered a sweet deal—a healthy cash bonus spread over two years, based on the value of the unvested stock options that they currently held. Designed to keep the employees at Ericsson, the total cash payment per employee—of which Qualcomm would fund 65.8 percent—was to be doled out in four installments of 20/40/20/20 percent of the total. Of the 1,053 employees affected, 1,016 of them took the deal under the Retention Bonus Plan (RBP). In return for joining the RBP, the employees agreed not to sue Qualcomm.

But some employees didn't like the deal. Ericsson did not have a stock option plan at the time, so the employees destined for the new organization were greatly concerned about the loss of their options that had not yet vested. Some of the employees had been hired by Qualcomm only recently, and the stock options had been an important factor in their decision to join the company. For these people, and for others who had sizable "paper" value tied up in the unvested options, the retention plan was a lose-lose scenario—go work for a company that has long been your staunchest competitor (Ericsson), and give up your chance to hit it big in Qualcomm stock. To a few employees, this scenario was just plain wrong—how could the company do this to them?

When the news and terms of the divestiture were communicated, many of the employees affected were dismayed at the loss of their unvested options—the initial understanding of many had been that their options would fully vest upon the sale. The problem involved the details of Qualcomm's stock option plan. The plan had a provision in it that employees' options would vest immediately if the control of the company were to change to another entity.

But the exact legal meaning of *control* was not well defined in the agreement, leaving room for ambiguity (depending on which side you were on). Since selling the infrastructure division to Ericsson was not changing the control structure of Qualcomm at all, the immediate vesting provision did not apply, according to the company. But for the employees who were being pushed to leave Qualcomm and join Ericsson, the effect of their change of employment was the same, and their interpretation was that, indeed, their "company" was changing control.

A former VP, Thomas Sprague, filed a lawsuit against Qualcomm on May 6, 1999, over the ambiguity of the stock option vesting. On July 30, 1999, an amended complaint was filed to extend the class to those who had signed the retention agreement, claiming that the signing was done under duress. After attempts to settle dragged on and on, the parties finally came to an agreement in 2001, under which Qualcomm was required to pay $11 million to 840 employees. But the settlement was split 86 percent to the employees who did not sign the RBP agreement and only 14 percent to those who did.

Unfortunately, this settlement did not end the dispute, and many more complaints were filed. Sprague and the other nonsigners got some measure of recompense, but the amount given to the 840 signers was so little that it might as well have been a loss. Some employees who were disgruntled by the small settlement and others who had not been party to the original suits went back to court to reopen an action against the company. Today, Qualcomm is still fighting several suits arising out of the Ericsson sale that have been consolidated into class actions. Apart from the litigation, Qualcomm so far has ended up digesting $74 million in compensation benefits related to the Ericsson deal, in its good faith efforts to accommodate the transferred employees. With many Qualcomm employees now millionaires thanks to stock options, though, the company is bound to be dogged by lawsuits by former (and even current) employees who want to join those elite ranks.

BUILDING A TEAM—INSIDE AND OUT

In addition to focusing on maintaining a world-class engineering team inside of Qualcomm, the company has recognized that its future success also hinges on developing a team with similar qualities outside the company. Much of the success in developing CDMA in the wireless industry in the 1990s came because of practical implementation help from scores of other organizations, such as PacTel and many Korean manufacturers and network operators. In the coming decade, Qualcomm is looking ahead to foster another complementary team of outside application developers to promote its BREW product—an open-source programming platform for CDMA.

In the high-tech segments of the electronics industries, the companies that see rapid adoption of their products are those that are most effective at giving design engineers the tools to use their products easily. If a chip manufacturer wants to sell millions of chips, for instance, it has to give its customers all the right incentives to design its chip into an end product.

In the rapidly expanding microcontroller market of the 1990s, for example, a small company called Microchip was pitted against behemoths like Intel and Motorola. The strategy that Microchip employed was to develop an extremely user-friendly development and debugging tool that could be used for its products—and then essentially give it away to developers. Design engineers saw how quickly and easily they could do their jobs with a tool that didn't need three levels of management approval. In new product applications, then, the designers usually opted to start with the Microchip tools, since the cost of entry was low compared to the power and functionality of the tool.

Once competency in a tool set is established, it's difficult for designers to move away from this platform they are familiar with. Familiarity with a development process and design flow becomes a strong habit for an engineer or computer scientist to break. Often, it takes a mandate from the higher ranks to force a designer away from a product that he's used before and knows how to work with. And most managers will not purposely force developers into unfamiliar territory, as they know that it will require time and resources to get the developers acquainted with new tools. Microchip was very successful with this strategy, cultivating a grass-roots developer community by using a technical focus, not a marketing focus.

Qualcomm also recognized that the developer community—and the development environment—holds the key to the wireless media environment of the future. The launching of the BREW platform sought to capitalize on the power of applications developers in guiding standards for the wireless Internet. BREW, first launched in 2001, not only gave developers and their companies compelling reasons to build content, but reasons to build it based on Qualcomm's technology.

To foster support in the wireless developer community, Qualcomm put significant resources into developing a user-friendly product with easy user access; it then basically planned on providing the best that its customers' money could buy. Following a model similar to Microchip's, Qualcomm developed a simplified BREW SDK (software development kit) and distributed it freely to any interested developers. Then, in an effort to entice developers to join the BREW community, Qualcomm spent millions on trade show advertising and yearly developer conferences. For a small fee (or no fee at all for key customers), Qualcomm would wine and dine developers, offering the best local entertainment and technical presentations from key Qualcomm engineers.

Qualcomm's BREW developer conferences have become almost legendary among developers for their posh treatment and luxurious amenities. The marketing and events team at Qualcomm holds little back and seems bent on outdoing the previous conference every year. All the tools and information that a developer needs are given freely at these events, and the entertainment is top notch. The setting, in beautiful, sunny San Diego, is itself enough to give developers from colder, wetter regions a reason to spend a few days listening to the company's pitch on BREW. For engineers, who are often stereotyped as having little social life outside of their work, it's almost impossible to go to the event and not have fun.

With its success in cultivating a vibrant and growing BREW developer community in the United States, Qualcomm is now moving to grow the external team internationally. Setting up regional conferences and training centers in countries such as China, the United Kingdom, and Romania, Qualcomm is targeting pockets of developers in order to get the number of BREW adopters up to critical mass. Without the support of the international developer community, BREW has no future, so Qualcomm will continue to invest in establishing development centers and labs around the world to facilitate its growth.

Through complementary internal and external efforts to promote technical innovation based on Qualcomm's designs, the company aims to secure the future, no matter where it may lead.

CHAPTER 20

Remaining a Technology Leader

–·––→

Positioning for 3G and Beyond

Given all the successes Qualcomm has enjoyed in its relatively short corporate life, many people question whether the company can live up to such a high standard going forward. Not surprisingly, some of those who have doubted the company's code-based wireless (CDMA) crusade all along remain skeptical about the future. As if the last fifteen years have been a fluke, some still hold that there's undoubtedly something coming that will pull the support out from under the CDMA house of cards, collapsing Qualcomm. The story of the company's continued hypergrowth has been just too good to be true, according to its critics.

Qualcomm has faced this type of skepticism literally from day one. At each seemingly insurmountable technical or business obstacle, the combined talent of the Qualcomm team and its extensive list of CDMA partners has come through to do things that many people said were impossible. In most areas of its business, Qualcomm has had a tremendous track record of success. In the areas where it has failed, it was quick to recover and learn from its mistakes.

As the wireless industry evolves in this new century, new problems and paradigms are arising to change the game. The way the industry is regulated in the United States and abroad has changed dramatically, and the global landscape continues to be a moving target. Of course, Qualcomm's business will continue to change—the model and strategies that it has used in the past may not play out as effectively going forward. While many investors and industry watchers maintain that Qualcomm has already "arrived," the company itself is not at all in agreement with this—significant challenges and opportunities lie ahead. What is certain is that the pace of activity and innovation in the company today has not abated.

Going forward beyond 2004, Qualcomm has put in place what it believes is the right mix of talent and resources to meet the challenges of the new wireless world. In fact, while this book has focused almost exclusively on Qualcomm's efforts in code-based wireless, the company has maintained significant activity in several other forms of communications: The visionaries in the company still consider CDMA only one area of opportunity in advanced communications. While their efforts in this area were far more successful than most imagined, there are several other related products that Qualcomm hopes will keep the company growing in the future.

To meet the varied challenges in communications, at the close of 2003, Qualcomm organized its business efforts into five divisions:

Qualcomm CDMA Technologies (QCT). This division designs and develops CDMA chipsets and accompanying software for wireless handsets and infrastructure equipment.

Qualcomm Digital Media (QDM). This division works with advanced media applications such as direct digital delivery of motion pictures and image compression. It also develops highly secure wireless networks for government or private use.

Qualcomm Internet Services (QIS). This division develops the technologies associated with the convergence of wireless data and voice technologies. It is primarily focused on the company's BREW wireless programming platform, but it also includes the QChat product, which is a push-to-talk (PTT) solution, and Eudora, an electronic mail software application.

Qualcomm Wireless Business Solutions (QWBS). This division primarily handles Qualcomm's satellite messaging business. This includes the OmniTRACS product and service groups domestically and internationally.

Qualcomm Wireless Systems (QWS). This division supports the GlobalStar efforts by supplying products and services for the system. Currently in bankruptcy, GlobalStar (and Qualcomm) is looking at several strategic options for this endeavor.

In addition to its operating divisions, Qualcomm also funds the Qualcomm Strategic Initiatives (QSI) to encourage the growth of CDMA around the world. This group selectively offers financing and other forms of capital support to a variety of ventures working with wireless equipment and services. In this way, the group seeds many strategic markets around the world to contribute to the long-term viability and growth of CDMA in all corners of the globe. Its operating financials are often broken out separately from the company's overall performance, so that investors can easily distinguish performance in each business area.

To clarify the performance of different aspects of the company's operations,

Qualcomm's revenue and earnings are broken down and reported for the following business segments:

QCT: Qualcomm CDMA Technologies (sales of chipsets and software)

QTL: Qualcomm Technology Licensing (worldwide license fees and royalties)

QWI: Qualcomm Wireless Internet (includes the QDM, QIS, and QWBS divisions)

QSI: Qualcomm Strategic Initiatives (strategic investment activities)

In order to continue the expansion and proliferation of its technologies in underserved areas of the world, Qualcomm has recently put significant resources into opening offices in Asia and now Europe. Qualcomm is also establishing several technical centers and joint ventures to extend the reach of CDMA and associated technologies. Qualcomm's CDMA experts are taking the initiative in working with carriers and equipment manufacturers around the world. While code-based wireless is already used in more than 200 million wireless devices worldwide, it still covers less than 20 percent of the total market, leaving many areas of the world open for growth. Renewed efforts to expand internationally will be key to the continued acceptance and proliferation of CDMA.

SOMETHING BREWING

Along with many other companies in the industry that are working to make 3G wireless services a reality, Qualcomm realized early on that wireless data represents the future. Efficient transmission of voice communications will remain the company's bread and butter for a long time, but the profit margins on voice services will eventually decline the way those for long distance in landline telephony have done. Data applications such as e-mail, games, and enterprise applications will be the future. Voice will become a commodity, and premium services and data will soon be where the real money will be made. But even today, the wireless data market is still in its infancy.

Much of the wireless industry also sees data services overtaking voice services in importance for its business. But Qualcomm has gone beyond embracing wireless data as its next core business; the company is once again attempting to lead the industry by advancing the wireless data market itself. In 2000, while just about everyone from Nokia to Sprint to Ericsson was calling data the future of wireless, Qualcomm was busy shaping how that future should play out, in the form of a full solution for end users.

Qualcomm has tried to leverage its expertise in total solutions to leapfrog ahead and provide every company on the value chain with a compelling alternative for offering wireless data to consumers. The company introduced its binary runtime environment for wireless (BREW) platform in January 2001, citing the need to deliver a full solution to the wireless data market that would compliment the company's products. The BREW platform includes both a technology component and a business component. The technology includes software for handsets and for servers belonging to the network operators that adopt the solution. The BREW software on the handset is essentially a tiny operating system that can download applications over the air from the network server. The software on the handset and that on the server work together, so a user can order an application—such as a game or a business tool—and be billed accordingly.

On top of the technology component, the BREW solution includes a provisioning and billing system that has already been set up for the service providers to use. In addition, Qualcomm will test and validate applications for use on any particular carrier's network and devices. With BREW, carriers won't have to cobble together products from several companies to handle each portion of the service—Qualcomm handles it all. And the company takes only a fraction of the revenue collected from the applications ordered, with most of it going to the developers of the applications. The business component of BREW solves a problem that has stymied growth in wireless data: By standardizing the distribution of applications, it offers more incentives for operators and the application developers to build and launch wireless data applications.

The problem with data applications up until 2001 was that the developer community was fragmented among different technologies. Many different operating systems are being used for wireless data applications on handsets around the world, and none of them are compatible with the others. Developers who are looking to write a software application are thus faced with questions about which version to write for and whether the population using that version is large enough to make it profitable. The most widely used operating environment for mobile applications on handsets is Sun Microsystems's Java, actually in a scaled-down version called J2ME, for Java2 Micro Edition—a thinner programming environment designed specifically for mobile devices. The problem is that Java is still just one programming language, not a total solution, requiring developers not only to write the code but to set up multiple partnerships in the industry in order to attain effective distribution.

With the BREW platform, Qualcomm again is offering a win-win solution—basically, everybody benefits. The key element of the solution is that it directly ties together the network operator (the one who is providing services to end customers) and the developer (the one who is building applications) through Qualcomm's distribution system. Qualcomm acts as the intermediary to smooth the process of getting a software application out of a content company and into a network operator's system, where end users can download it and pay for its use. Developers can easily see how to make money on their applications, while operators can see a simplified way to get access to applications (tested and verified by Qualcomm) that can run on the devices they offer.

With the BREW system, Qualcomm is working to overcome an early problem with wireless data services—garnering a critical mass of developers for a device platform. Qualcomm identified the major obstacles that kept developers from flocking to a platform and developing content for it—projecting revenue and getting paid. Most content delivery models in place with Java or other systems provided little financial incentive for developers, and the method of compensation was sometimes not even consistent with the popularity of the content. In Qualcomm's BREW system, developers can have the distribution of their content managed and billed for by Qualcomm. The revenue split between all the companies is set up in advance, but Qualcomm stipulates that the developer keeps the majority of the revenue from each download—usually 80 percent—while the carrier and Qualcomm split the rest.

Originally, Qualcomm offered BREW as an option only for CDMA network operators, touting it as an advantage for these operators. The company has since opened up BREW for use on any mobile network, regardless of technology. Because of the company's legacy in CDMA, many critics were quick to point out that once again Qualcomm was trying to use BREW to steamroll the industry into using its proprietary solution. In order to help proliferate BREW and avoid this controversy, Qualcomm changed its strategy to encompass competing GSM (global system for mobile) and other TDMA (time-based wireless) networks. The company has also attempted to avoid the suggestion that BREW is battling against Java by integrating a Java Virtual Machine (operating system) into BREW. This way, the millions of Java developers around the world can also reap the benefits offered by the BREW distribution and billing model.

Going forward in 2005, Qualcomm is continuing to pour resources into advancing its BREW solution. It has successfully courted more than a dozen network operators from around the world, and more than one hundred different handset models are capable of accessing the BREW application service. Each year, Qualcomm holds the BREW developers conference in San Diego, inviting application developers from around the world for two days of intensive learning and demonstration of just what BREW has to offer. The event is not all work, though—it includes a BREWfest party featuring live performance from top bands (Kool & The Gang appeared in 2003) and plenty to drink and eat. With a business conference like this one, it's no wonder BREW has been very successful at garnering developers and business partners.

EMERGING MARKETS: THE NEXT FRONTIER

When Qualcomm first entertained the idea of using spread spectrum in mobile applications, cellular was the most popular option, but not necessarily the one with the largest potential. While the company was actively pursuing the standardization of CDMA for cellular applications, it was also spending significant resources on developing similar phones and other equipment for wireless local loop (WLL) and other mobile systems. The WLL market is far bigger than cellular, since many nations do not yet have a wired infrastructure in place to provide residents with basic telephone service. Qualcomm realized that CDMA was the optimum way for governments to rapidly deploy advanced communications for their populace, and in 1993 it was successful in signing agreements to pursue its solution in China, Russia, Chile, Malaysia, and India.

The development and deployment of WLL systems has taken much longer than anticipated, though. Nearly a decade after it first initiated CDMA trials in various emerging markets around the world, Qualcomm is finally starting to show traction in terms of volume commercial product deliveries in a few countries. In China, Qualcomm's WLL solution has given way to its break into the cellular market there—now the largest cellular market in the world. The company's success in finally breaking into China (described in Chapter 17) was a major factor in the amazing rise in the price of the company's stock in 1999. To date, Qualcomm has benefited from more than 20 million Chinese adopters of its cellular CDMA technology.

Right alongside China, India was another major target in Qualcomm's sights for WLL systems. With a huge population and a similarly low penetration rate, India was another great opportunity to get CDMA technology in on the ground floor of a communications revolution. As in China, GSM dominated India's second-generation mobile networks, with more than 15 million total subscribers by the end of 2003. But a new twist in the story has come about, thanks to dramatic changes in government regulation—changes that finally opened the doors for CDMA. The boon to Qualcomm came when the government of India initiated efforts to boost its teledensity through the New Telecom Policy of 1999. This new set of rules opened the floodgates in India for investment in local mobile networks to compete with cellular services.

The new regulatory policies permitted private companies such as Reliance Infocomm to operate limited-mobility networks in major urban and rural areas under basic telephone service licenses. The limited-mobility networks allow users to roam only over short distances, while networks licensed by cellular operators (using GSM) allow users to roam over wide areas. But for many Indians, limited mobility is a negligible factor, so adoption of such services has been swift. Qualcomm has gone to great lengths to support Reliance and other fixed operators in their efforts to break open the Indian mobile communications market. It has developed WLL hardware and systems based upon CDMA technology, and it even elected to invest up to $200 million in Reliance; however, the milestones outlined in the agreement were apparently not met, as Qualcomm announced in 2002 that the funding did not take place.

Of course, the major upheaval in the Indian market incited by the new regulations has led to a litany of controversy and litigation. The problem centers on the fact that the WLL services are so close to the standard cellular services that users see little differentiation between the two. The WLL services can also be sold more cheaply, since companies offering WLL service don't need to pay for cellular licenses. This inconsistency led many cellular operators to cry foul when Reliance Infocomm and other operators announced plans to launch limited-mobility services based on CDMA. It is reported that Indian cellular operators and their investors have spent 250,000 million rupees (roughly $5 billion) to build out their networks. The business model and protection guaranteed by the license for cellular services have now been summarily thrown out the window by the new telecom policy.

After some tense court battles over the unfair nature of WLL's entrance into the mobile market, the Indian authorities ruled in favor of the fixed operators, and Reliance launched its CDMA services as of May 2003. While it took longer than many anticipated to clear the regulatory hurdles, the rapid ramp-up of subscribers in the various regions of the country (similar to that in China) to over 5 million by the end of 2003 made up for the lag. Going forward, the Indian market via WLL may be one of the best long-term revenue streams for Qualcomm.

In addition to China and India, Qualcomm has also been making inroads recently in other emerging markets, such as Russia and Latin America. In Russia, in addition to WLL systems, Qualcomm has also recently been aiding in the launch of networks using the 450-MHz spectrum, which was once used for early first-generation technologies but has gone unutilized in second-generation (2G) and third-generation (3G) systems. Since many European nations do not use this area of spectrum for GSM technology, Qualcomm is hoping that CDMA in the 450-MHz band may be a way to finally break into the European stronghold. The upheaval in the Indian market has shown that such things are possible if a government is motivated to spur competition. Many industry analysts are now suggesting that CDMA450 will be much more than just a niche technology in a few remote markets, as was once thought.

STEALING FROM THE GSM CANDY STORE

Critics of Qualcomm have long complained that while the company has been successful in introducing CDMA (or at least more successful than anticipated), the adoption of code-based wireless has still lagged behind GSM by a tremendous margin. Qualcomm investors eager to reach the $1,000-per-share (presplit) milestone, set by Paine Webber analyst Walter Piecyk in 1999, have continued to look for ways in which the company can break into the European stronghold, which many see as the key to CDMA's eventually overtaking GSM. While Qualcomm executives have been insistent that CDMA will be the dominant technology in the future, how soon it will get there is still open to debate. With the choices for 3G systems all using various flavors of CDMA, it will happen. But in the meantime there are lots of lost opportunities as GSM continues to expand.

The principal problem in propagating CDMA technology into next-generation wireless networks is that the core of the majority of the existing networks—the wired switching gear—is based on the GSM-MAP (GSM mobile application protocol) specification, which traditionally has been incompatible with CDMA equipment. Qualcomm's solution to enable CDMA to be easily introduced into any network around the globe (including GSM) involves a product called GSM1x. Essentially, this product puts a CDMA2000 1x air interface on top of the GSM-MAP network. It also provides for multimode handsets that can operate in both the GSM and CDMA modes at various frequencies.

The major selling point to GSM operators is that the benefits of CDMA can now be easily laid on top of the core networks that they already have in place. In the past, moving to CDMA technology meant that a GSM-MAP operator basically had to build a new network based upon ANSI 41 from the ground up—a huge undertaking with prohibitive costs. With GSM1x, the operator leaves all the features and services of its GSM network intact for its current users. But it gains the capacity advantages of CDMA, as well as the possibility of launching BREW services or even upgrading to Qualcomm's next-generation 1xEV-DO, with data speeds of up to 3.1 Mbps.

Qualcomm's GSM1x solution has evolved over the years, but the big push to market the solution came in 2002. With the realization that CDMA could not proliferate by displacing GSM in areas where it was entrenched, the integration solution came to be seen as a better path to follow. In addition, GSM network operators were stalling on their way to 3G by adopting an inferior GPRS data upgrade, while CDMA network operators were flourishing with Qualcomm's 1x solution. Qualcomm hoped to tantalize GSM operators with the benefits that CDMA was showing around the world as a next-generation solution.

Another early push for harmonizing CDMA and GSM networks into an integrated GSM1x platform came from Asian markets, where operators were dealing with both GSM and CDMA networks that couldn't support cross-roaming. Chinese operators had made it clear to Qualcomm that roaming between the two types of networks was important, and the Chinese communications industry went on to make it a mandatory requirement. This meant that at a minimum, CDMA phones had to be capable of accepting a user's identity module, called a SIM (subscriber identity module) card. The SIM is a removable chip that contains all the user's identification and billing information.

In response, Qualcomm and the CDMA Development Group (CDG) went to work on developing and specifying a removable identity function in CDMA handsets. They developed and tested a R-UIM (removable user identity module) in a Samsung handset in August 2001, showing that this level of convergence was possible. With this solution, users could roam across both types of networks and retain their contact and billing information with their primary provider.

To date, the most progress with the GSM1x solution has been made in China with China Unicom. Qualcomm has successfully completed the first phase of trials with China Unicom and anticipates having commercial networks up and running soon. If Qualcomm is successful in penetrating China with the GSM1x solution, operators in other countries may be encouraged to adopt the technology as well in order to provide their GSM networks with the benefits of CDMA. Each GSM1x network that is built out gives Qualcomm millions of opportunities to sell subscribers a handset that uses its patented technology and chipset.

TRANSFORMING THE BUSINESS

In order to reach its current level, Qualcomm has had to go through several major—and often painful—corporate transformations. Taking an advanced idea from paper to commercial reality stretched the abilities of Jacobs and the executive staff and forced them to move into many unfamiliar areas. When they had to move quickly into the cellular industry, they forged many new critical partnerships to help them propagate their code-based wireless solution. When they had to manufacture millions of products to support that industry, they once again worked overtime to negotiate joint ventures that provided the necessary resources. When they had to navigate legal and political minefields, they successfully sought appropriate outside counsel and advice.

As Qualcomm now looks forward, it is once again faced with a different market driven by different demands. CDMA has been widely accepted, and steady growth has ensued. The standards for 3G networks have been cemented, and they all include CDMA, for which Qualcomm has already renewed its licensing deals with manufacturers. Everything on the licensing front appears secure for the time being, pending any major legal challenges to the company's intellectual property rights (IPR). But two major challenges face the company going forward—the speed of proliferation of CDMA and its dominance of the market for CDMA chipsets.

Even though CDMA is destined to be the future of mobile networks, progress toward that goal has been miserably slow in many areas of the world. Especially with GSM operators, the wideband or W-CDMA version of 3G networks (called UMTS, or universal mobile telecommunications system) has had its launch dates postponed time and time again. While many in the industry had planned on having UMTS launched and in wide use by now, the technology still is available to only a fraction of the wireless subscriber base. What's more disconcerting, though, is that many operators, such as AT&T Wireless and Cingular in the United States, are launching an interim solution for their GSM networks called EDGE (enhanced data rate for GSM evolution). This upgrade allows high-speed data capabilities similar to the initial version of Qualcomm's CDMA2000 1x solution deployed by many CDMA carriers, but it includes none of Qualcomm's intellectual property. This delay in the adoption of W-CDMA has delayed royalties that many Qualcomm investors were hoping the company would be collecting by now.

Once thought of as a niche technology, EDGE has become a more widespread choice for network operators around the world. A few years ago, Jacobs even went so far as to say that he thought EDGE would never see commercial use. Many others agreed with him, as it seemed that UMTS was just around the corner, making EDGE a moot option. But now things have changed, and EDGE threatens to slow the progress of the wireless world toward CDMA. The CDG and other parties with a vested interest in code-based wireless have come out in force to deter the widespread adoption of EDGE in GSM networks, but a few operators have already launched the service. In the near term, EDGE remains one of the most serious threats to CDMA simply because it delays overall progress toward a ubiquitous CDMA world.

But while EDGE is more of a marketing challenge to Qualcomm and CDMA promoters, another threat to the company's core business is driving more fundamental changes in the approach Qualcomm is taking to selling chipsets. Up until 2003, Qualcomm had little competition for its CDMA ASICs (application-specific integrated circuits) and associated chipsets. It has developed this as a major core competency, and chipsets are a major component of its business (providing 61 percent of total revenues, or $2.4 billion, in 2003, for example). But other equipment manufactures such as Nokia and Samsung have now successfully developed competitive chipsets for the CDMA2000 protocols. While

Qualcomm has traditionally held more than 90 percent of the CDMA chipset market, the company acknowledges that this will fall in future periods.

Basically, Qualcomm is seeing the natural ebbing of its first-mover advantage in code-based wireless. The company's lone pioneering efforts in CDMA are behind it, and while it still holds an unbalanced majority of the knowledge concerning the implementation of advanced versions of CDMA, other companies are moving up fast to provide competitive products and solutions. Qualcomm is therefore slowly transforming its business to rely less on this first-mover advantage and instead to compete more head-to-head with its peers based on the features and value of its products. Therefore, Qualcomm's lead in CDMA products will be maintained by staying on the cutting edge, offering designs that are at least a generation ahead of competitors' designs in terms of cost and features. To accomplish this, Qualcomm is relying on its superior intellectual property and maintaining huge investments in research and development. In fact, the company has announced that spending to produce superior ASICs and software for W-CDMA networks and handsets will increase substantially.

The company is now very active in producing a variety of chipset solutions to span the entire wireless market—not just CDMA. As the market for GSM and other time-based wireless networks boomed in the late 1990s, Qualcomm realized that integration of these technologies with CDMA would be essential. Since that time, the company has secured the necessary talent and rights to include GSM and other protocols in its CDMA products. Its multimode chipset solutions are now being extensively tested and qualified on numerous networks around the world. This effort to integrate CDMA with other competing technologies signals a major shift in Qualcomm's business strategy going forward.

With its efforts to move from a CDMA-centric product model to a blended, technology-neutral model, Qualcomm will now be faced with increased competition for its chipset products. Because of its competence in all things CDMA, though, the company still expects to maintain a significant share of the chipset market for wireless devices. In particular, the company has set the lofty goal of capturing 50 percent of the W-CDMA chipset market based on its confidence in a recent generation of MSM62xx chips that are being tested by several network operators.

These efforts to supply products across more technology platforms are also designed to help reduce Qualcomm's reliance on a few customers for the bulk of its revenue and profits. In 2003, more than 50 percent of the company's total revenue came from four companies—Samsung, LG Electronics, Motorola, and Kyocera. Samsung alone provided 17 percent of the company's revenue stream, causing concern among Qualcomm investors (Samsung has made significant efforts in producing its own CDMA chips and has made great progress in the GSM market as well). With the changes being brought about by the third-generation of wireless services—and the accompanying integration of technologies—Qualcomm is shifting its strategy to permeate the market beyond its traditional CDMA lines. Its prowess will once again be tested by its ability to adapt to the new environment and effectively court new customers. Based on the company's past successes and tenacious attitude, Qualcomm certainly has an above-average chance to once again defy the odds and meet its lofty goals, regardless of the formidable and daunting challenges it now faces—along with the entire wireless industry into the future.

Timeline of Selected Key Events

1942

Hedy Lamarr and George Antheil are awarded a patent for their "Secret Communications System," which—for the first time—depicts a technique for frequency hopping, a fundamental concept behind many methods of modern communications.

1948

Claude Shannon publishes *A Mathematical Theory of Communication*, a groundbreaking work that paved the way for a new field of study, information theory.

1957

After receiving a master's degree in electrical engineering from MIT, Andrew Viterbi moves to California and starts work on the U.S. satellite program at JPL.

1959

After receiving his doctorate from MIT, Irwin Jacobs joins the teaching staff alongside Claude Shannon to continue exploring new ground in information theory.

1964

Irwin Jacobs takes a one-year leave of absence from teaching to work as a research fellow at JPL, where he spends a significant amount of time alongside fellow MIT graduate Andrew Viterbi.

1966

Irwin Jacobs leaves MIT for California to help build a new electrical engineering department at UCSD.

1968

Linkabit is formed by Irwin Jacobs, Andrew Viterbi, and Len Kleinrock, to pool their resources as consultants in communications technology.

1972

Irwin Jacobs resigns from teaching to dedicate his efforts to running the fast-growing Linkabit.

1980

Linkabit is purchased by M/A-COM.

1983

The first (analog) cellular networks are commercially deployed in the United States.

1985

April—Jacobs leaves Linkabit, which had grown to over 1,400 employees. Viterbi and several other key employees quit within weeks of Jacobs's departure.

July—Qualcomm is cofounded by seven ex-Linkabit colleagues: Irwin Jacobs, Andrew Viterbi, Adelia Coffman, Harvey White, Andrew Cohen, Klein Gilhousen, and Franklin Antonio.

Omninet awards a contract to Qualcomm to develop what was to become OmniTRACS for the trucking industry.

1986

October—Qualcomm files for a patent on using CDMA in a mobile communications application.

1987

September—Qualcomm records $6.55 million in revenues and $208,000 in net income for its first full year (fiscal 1987).

1988

August—Qualcomm and Omninet merge, with Omninet officers taking three board seats.

September—The OmniTRACS product is commercially introduced.

September—The CTIA releases its User Performance Requirements for digital cellular technology.

October—The first OmniTRACS contract is signed with Schneider National.

October—Qualcomm first introduces the concept of cellular CDMA.

1989

January—The TIA selects TDMA as the basis for the next-generation cellular standard in the United States.

February—Qualcomm visits PacTel to pitch the idea of CDMA for cellular networks.

April—PacTel commits $1 million to Qualcomm to fund CDMA prototype development.

April—Qualcomm sells 2,500,000 shares of Series B preferred stock for $8 per share.

September—Qualcomm sells Series C preferred stock for $8 per share.

November—First-ever CDMA field trial is held in San Diego with PacTel Cellular.

November—Qualcomm files in the United States for three fundamental patents on CDMA.

1990

February—Field trial of CDMA in New York with NYNEX Mobile commences.

March—The TIA approves the IS-54 standard (which uses TDMA) in North America.

July—NYNEX initiates advance payments of $2.25 million to Qualcomm for future credit on CDMA equipment.

August—Qualcomm commences operation of OmniTRACS in Canada with Cancom.

August—Qualcomm signs a multimillion-dollar deal with AT&T, NYNEX, and Ameritech to develop and provide CDMA technology.

December—NYNEX requests that the advance from July be repaid.

1991

January—Commercial operation of OmniTRACS commences in Europe.

May—Qualcomm enters into a joint CDMA development agreement with ETRI (South Korea).

September—Qualcomm records $1.1 million in monthly service revenue for OmniTRACS.

November—Qualcomm files with the FCC for an experimental license for CDMA in PCS systems.

November—Large-scale CDMA field trial is held in San Diego—five cells, nine sectors, and seventy mobile units.

December—Qualcomm IPO nets the company $68 million (73.6 million shares offered @ $1.00 per share).

1992

January—The CTIA reaffirms its support for the TDMA standard in the United States; an open forum for WBSS is recommended.

March—Qualcomm is awarded a patent for the CDMA soft-handoff method.

April—Qualcomm signs a CDMA license agreement with Nokia, the world's second largest handset manufacturer at the time.

May—Field demos of CDMA with Deutsche Bundespost Telekom in Germany take place.

June—The CTIA asks the TIA to expedite the adoption of the CDMA standard in North America.

September—US West New Vector announces the purchase of CDMA for the Seattle market in late 1993.

1993

March—Qualcomm conducts its first meetings with Chinese officials to discuss CDMA.

March—Bell Atlantic Mobile (BAM) chooses CDMA for its cellular network.

March—South Korea adopts CDMA as the platform for the nation's wireless services.

March—Four South Korean manufacturers sign CDMA support agreements with Qualcomm.

July—Secondary public offering nets $151 million (46.4 million shares @ $3.44).

July—The TIA adopts CDMA as a North American standard (IS-95A).

August—Congress and President Clinton authorize auctions of spectrum in PCS bands.

December—Qualcomm signs an agreement in Beijing to conduct CDMA field trials.

December—The CDMA Development Group (CDG) is founded.

1994

February—QPE, a joint venture with Sony, is formed to manufacture CDMA phones.

April—Qualcomm begins testing CDMA networks in China.

October—Qualcomm announces the successful completion of Chinese field tests of CDMA.

December—Qualcomm and Northern Telecom create a strategic alliance to market and manufacture CDMA infrastructure equipment.

1995

June—PCS PrimeCo selects CDMA as the basis for its PCS network.

July—Sprint PCS adopts CDMA as the technology for its PCS network.

July—Allen Salmasi leaves Qualcomm to become CEO of Nextwave Telecom.

August—Public offering nets $486 million (92 million shares @ $5.47).

October—First commercial launch of a CDMA network in Hong Kong.

December—Auction of C-block PCS licenses begins after months of delay in litigation.

1996

January—CDMA-based networks are commercially launched in South Korea.

February—The United States passes the Telecommunications Act of 1996 to deregulate telecommunications and spur competition.

November—China's Great Wall Mobile Communications drafts a plan to build a CDMA network.

November—PrimeCo (now Verizon Wireless) launches cdmaOne in fifteen U.S. markets.

1997

February—Qualcomm agrees to contribute $18 million to gain the naming rights for San Diego's Qualcomm Stadium (previously Jack Murphy Stadium) until 2017.

April—Qualcomm launches the Q Phone.

May—Qualcomm signs a deal to sell wireless phones to Great Wall in China.

November—Great Wall begins installing a trial CDMA network.

1998

January—There are now 7.8 million CDMA subscribers worldwide, representing a 3.7 percent market share.

March—China postpones approval of Qualcomm's manufacturing plants, delaying regional CDMA phone systems in Xian, Beijing, Shanghai, and Guangxi.

April—The TIA endorses CDMA2000 as the 3G solution for the International Telecommunications Union (ITU).

September—Leap Wireless spin-off is completed.

December—U.S. trade representatives file a complaint with the EC over third-generation (3G) standards policies in Europe.

1999

March—Qualcomm and Ericsson reach a major agreement to cross-license CDMA, removing a major roadblock to CDMA's acceptance as a 3G standard.

April—Qualcomm's stock jumps on reports that China's telecom ministry plans to buy $500 million worth of CDMA equipment.

May—The United States accidentally bombs the Chinese embassy in Bosnia during Bosnian conflict, putting a chill on U.S.–China relations.

July—Public offering nets $1.1 billion (28 million shares @ $39.13).

October—GlobalStar officially rolls out service on a regional basis.

November—The United States agrees to support China's entry into the World Trade Organization.

December—Qualcomm sells its phone manufacturing capabilities to Kyocera.

2000

January—Qualcomm agrees to acquire SnapTrack, a developer of GPS technology, for $1 billion in stock.

February—Qualcomm drafts a deal with Unicom for a nationwide CDMA network. Within days, news reports state that the Chinese government has delayed the CDMA network indefinitely.

March—Chinese Premier Zhu Rongji denies any delay in rolling out CDMA.

March—Cofounder Andrew Viterbi retires from Qualcomm.

June—Qualcomm licenses CDMA technology to eight Chinese manufacturers.

September—Senate approves normalizing trade relations with China, an important step for entry into the WTO.

October—SK Telecom launches the world's first 3G CDMA2000 1X commercial service.

December—China's telecom ministry backs deployment of a nationwide CDMA network.

2001

January—Qualcomm introduces BREW applications platform.

March—Unicom invites companies to bid on multibillion-dollar CDMA network.

April—A U.S. spy plane collides with a Chinese fighter jet and lands in China.

May—Unicom postpones awarding CDMA contracts.

May—Unicom signs CDMA equipment contracts worth $1.5 billion with Ericsson, Motorola, and others.

May—Qualcomm holds the inaugural BREW developers' conference.

August—Qualcomm ships its 500 millionth CDMA chip.

September—CDMA surpasses 100 million subscribers worldwide.

November—China is accepted into the WTO. Unicom says it will deploy its CDMA network in January.

December—President Bush formalizes permanent normal trade status with China.

2002

January—Unicom launches a national CDMA wireless network.

January—SK Telecom launches CDMA2000 1xEV-DO in South Korea.

October—Monet Mobile launches the first CDMA2000 1xEV-DO commercial network in the United States.

2003

February—Qualcomm announces its first dividend payment to stockholders.

February—Qualcomm announces the first commercial trial of GSM1x with China Unicom.

May—China Unicom reaches 10 million CDMA subscribers.

September—Qualcomm ships its one billionth CDMA chip.

October—More than 50 million BREW applications are downloaded.

2004

January—Qualcomm announces that 12 percent of its royalty income is coming from W-CDMA products.

January—Verizon Wireless announces that it will launch a nationwide CDMA 1xEV-DO network in the United States.

February—Qualcomm hosts the inaugural European BREW developers' conference in London.

March—CDMA surpasses 200 million subscribers worldwide.

June—SprintPCS reverses its earlier decision and commits to launching CDMA 1xEV-DO.

June—China announces the successful testing of TD-SCDMA phones and pledges a commercial launch in June 2005.

July—Court rules that Texas Instruments breached patent portfolio agreement with Qualcomm.

August—Qualcomm drops suit against Texas Instruments to avoid disclosing license terms.

Notes

⟶

1. The concept of entropy was originally developed in physics to measure the degree of disorder of a thermodynamic system. Shannon's surprising insight was that more entropy or disorder was required in order to transmit information. Less entropy, or less disorder, meant more uniformity that conveyed less information.

2. Expounded in Clayton Christensen's books *The Innovator's Dilemma* and *The Innovator's Solution* is the intoxicating idea that you don't have to be best in order to win. Indeed, the effort to be best may create a failure framework that renders you vulnerable to disruption from smaller companies wielding inferior products in markets that you do not even serve. A popular professor at Harvard Business School and a mesmerizing speaker at companies around the world, Christensen offers the prime insight that technology overshoot—providing more performance and costly features than customers need—opens the way for entrepreneurs to attack established companies from below.

    Turning on its head the usual assumption that a technology must be as much as ten times superior to defeat an incumbent, Christensen showed that under conditions of overshoot, a disruptive technology can win while supplying ten times less performance. Since Christensen's books, marketeers have claimed disruptive magic for every new gizmo that supposedly, by Robert I. Cringely's definition, "puts an end to the good life for technologies that preceded it."

3. Intel is the key backer of WiMax, and Nextel has excited Flarion sponsors with a high-profile market test of its "flash-OFDM" system. Two heavyweights, to be sure. But neither system can claim anything close to the ten times advantage many experts consider to be required to overtake the market. Some analysts claim that CDMA2000 is bogged down "in the hundreds of kilobits range," while WiMax, Wi-Fi, and OFDM offer many megabits of capacity. But the reverse is probably true. As Qualcomm upgrades CDMA2000 EV-DO to Release A, which offers 3.1 Mbps downstream and 1.8 Mbps upstream, along with 30 milliseconds of latency, all over many mobile square kilometers of coverage area, Wi-Fi remains a LAN (local area network) technology; WiMax remains in the laboratory, now slated for action in 2006 or 2007; and Flarion's chief marketing attribute is that it is not a royalty-reaping gorilla like Qualcomm.

4. Bill Joy's statement was made at Esther Dyson's PC Forum conference in Scottsdale Arizona in 1990.

5. Today, software on individual machines still bogs down in the macrocosmic swamps of complexity. But on the Net, yields rise exponentially in proportion to the number and power of the machines on the network. Initially designed for the cramped memory spaces of personal digital assistants, Sun's Java programming language began the software revolution in wireless. Today there are about 100 million handsets bearing Java virtual machines that can execute any applet written in that increasingly popular language. But Java suffers from its strengths. It is a language and a virtual machine, not a full-fledged new system.

CHAPTER 1

1. Elizabeth Weise, "Hedy Lamarr—Inventor, A Sultry Screen Star Who Didn't Just Act—She Invented," March 10, 1997. Also see http://wireless.oldcolo.com/course/hedy.htm.

2. "Andrew Viterbi, Electrical Engineer," an oral history conducted in 1999 by David Morton, IEEE History Center, Rutgers University, New Brunswick, N.J.

3. Interview with the author. Unless otherwise cited, all further highlighted quotations also come from interviews conducted by the author.

CHAPTER 2

1. "Andrew Viterbi, Electrical Engineer," an oral history conducted in 1999 by David Morton, IEEE History Center, Rutgers University, New Brunswick, N. J.

2. Timothy J. McClain, "San Diego's Economic Romance with Telecommunications," *San Diego Metropolitan Magazine*, May 1998. Available at http://www.sandiegometro.com/1998/may/telecom.html.

3. "San Diego: Capital of the Wireless Future," *Wireless Future Magazine*, November–December 2002.

CHAPTER 4

1. Timothy J. McClain, "San Diego's Economic Romance with Telecommunications," *San Diego Metropolitan Magazine*, May 1998. Available at http://www.sandiegometro.com/1998/may/telecom.html.

2. Carol Schmidt, MSU Communications Services, "Gilhousens Give $5 million to MSU College of Engineering," source: http://www.montana.edu/foundation/gilhousen_story.htm.

3. Charles Petrie, "George Gilder—On the Bandwidth of Plenty," *Internet Computing*, December 9, 1996.

4. McClain, "San Diego's Economic Romance."

CHAPTER 6

1. W. D. White, "A Conversation with Claude Shannon," interview conducted by R. Price, edited by F. Ellersick, *IEEE Communications Magazine*, vol. 22. No. 5, May 1984, pp. 123–126.

CHAPTER 9

1. While the industry pundits questioned Iridium and Globalstar, an even more ambitious venture was still to come—a vision from the minds of Craig McCaw and Bill Gates called Teledesic. In 1994, McCaw and Gates proposed to the FCC an amazing system of 840 low-earth-orbit satellites streaming broadband voice and data services around the globe by 2001 (at the time, little more than 300 satellites were active worldwide). This system was not designed to support mobile users, but rather urban and rural homes and businesses that needed an alternative to landline services.

CHAPTER 11

1. Charles Petrie, "George Gilder—On the Bandwidth of Plenty," *Internet Computing*, December 9, 1996.

2. Bradley J. Fikes, "How Mighty Qualcomm Got That Way," *North County Times*, January 2000. Available at http://www.nctimes.net/news/010200/b.html.

CHAPTER 13

1. Kevin Maney, "Qualcomm Poised to Take Off—If Cell Phone Market Does," *USA Today*, April 22, 2003.

2. Timothy J. McClain, "Qualcomm's Irwin Jacobs: After Building a San Diego Industry, He's Taking On the World," *San Diego Metropolitan Magazine*, February 1997. Available at http://www.sandiegometro.com/1997/feb/coverstory.html.

3. Russ Arensman, "Meet the New Qualcomm," *Electronic Business*, March 1, 2000.

CHAPTER 16

1. Dan Briody, "Qualcomm Faces the China Syndrome," *Red Herring*, February 13, 2001.

2. Bill Roberts, "Riding the Big Wireless Wave," *Electronic Business*, July 1, 2003.

CHAPTER 17

1. Dean Calbreath and Jennifer Davies, "Qualcomm's Persistence Pays Dividends in China," Copley News Service, January 28, 2002. Available at http://www.irps.ucsd.edu/about/innews2002/copley012802.php.

2. Ibid.

3. Ibid.

4. Dan Briody, "Qualcomm Faces the China Syndrome," *Red Herring*, February 13, 2001.

Glossary of Key Acronyms and Terms

1G First-generation wireless, characterized by analog, voice-only transmission.

1xEV-DO 1x evolution—data optimized. An improved version of 1xRTT, initially offering high-speed data capabilities up to 2.4 Mbps in a dedicated 5-MHz frequency band; commercialized in 2001.

1xEV-DV 1x evolution—data and voice. A future version of 1xRTT that promises peak data rates of 3.1 Mbps. This differs from 1xEV-DO in that data and voice information dynamically share the same frequency spectrum. Currently being tested, this technology should be commercialized by 2006.

1xRTT An evolutionary step in the CDMA2000 family of standards that increased the capacity of earlier systems and provided for 144 Kbps of data; commercialized in 2000. Also referred to as 1x.

2G Second-generation wireless, phased in during the 1990s, going from analog to all-digital transmission with minimal data capabilities.

3G Third-generation wireless, which includes high-speed data capabilities enabling broadband multimedia and global roaming.

ACTS Advanced Communications Technologies and Services, a group funded by the European Commission.

AGC Automatic gain control.

AMPS Advanced mobile phone system, an early cellular standard based on analog technology.

analog Pertaining to data or signals using continuous-wave input and output. See also *digital*.

ANSI-41 The network interface standard for air interface protocols such as GSM and IS-95 (CDMA), used primarily in North America.

ASIC Application-specific integrated circuit; for example, those used in mobile phones, automobiles, and so on.

ASP Average selling price, on which intellectual property royalties are calculated.

BREW Binary run-time environment for wireless, an open-source programming platform developed by Qualcomm for code-based wireless (CDMA).

BTS Base transceiver station.

CAI Common air interface, a protocol for radio communications.

CDG CDMA Development Group, a group formed by Qualcomm and its initial partners, like PacTel, in 1993, to evangelize CDMA to the cellular industry.

CDMA Code-division multiple access; also referred to in this book as *code-based wireless.*

CDMA2000 The code-based wireless (CDMA) version for 3G, developed to meet the goals of IMT-2000.

cell The calling area controlled by a base transceiver station (BTS).

CEPT Conference of European Posts and Telecommunications.

code-based wireless Wireless technology based on CDMA.

CTIA Cellular Telecommunications & Internet Association, previously the Cellular Telecommunications Industry Association.

digital Pertaining to data or signals consisting of discrete states, often represented as a stream of 0s and 1s. See also *analog.*

DoD U.S. Department of Defense.

DOJ U.S. Department of Justice.

EDGE Enhanced data rate for GSM evolution, an intermediate upgrade for 2G versions of GSM, providing data capabilities.

ETRI South Korean Electronics and Telecommunications Research Institute.

ETSI European Telecommunications Standards Institute.

EU European Union.

FDMA Frequency-division multiple access; also referred to in this book as *frequency-based wireless.*

First-generation wireless See *1G.*

FRAMES Future Radio Wideband Multiple Access System, a project set up under the ACTS group in Europe.

frequency hopping Radio transmission in which the signal hops over a number of preset frequencies; originally developed for military applications to prevent signal jamming and later applied to commercial wireless.

frequency-based wireless Wireless technology based on FDMA.

GPS Global positioning system.

GPRS General packet radio service.

GSM Global system for mobile communications (originally *groupe special mobile*), a digital standard using time-based wireless (TDMA) that was adopted by the European Union.

GSM-MAP The network interface standard for the global system of mobile communications (GSM) used commonly in Europe.

hard handoff Passing a mobile transmission from one radio tower to another with no overlap between the towers handling the signals. See also *soft handoff*.

iDEN Integrated digital enhanced network, Motorola's proprietary technology utilizing time-based wireless (TDMA).

IEEE Institute of Electrical and Electronics Engineers.

i-Mode A wireless Internet service introduced in 1999 in Japan by NTT DoCoMo.

IMT-2000 International mobile telecommunications in 2000, a road map for future wireless services established by the International Telecommunications Union (ITU).

IP (1) Intellectual property; (2) Internet protocol.

IPR Intellectual property rights.

IS-54 The initial standard for digital time-division multiple access (TDMA) wireless, issued by the TIA.

IS-95 The initial standard for code-based (CDMA) wireless, issued by the TIA in 1993.

IS-95A Revised standard for code-based wireless (CDMA), issued by the TIA in 1995.

IS-95B Revised standard for code-based wireless (CDMA), including 64-Kbps data transmission, issued by the TIA in 1999.

IS-136 A standard using TDMA that followed and improved upon IS-54.

ITU International Telecommunications Union, based in Geneva, Switzerland; originally founded in 1865 as the International Telegraph Union.

JPL NASA's Jet Propulsion Laboratory; affiliated with the California Institute of Technology in Pasadena.

KMT Korean Mobile Telecom.

LEO Low earth orbit.

Linkabit The first company formed by Irwin Jacobs, Andrew Viterbi, and Len Kleinrock in 1968.

LMNQ A consortium of Lucent, Motorola, Nortel, and Qualcomm, established in 1997 to develop 3G standards for code-based wireless (CDMA).

M/A-COM Name derived from Microwave Associates Conglomerate; the company that purchased Linkabit in 1980.

MFRR Most favorable royalty rate, applied to IP licensing agreements.

MII Ministry of Information Industry of Mainland China; renamed from the Ministry of Post and Telecommunications.

MoC South Korean Ministry of Communications.

MTS Mobile telephony system, adopted in the United States after World War II; a predecessor of cellular.

N-AMPS Narrowband advanced mobile phone service.

OHG Operators Harmonization Group, established in 1998 by mobile communications operators to harmonize 3G proposals submitted to the ITU.

OmniTRACS Two-way satellite-based tracking and communication system developed by Qualcomm for the trucking industry in the late 1980s.

PCS Personal communications services.

PLA People's Liberation Army of Mainland China.

POP (1) Persons of population, or potential customers in a region licensed to a network operator; (2) point of presence, or equipment located at a network node.

prior art Concepts, including technical specifications and drawings, submitted with previous patent applications.

PSTN Public switched telephone network.

QPE Qualcomm Personal Electronics, a joint venture with Sony started in 1994.

RF Radio frequency.

R-UIM Removable user identity module card.

SDO Standards development organization.

second-generation wireless See *2G*.

SIM Subscriber identity module card.

SMS Short messaging services available on digital systems; for example, text messaging.

soft handoff Passing a mobile transmission from one radio tower to another with a brief overlap as both towers process the signals. See also *hard handoff*.

spread spectrum A method of radio transmission in which a signal is carried across a wide band of frequencies simultaneously; originally developed to avoid detection in military communications.

TDMA Time-division multiple access; also referred to in this book as *time-based wireless*.

teledensity The number of telephones per capita, a measure of the degree of development of a country's communications infrastructure.

third-generation wireless See *3G*.

TIA Telecommunications Industry Association.

time-based wireless Wireless technology based on TDMA.

TSSC Technical Standards Subcommittee of the TIA.

UMTS Universal mobile telecommunications system, a wideband CDMA version for 3G in Europe.

UPR User performance requirements.

USPTO U.S. Patent and Trademark Office.

VLSI Very large-scale integration of computer circuits.

vocoder Voice encoder used in digital systems.

VRC Variable-rate encoder.

WAP Wireless application protocol.

WBSS Wideband spread spectrum.

W-CDMA Wideband code-division multiple access (CDMA), a standard for 3G wireless developed in Europe.

WLL Wireless local loop.

WTO World Trade Organization.

Bibliography

--·-·--·-·--·-·--·-·--·-·--·-·--·-·--·-·--·-·--·-·--·-·--·-·--·-·--→

"Andrew Viterbi, Electrical Engineer," an oral history conducted in 1999 by David Morton, IEEE History Center, Rutgers University, New Brunswick, NJ.

"Bell Atlantic Mobile chooses CDMA." *Telephony*, March 8, 1993.

"Digital Cellular Debate Remains Heated Despite CDMA's Success." *Telephony*, June 28, 1993.

"Foreign Experience Wins Over China Unicom in CDMA Bids." *China Online*, May 16, 2001. Available at http://www.chinaonline.com/industry/telecom/ NewsArchive/cs-protected/ 2001/May/B201051411.asp.

"Industry Group Clears CDMA as Standard for Cellular Systems." *Wall Street Journal*, July 19, 1993.

"Irwin M. Jacobs, Electrical Engineer," an oral history conducted in 1999 by David Morton, IEEE History Center, Rutgers University, New Brunswick, N.J., U.S.A.

"Nokia and Qualcomm Ink Deal." *Telephony*, April 20, 1992.

"On the Road to Success with RLE's Alumni Company Founders." *RLE Currents*, vol. 8, no. 1 (Spring 1996). Available at http://rleweb.mit.edu/publications/ currents/8-1cov.htm#jaco.

"Spread Betting." *The Economist*, June 19, 2003.

Aley, James. "Heads We Win, Tails We Win." *Fortune*, March 3, 2003.

Andrews, Edmund L. "In Auctions of Airwaves, the Sky Seems to Be the Limit." *New York Times*, February 26, 1996.

Arensman, Russ. "Meet the New Qualcomm." *Electronic Business*, March 1, 2000.

Arnold, Wayne. "Cellular Operators in Europe, Asia Plan Statement on Ericsson-Qualcomm Battle." *Wall Street Journal*, December 18, 1998.

Ausubel, Lawrence M., Peter Cramton, R. Preston McAfee, and John McMillan, "Synergies in Wireless Telephony: Evidence from the Broadband PCS Auctions." *Journal of Economics and Management Strategy*, vol. 6, no. 3 (1997), 497–527.

Backover, Andrew. "Nextwave Stubbornly Clings to Life." *USA Today*, July 2, 2001.

Bekkers, Rudi, Geert Duysters, and Bart Verspagen. "Intellectual Property Rights, Strategic Technology Agreements and Market Structure. The Case of GSM." Eindhoven Centre for Innovation Studies, Eindhoven University of Technology, Eindhoven, the Netherlands, September 2000.

Bellisio, J. A., "Report: Sixth Meeting of the FCC Technological Advisory Council." Federal Communications Commission, October 22, 2000.

Briody, Dan. "Qualcomm Faces the China Syndrome." *Red Herring*, February 13, 2001.

Calbreath, Dean, and Jennifer Davies. "Qualcomm's Persistence Pays Dividends in China." Copley News Service, January 28, 2002. Available at http://www-irps .ucsd.edu/about/innews2002/copley012802.php.

Carlson, Caron. "Europe Requests Proof of 3G Charges." *Wireless Week*, February 1, 1999. Available at http://www.wirelessweek.com/article/CA3907.

Carlson, Caron. "Study: Europe, U.S. Won't Budge on 3G." *Wireless Week*, January 25, 1999. Available at http://www.wirelessweek.com/article/CA3952.

Chao, Julie. "Qualcomm's Prospects Suddenly Become Very Good." *Wall Street Journal*, June 7, 1995.

Chaudhury, Prodip, Werner Mohr, and Seizo Onoe, "The 3GPP Proposal for IMT-2000." *IEEE Communications Magazine*, December 1999.

Choi, Hae Won, Pui-Wing Tam, and Khanh Tranin. "Korean Cell Firms Wary of U.S. Standard." *Wall Street Journal*, July 10, 2000.

Cowhey, Peter F., Jonathan D. Aronson, and John E. Richards. "The Peculiar Evolution of 3G Wireless Networks: Institutional Logic, Politics, and Property Rights." (working paper), February 25, 2003. Found at http://www-cepr .stanford.edu/programs/SST_Seminars/Cowhey.pdf.

Cunningham, Ralph. "License or Be Damned." *Managing Intellectual Property*, July/August 1999.

Daniels, Guy. "Qualcomm vs. the Koreans." *Telecom Insider*, October 12, 2001.

Declaration of Walter Hanig to the Superior Court of the State of California, County of San Diego, Central Division. Case No. 763814, May 25, 2001. Available at http://www.a-k.com/client_declaration.pdf.

Donald Schilling, Electrical Engineer, an oral history conducted in 1999 by David Hochfelder, IEEE History Center, Rutgers University, New Brunswick, N.J., U.S.A.

Farquhar, Michele C., Memorandum Opinion and Order, "In re Applications of NextWave Personal Communications, Inc. for Various C-Block Broadband PCS

Licenses." Federal Communications Commission, February 14, 1997. Available at http://www.fcc.gov/Bureaus/Wireless/Orders/1997/da970328.txt.

Fikes, Bradley J. "How Mighty Qualcomm Got That Way." *North County Times*, January 2000. Available at http://www.nctimes.net/news/010200/b.html.

Forney, Matt. "Walled Out: For Qualcomm, China Has Beckoned Twice and Then Hung Up." *Wall Street Journal*, July 13, 2000.

Forney, Matt, and Peter Wonacott. "China Telecom Firm's U.S. Deal at Risk—Unicom, Slated for Listing, Looks Unlikely to Use Qualcomm Technology." *Wall Street Journal*, May 25, 2000.

Frezza, Bill. "CDMA: The Revenge of the Nerds." *Network Computing*, April 1997. Available at http://www.networkcomputing.com/807/807colfrezza.html.

Frezza, Bill. "CDMA: Blazing a Trail of Broken Dreams." *Network Computing*, April 1996. Available at http://www.networkcomputing.com/706/706frezza.html.

Frezza, Bill. "The Future Unplugged: I Want My STV." *Network Computing*, October 1995. Available at http://www.networkcomputing.com/613/613frezza.html.

Frezza, Bill. "Succumbing to Techno-Seduction." *Network Computing*, April 1995. Available at http://www.networkcomputing.com/604/604frezza.html.

Gilder, George. *Telecosm: How Infinite Bandwidth Will Revolutionize Our World*. New York: Free Press, 2000.

Gilder, George. "The New Rule of Wireless." *Forbes ASAP*, March 1, 1993.

Gilhousen, Klein, Irwin M. Jacobs, Roberto Padovani, Andrew J. Viterbi, Lindsay A. Weaver, Jr., and Charles E. Wheatley III. "On the Capacity of a Cellular CDMA System." *IEEE Transactions on Vehicular Technology*, vol. 40, no. 2 (May 1991).

Gleick, James. "Patently Absurd." *The New York Times Magazine*, March 12, 2000. Available at http://www.nytimes.com/library/magazine/home/20000312mag-patents.html.

Gohring, Nancy. "Fool's Gold: Many Risk-Taking Dreamers Were Lured to Wireless by the Promise of C Block Riches." *Telephony*, September 21, 1998. Available at http://telephonyonline.com/ar/telecom_fools_gold_risktaking/index.htm.

Hardy, Quentin. "Qualcomm, Ericsson Are Close to Pact to End Long-Running Patent Dispute." *Wall Street Journal*, February 22, 1999.

Hardy, Quentin. "Jacobs's Patter: An Inventor's Promise Has Companies Taking Big Cellular Gamble." *Wall Street Journal*, September 6, 1996.

Hardy, Quentin, and Leslie Cauley. "Qualcomm Set to Get Support of Key Group." *Wall Street Journal*, June 5, 1995.

International Telecommunication Union, "ITU Warns That CDMA-Based RTT Proposals for IMT-2000 Could Be Excluded from Further Consideration if IPR

Stalemate Is Not Resolved by the Year End." Press release, December 7, 1998. Available at http://www.itu.int/newsarchive/press_releases/1998/34.html.

Jacobs, Jeff. "London Investor Day." PowerPoint Presentation, November 12, 2003.

Jacobs, Paul. "London Investor Day." PowerPoint Presentation, November 19, 2002.

Jerome, Marty. "Air War." *Byte.com*, August 1997. Available at http://www.byte.com/art/9708/sec7/art1.htm.

Johnston, Carl, Michael Overdorf, and Clayton Christensen. "Disrupting Mobile Commerce." March 2001. Available at http://www.innosight.com/documents/Mobile Commerce.pdf.

Keller, John J., and Mary Lu Carnevale. "AT&T, Two Bell Firms Plan Technology to Boost Capacity of Cellular Systems." *Wall Street Journal*, August 2, 1990.

Kelly, Kevin. Testimony Before the Subcommittee on Trade of the House Committee on Ways and Means Hearing on Trade Relations with Europe and the New Transatlantic Economic Partnership, July 28, 1998. Available at http://waysand means.house.gov/legacy/trade/105cong/7-28-98/7-28kell.htm.

Kharif, Olga. "Qualcomm's Mixed Signals." *BusinessWeek Online*, May 8, 2003. Available at http://www.businessweek.com/technology/content/may2003/tc2003058_1563_tc05 5.htm.

LaForge, Perry M. "Global View of CDMA History for TDMA Operators." CDMA Development Group, March 2001. Available at http://www.cdg.org/resources/Guest_column.asp?columnid=8.

Lee, William C. Y. *Lee's Essentials of Wireless Communications*. New York: McGraw-Hill, 2000.

Lindstrom, Ann H. "Qualcomm, Korea Start CDMA Project." *Telephony*, June 3, 1991.

Lynch, Grahame. *Bandwidth Bubble Bust: The Rise and Fall of the Global Telecom Industry*. Lincoln NE: Author's Choice Press, 2001.

M•CAM, Inc. "The Problems with Patents and the Impact on the Investing Public." July 23, 2001. Available at http://www.m-cam.com/downloads/MCAMReport.pdf.

M•CAM, Inc. "Intellectual Property Analysis of Qualcomm's Mobile Wireless Patent Portfolio (CDMA)." March 9, 2001. Available at http://www.m-cam.com/patentlyobvious/20010309_qualcomm.pdf.

Mason, Charles F. "A Niche Market in the US." *Telephony*, June 20, 1994.

Mason, Charles F. "How CDMA Came from Behind and Overtook TDMA (Part I)." *Telephony*, June 21, 1993.

Mason, Charles F. "CTIA Board Reaffirms TDMA, Qualcomm Suffers Setback." *Telephony*, January 13, 1992.

Mathieson, Rick. "Making Waves in San Diego: The Wireless Coast Comes of Age." *Mpulse*, January 2002. Available at http://www.cooltown.com/mpulse/0102-sandiego.asp.

McClain, Timothy J. "San Diego's Economic Romance with Telecommunications." *San Diego Metropolitan Magazine*, May 1998. Available at http://www.sandiegometro.com/1998/may/telecom.html.

McClain, Timothy J. "Qualcomm's Irwin Jacobs: After Building a San Diego Industry, He's Taking On the World." *San Diego Metropolitan Magazine*, February 1997. Available at http://www.sandiegometro.com/1997/feb/coverstory.html.

McGough, Robert, and Quentin Hardy. "Is Qualcomm Mixing Signals on Korea Sales?" *Wall Street Journal*, May 18, 1999.

Murray, James B. *Wireless Nation: The Frenzied Launch of the Cellular Revolution.* Cambridge, MA: Perseus Publishing, October 2002.

NextWave Telecom, "Statement of Raymond P. Dolan, NextWave Chief Operating Officer, presented to Senate Budget Committee." February 10, 2000. Available at http://www.nextwavetel.com/news/press_releases/pr_0211000.html.

O'Shea, Dan. "Northern Telecom Backs Qualcomm, CDMA." *Telephony*, December 12, 1994.

Padovani, Roberto. "Beyond 3G—CDMA Evolution." PowerPoint Presentation to the San Diego Telecom Council SIG, June 18, 2002.

Palmintera, Diane, Joan Bannon, Marci Levin, and Arturo Pagan. "Developing High-Technology Communities: San Diego." Innovation Associates, Inc., Reston, VA. Available at http://www.innovationassoc.com/documents/SD_Report.pdf, April 2000.

Petrie, Charles. "George Gilder—On the Bandwidth of Plenty." *Internet Computing*, December 9, 1996.

Pickholtz, Raymond L., Laurence B. Milstein, and Donald L. Shilling, "Spread Spectrum for Mobile Communications," *IEEE Transactions on Vehicular Technology*, vol. 40, no. 2 (May 1991).

Pulliam, Susan. "Qualcomm's Digital Technology Wins Praise, but Marketing Delays Are Raising Questions." *Wall Street Journal*, October 11, 1994.

QPSX. "IP Based Business Strategies: Qualcomm and Interdigital Capitalize on Digital Wireless Inventions." March 27, 2001. Available at www.qpsx.com.au/download/Qualcomm&Interdigital.pdf.

QPSX. "Trends in Patents: Qualcomm Wields Its Patent Power." March 27, 2001. Available at http://www.qpsx.com.au/download/QualcommWields.pdf.

Qualcomm Incorporated. "Qualcomm Makes Commitment for $300 Million Strategic Investment in NextWave Telecom." Press release, August 16, 2001. Available at http://www.qualcomm.com/press/releases/2001/press58.html.

Qualcomm Incorporated. "The Economics of Wireless Mobile Data." (corporate white paper), March 15, 2001. Available at http://www.qualcomm.com/main/whitepapers/WirelessMobileData.pdf.

Qualcomm Incorporated. "QUALCOMM Responds to Ericsson's Proposal for Harmonization." Press release, December 10, 1998. Available at http://www.qualcomm.com/press/releases/1998/press581.html.

Qualcomm Incorporated. "Ericsson Drops Three Essential Patents from Lawsuit Against Qualcomm and Surrenders Two Others." Press release, October 20, 1998. Available at http://www.qualcomm.com/press/releases/1998/press777.html.

Qualcomm Incorporated. "QUALCOMM Provides IPR Position to ITU for Third-Generation Proposals." Press release, October 13, 1998. Available at http://www.qualcomm.com/press/releases/1998/press779.html.

Qualcomm Incorporated. "Qualcomm Responds to ETSI on Third Generation Technology Issues." Press release, August 6, 1998. Available at http://www.qualcomm.com/press/releases/1998/press813.html.

Qualcomm Incorporated. "Qualcomm Supports Converged Standard for IMT-2000." Press release, June 2, 1998. Available at http://www.qualcomm.com/press/releases/1998/press849.html.

Qualcomm Incorporated, 10K SEC filings, 1996–2003. Available at http://www.qualcomm.com/IR/.

Qualcomm Incorporated. "CDMA vs. GSM." January 1995.

Qualcomm Incorporated. "Economics of PCS: A Tale of Two Networks." November 1994.

Qualcomm Incorporated. Annual reports to shareholders, 1991–2003.

Rivette, Kevin G., and David Kline. *Rembrandts in the Attic: Unlocking the Hidden Value of Patents*. Boston: Harvard Business School Press, 1999.

Roberts, Bill. "Riding the Big Wireless Wave." *Electronic Business*, July 1, 2003.

Scibor-Marchocki, Romuald Ireneus. "A Tribute to Hedy Lamarr." Available at http://www.rism.com/atribute.htm#sonobuoy.

Shapiro, Carl. "Navigating the Patent Thicket: Cross Licenses, Patent Pools and Standard-Setting." NBER Conference on Innovation Policy and the Economy, March 2001.

Simard, Caroline, and Joel West. "The Role of Founder Ties in the Formation of San Diego's 'Wireless Valley.'" May 12, 2003. Available at www.business.auc.dk/druid/conferences/summer2003/papers/SIMARD_WEST.pdf.

Sosbe, Tim. "Tamar Elkeles: Technology and Training at QUALCOMM." *Chief Learning Officer*, September 2003. Available at http://www.clomagazine.com/content/templates/clo_cloprofile.asp?articleid= 254&zoneid=4.

Southgate, David. "A Best-of-Breed in Staff Retention." *TechRepublic*, April 29, 2002. Available at http://techrepublic.com.com/5100-6297-1048261.html.

Steinbock, Dan. *Wireless Horizon*. New York: AMACOM, July 2002.

Steinbock, Dan. *The Nokia Revolution: The Story of an Extraordinary Company That Transformed an Industry*. New York: AMACOM, May 2001.

Sung-jin, Yang. "GSM Royalty Payment in Dispute." *Korea Herald*, April 24, 2003. Available at http://www.ica.or.kr/en/krit_01_read.asp?board_seq=201&seq= 371&page; eq18.

Tam, Pui-Wing. "Qualcomm Ordered to Share Royalties from CDMA Sales." *Wall Street Journal*, December 12, 2000.

Tiedemann, Ed. "CDMA Standards History." PowerPoint Presentation, November 17, 2003.

Tiedemann, Ed. "Cdma2000 1X: New Capabilities for CDMA Networks." *IEEE Vehicular Technology Society News*, November 2001.

Tiedemann, Ed. "IMT-2000 Standards." PowerPoint Presentation, November 28, 2000.

Tiedemann, Ed. "CDMA—The Third Generation Technology (The Status of cdma2000 Development)." PowerPoint Presentation, April 2000.

Tiedemann, Ed. "Current Standards Stats." PowerPoint Presentation, September 1999.

Tiedemann, Ed. "Views on Third Generation Systems (North American, cdmaOne™: The OHG Output." PowerPoint Presentation, June 1999.

Tiedemann, Ed, Yu-Cheun Jou, and Joseph P. Odenwalder. "The Evolution of IS-95 to a Third Generation System and to the IMT-2000 Era." PowerPoint Presentation, November 26, 2003.

Titch, Steven. "Blind Faith." *Telephony Online*, September 8, 1997. Available at http://telephonyonline.com/ar/telecom_blind_faith_leading/.

Titch, Steven. "PacTel Gives Qualcomm a Look." *Telephony*, November 30, 1992.

Treacy, Michael, and Fred Wiersema. *The Discipline of Market Leaders: Choose Your Customers, Narrow Your Focus, Dominate Your Market*. New York: Perseus Publishing, January 1997.

Viterbi, Andrew J. "Wireless Digital Communication: A View Based on Three Lessons Learned." *IEEE Communications Magazine*, September 1991.

Viterbi, Andrew J. "Very Low Rate Convolutional Codes for Maximum Theoretical Performance of Spread-Spectrum Multiple-Access Channels." *IEEE Journal on Selected Areas in Communications*, vol. 8, no. 4 (May 1990).

Viterbi, Andrew J. "When Not to Spread Spectrum—a Sequel." *IEEE Communications Magazine*, vol. 23, no. 4 (April 1985).

Viterbi, Andrew J. "Spread Spectrum Communications—Myths and Realities." *IEEE Communications Magazine*, May 1979.

Weise, Elizabeth. "Hedy Lamarr, Inventor: A Sultry Screen Star Who Didn't Just Act—She Invented." March 10, 1997. Available at http://wireless.oldcolo.com/hedy.txt.

Welch, Matt. "Birth of a Blueprint: Profile Internet Father, Leonard Kleinrock." Available at http://www.mattwelch.com/ZoneSave/Kleinrock.htm.

West, Joel, and Justin Tan. "Qualcomm in China." *Asian Case Research Journal*, December 2002.

Yang, Heedong, Youngjin Yoo, Kalle Lyytinen, and Joong-Ho Ahn. "Diffusion of Broadband Mobile Services in Korea: The Role of Standards and Its Impact on Diffusion of Complex Technology System." Available at http://weatherhead.cwru.edu/pervasive/Paper/UBE%202003%20-%20Yoo.pdf.

Index